EVERYDAY
slow
cooker
& ONE DISH RECIPES

HUNDREDS OF EASY, ECONOMICAL & FAMILY-FRIENDLY MEALS AT YOUR FINGERTIPS!

Busy schedules, long hours at work and tight budgets are three reasons why folks are looking for a convenient and affordable way to put a wholesome dinner on the table. Look no further, because you will be thrilled with the recipes featured in *Taste of Home Everyday Slow Cooker & One Dish Recipes*. Busy cooks will love these yummy home-style dishes, because they require less time to prepare, and cleanup is a cinch!

Those with hectic days can breathe a sigh of relief—this book offers plenty of fast, delicious dinners! Inside you'll find more than 325 recipes and tips that offer simplicity when it comes to getting supper on the table.

This beautiful book is divided into three main sections: Slow Cookers, Stovetop Suppers and Oven Entrees. IT'S LIKE THREE BOOKS IN ONE! And each section has chapters, such as beef & ground beef, poultry, pork and more.

SLOW COOKER. This humble cooking appliance has become one of the most popular in America—and for good reason! A slow cooker does all the work for you! While you're away, your favorite meal simmers at home to mouthwatering perfection. The affordable appliance is easy to use…just set it and forget it! In addition, slow cookers are economical because they take affordable cuts of meat, such as beef stew meat or chicken thighs, and turn them into tender, delicious sensations.

The slow cooker recipes range from tasty appetizers to comforting entrees. You'll find side dishes perfect for potlucks, as well as recipes for toasty beverages and desserts. Plus, this book features 50 BRAND-NEW, NEVER-BEFORE-PUBLISHED SLOW COOKER RECIPES!

To get the best out of your slow cooker, refer to Slow Cooking 101 on page 240. This six-page section offers tip and hints so that every slow cooker recipe you create turns out perfect!

STOVETOP SUPPERS. This section is full of one-pot meals you can throw together in a snap. Quick, easy and family-friendly, they require little cleanup because they usually take advantage of a skillet or Dutch oven. These super-easy dinners are sure to satisfy.

OVEN ENTREES. The final section of this warm and inviting cookbook features stick-to-your-ribs oven specialties. You'll enjoy satisfying casseroles, such as baked pastas, as well as beef and pork roasts, potpies, pizzas and much more. These meal-in-one sensations make perfect family fare, and they are especially well suited for potlucks, church suppers, banquets and other covered-dish dinners.

For a break from meat-and-potato meals, check out the Fish & Seafood chapters of the Stovetop Suppers and Oven Entrees sections. You'll find unique recipes for wholesome yet different choices for dinner.

Each recipe in this amazing book has been tested by the Taste of Home Test Kitchen for accuracy and flavor. Recipes on the lighter side include Nutrition Facts and Diabetic Exchanges, and they are conveniently marked with an asterisk after the recipe title.

Set your slow cooker, grab your favorite skillet or preheat the oven, because it's time to get started! After one bite of any of these delights, you'll see how easy it is to make lasting memories at the dinner table!

SENIOR VICE PRESIDENT, EDITOR IN CHIEF: Catherine Cassidy

VICE PRESIDENT, EXECUTIVE EDITOR/BOOKS: Heidi Reuter Lloyd

FOOD DIRECTOR: Diane Werner RD

SENIOR EDITOR/BOOKS: Mark Hagen

EDITOR: Krista Lanphier

ART DIRECTOR: Gretchen Trautman

CONTENT PRODUCTION SUPERVISOR: Julie Wagner

DESIGN LAYOUT ARTIST: Kathy Crawford

PROJECT GRAPHIC DESIGN ASSOCIATE: Kathy Pieters

PROOFREADERS: Linne Bruskewitz, Amy Glander

RECIPE ASSET SYSTEM MANAGER: Coleen Martin

PREMEDIA SUPERVISOR: Scott Berger

RECIPE TESTING AND EDITING: Taste of Home Test Kitchen

FOOD PHOTOGRAPHY: Taste of Home Photo Studio

ADMINISTRATIVE ASSISTANT: Barb Czysz

COVER PHOTOGRAPHER: Rob Hagen

COVER FOOD STYLIST: Alynna Malson

COVER SET STYLIST: Jennifer Bradley Vent

NORTH AMERICAN CHIEF MARKETING OFFICER: Lisa Karpinski

VICE PRESIDENT/BOOK MARKETING: Dan Fink

CREATIVE DIRECTOR/CREATIVE MARKETING: Jim Palmen

THE READER'S DIGEST ASSOCIATION, INC.

PRESIDENT AND CHIEF EXECUTIVE OFFICER: Mary G. Berner

PRESIDENT, NORTH AMERICAN AFFINITIES: Suzanne M. Grimes

FRONT COVER: Beef Roast Dinner (p. 37).

BACK COVER, LEFT TO RIGHT: Spinach Alfredo Lasagna (p. 32), Prosciutto Pasta Toss (p. 139) and Pork Parmigiana (p. 222).

International Standard Book Number (10): 0-89821-812-8

International Standard Book Number (13): 978-0-89821-812-1

Library of Congress Number: 2010924672

Printed in U.S.A.

For other Taste of Home books and products, visit **ShopTasteofHome.com.**

table of contents

SLOW COOKER

Soups & Sandwiches

20

19

9

Soups and sandwiches are longtime staples we will always rely on. Slow-cooked soups simmer for hours and are just the ticket for a warm and comforting meal. And a slow cooker turns meat into tender fillings for robust sandwiches. You'll enjoy the satisfying, easy-to-make recipes in this chapter.

Southwestern Pork and Squash Soup

Molly Newman
PORTLAND, OREGON

My family loves this stew. The leftovers are even better the next day! We each enjoy eating a bowl with fresh corn muffins hot from the oven.

Southwestern Pork And Squash Soup*

PREP: 20 min. ■ **COOK:** 4 hours

1 pound pork tenderloin, cut into 1-inch cubes
1 medium onion, chopped
1 tablespoon canola oil
3 cups reduced-sodium chicken broth
1 medium butternut squash, peeled and cubed
2 medium carrots, sliced

1 can (14-1/2 ounces) diced tomatoes with mild green chilies
1 tablespoon chili powder
1 teaspoon ground cumin
1 teaspoon dried oregano
1/2 teaspoon pepper
1/4 teaspoon salt

■ In a large skillet, brown pork and onion in oil; drain. Transfer to a 4- or 5-qt. slow cooker. Stir in the remaining ingredients. Cover and cook on low for 4-5 hours or until meat is tender.

Yield: 6 servings.

✻**Nutrition Facts:** 1-1/2 cups equals 220 calories, 5 g fat (1 g saturated fat), 42 mg cholesterol, 708 mg sodium, 26 g carbohydrate, 7 g fiber, 19 g protein. **Diabetic Exchanges:** 2 lean meat, 4 vegetable, 1/2 fat.

Manhattan Clam Chowder*

Mary Dixon
NORTHVILLE, MICHIGAN

I came up with this simple, delicious soup years ago when my husband and I both worked. It's easy to dump the ingredients into the slow cooker in the morning and wonderful to come home to the aroma of a homemade dinner.

PREP: 10 min.
COOK: 8 hours

3 celery ribs, sliced
1 large onion, chopped
1 can (14-1/2 ounces) sliced potatoes, drained
1 can (14-1/2 ounces) sliced carrots, drained
2 cans (6-1/2 ounces *each*) chopped clams
2 cups tomato juice
1-1/2 cups water
1/2 cup tomato puree
1 tablespoon dried parsley flakes
1-1/2 teaspoons dried thyme
1 teaspoon salt, optional
1 bay leaf
2 whole black peppercorns

■ In a 3-qt. slow cooker, combine all ingredients. Cover and cook on low for 8-10 hours or until vegetables are tender. Discard bay leaf and peppercorns.

Yield: 9 servings.

✻**Nutrition Facts:** One 1-cup serving (prepared with no-salt-added tomato juice and without salt) equals 123 calories, 1 g fat (0 saturated fat), 27 mg cholesterol, 330 mg sodium, 17 g carbohydrate, 0 fiber, 12 g protein. **Diabetic Exchanges:** 1 very lean meat, 1 starch, 1 vegetable.

Norma Reynolds
OVERLAND PARK, KANSAS

This satisfying, homemade soup with a hint of cayenne is full of vegetables, chicken and noodles.

Hearty Chicken Noodle Soup

Hearty Chicken Noodle Soup

PREP: 20 min. ■ **COOK:** 5-1/2 hours

- 12 fresh baby carrots, cut into 1/2-inch pieces
- 4 celery ribs, cut into 1/2-inch pieces
- 3/4 cup finely chopped onion
- 1 tablespoon minced fresh parsley
- 1/2 teaspoon pepper
- 1/4 teaspoon cayenne pepper
- 1-1/2 teaspoons mustard seed
- 2 garlic cloves, peeled and halved
- 1-1/4 pounds boneless skinless chicken breast halves
- 1-1/4 pounds boneless skinless chicken thighs
- 4 cans (14-1/2 ounces *each*) chicken broth
- 1 package (9 ounces) refrigerated linguine

■ In a 5-qt. slow cooker, combine the first six ingredients. Place mustard seed and garlic on a double thickness of cheesecloth; bring up corners of cloth and tie with kitchen string to form a bag. Place in slow cooker. Add chicken and broth. Cover and cook on low for 5-6 hours or until chicken juices run clear.

■ Discard spice bag. Remove chicken; cool slightly. Stir linguine into soup; cover and cook for 30 minutes or until tender. Cut chicken into pieces and return to soup; heat through.

Yield: 12 servings (3 quarts).

Shredded Turkey Sandwiches*

Jacki Knuth
OWATONNA, MINNESOTA

This easy and simple slow-cooked sandwich gets its flavor from onion soup mix and beer. In total, it only takes five ingredients to make the recipe!

PREP: 15 min.
COOK: 7 hours

- 2 boneless skinless turkey breast halves (2 to 3 pounds *each*)
- 1 bottle (12 ounces) beer *or* nonalcoholic beer
- 1/2 cup butter, cubed
- 1 envelope onion soup mix
- 24 French rolls, split

■ Place turkey in a 5-qt. slow cooker. Combine beer, butter and soup mix; pour over meat. Cover and cook on low for 7-9 hours or until meat is tender.

■ Shred the meat and return to the slow cooker; heat through. Serve on rolls.

Yield: 24 servings.

* Nutrition Facts: 1 sandwich equals 294 calories, 7 g fat (3 g saturated fat), 57 mg cholesterol, 476 mg sodium, 31 g carbohydrate, 1 g fiber, 24 g protein. **Diabetic Exchanges:** 3 lean meat, 2 starch, 1/2 fat.

Sauerkraut Sausage Soup

Elizabeth Goetzinger
LEWISTON, IDAHO

I've taken this delicious soup to church gatherings and family reunions, and it always receives great compliments. Everyone loves it!

PREP: 25 min.
COOK: 8 hours

- 6 small red potatoes, quartered
- 3 medium carrots, halved and cut into 1/4-inch slices
- 1 medium onion, cut into thin wedges
- 1 can (14 ounces) sauerkraut, rinsed and well drained
- 1 tablespoon brown sugar
- 1 tablespoon spicy brown mustard
- 1 teaspoon caraway seeds
- 1 pound smoked kielbasa *or* Polish sausage, cut into 1-inch slices
- 2 cans (14-1/2 ounces *each*) reduced-sodium chicken broth

■ In a 3- or 4-qt. slow cooker, combine potatoes, carrots and onion. Combine the sauerkraut, brown sugar, brown mustard and caraway seeds; spoon over vegetables. Top with sausage and broth. Cover and cook on low for 8-9 hours or until the vegetables are tender.

Yield: 6 servings.

Hawaiian Kielbasa Sandwiches

Judy Dames
BRIDGEVILLE, PENNSYLVANIA

If you are looking for a different way to use kielbasa, the sweet and mildly spicy flavor of these filling sandwiches is a nice change of pace.

Hawaiian Kielbasa Sandwiches

PREP: 15 min. ■ **COOK:** 3 hours

- 3 pounds smoked kielbasa *or* Polish sausage, cut into 3-inch pieces
- 2 bottles (12 ounces *each*) chili sauce
- 1 can (20 ounces) pineapple tidbits, undrained
- 1/4 cup packed brown sugar
- 12 hoagie buns, split

■ Place the kielbasa in a 3-qt. slow cooker. Combine the chili sauce, pineapple and brown sugar; pour over kielbasa. Cover and cook on low for 3-4 hours or until heated through. Serve on buns.

Yield: 12 servings.

Constance Sullivan
OCEANSIDE, CALIFORNIA

Here's a hearty soup that is delicious and chock-full of vegetables, like mushrooms, leeks and carrots. It really hits the spot on a chilly day. I like to eat it with a chunk of crusty bread smothered in butter. The soup also makes great leftovers for lunch the next day.

Mushroom Barley Soup

PREP: 25 min. + soaking ■ COOK: 5 hours

- 1/2 cup dried great northern beans
- 1 pound sliced fresh mushrooms
- 2 cups chopped onions
- 1 medium leek (white portion only), sliced
- 1 to 2 garlic cloves, minced
- 2 tablespoons butter
- 2 cartons (32 ounces *each*) chicken broth
- 3 celery ribs, thinly sliced
- 3 large carrots, chopped
- 1/2 cup medium pearl barley
- 2 teaspoons dried parsley flakes
- 1-1/2 teaspoons salt
- 1 bay leaf
- 1/4 teaspoon white pepper

■ Soak the beans according to package directions. Meanwhile, in a large skillet, cook the mushrooms, onions, leek and garlic in butter over medium heat until tender.

■ Transfer to a 6-quart slow cooker. Drain and rinse the beans, discarding liquid. Add the beans, broth, celery, carrots, barley, parsley, salt, bay leaf and pepper. Cover and cook on low for 5 to 6 hours or until beans and vegetables are tender. Discard bay leaf.

Yield: 12 servings (3 quarts).

Hot Ham Sandwiches

Susan Rehm
GRAHAMSVILLE, NEW YORK

I came up with this crowd-pleasing recipe when trying to re-create a favorite sandwich from a restaurant near my hometown. Flavored with sweet relish, the ham sandwiches are oh-so-easy.

PREP: 10 min. ■ COOK: 4 hours

- 3 pounds thinly sliced deli ham (about 40 slices)
- 2 cups apple juice
- 2/3 cup packed brown sugar
- 1/2 cup sweet pickle relish
- 2 teaspoons prepared mustard
- 1 teaspoon paprika
- 12 kaiser rolls, split
- Additional sweet pickle relish, optional

■ Separate ham slices and place in a 3-qt. slow cooker. Combine the apple juice, brown sugar, relish, mustard and paprika. Pour over ham.

■ Cover and cook on low for 4-5 hours or until heated through. Place 3-4 slices of ham on each roll. Serve with additional relish if desired.

Yield: 12 servings.

Spicy Pork Chili

Taste of Home Test Kitchen
Tender pork adds extra heartiness to this slow-cooked chili. You can use pork tenderloin, boneless pork roast or boneless pork chops in the recipe.

PREP: 10 min.
COOK: 6 hours

- 2 pounds boneless pork, cut into 1/2-inch cubes
- 1 tablespoon canola oil
- 1 can (28 ounces) crushed tomatoes
- 2 cups frozen corn
- 1 can (15 ounces) black beans, rinsed and drained
- 1 cup chopped onion
- 1 cup beef broth
- 1 can (4 ounces) chopped green chilies
- 1 tablespoon chili powder
- 1 teaspoon minced garlic
- 1/2 teaspoon salt
- 1/2 teaspoon cayenne pepper
- 1/2 teaspoon pepper
- 1/4 cup minced fresh cilantro
- Shredded cheddar cheese, optional

■ In a large skillet, cook pork in oil over medium-high heat for 5-6 minutes or until browned. Transfer pork and drippings to a 5-qt. slow cooker. Stir in the tomatoes, corn, beans, onion, broth, chilies, chili powder, garlic, salt, cayenne and pepper.

■ Cover and cook on low for 6-7 hours or until pork is tender. Stir in cilantro. Serve with cheese if desired.

Yield: 6 servings.

SLOW COOKER Soups & Sandwiches

Montana Wildfire Chili

Donna Evaro
GREAT FALLS, MONTANA

This thick and chunky chili has some kick to it. I like to top it with shredded cheddar and then serve it with a side of corn bread.

PREP: 30 min. ■ COOK: 5 hours

- 2 pounds ground beef
- 1 large sweet onion, chopped
- 1 medium sweet red pepper, finely chopped
- 1 medium sweet yellow pepper, finely chopped
- 2 cans (16 ounces *each*) chili beans, undrained
- 2 cans (14-1/2 ounces *each*) stewed tomatoes, drained
- 1/2 cup tomato juice
- 2 jalapeno peppers, seeded and minced
- 2 garlic cloves, minced
- 2 teaspoons ground cumin
- 2 teaspoons chili powder
- 1 teaspoon salt
- 1 teaspoon cayenne pepper

■ In a large skillet, cook the beef, onion and peppers over medium heat until the meat is no longer pink; drain.

■ Transfer to a 4- or 5-quart slow cooker. Stir in the beans, tomatoes, tomato juice, jalapenos, garlic, cumin, chili powder, salt and cayenne. Cover and cook on low for 5-6 hours or until heated through.

Yield: 8 servings (2-1/2 quarts).

Editor's Note: When cutting hot peppers, disposable gloves are recommended. Avoid touching your face.

When handling jalapeno peppers,

always wear plastic gloves. If you have to cut a large number of peppers, try this: First cut off the tops of the peppers, then slice them in half the long way. Use the small end of a melon baller to easily scrape out the seeds and membranes. It speeds the job along and keeps you from accidentally slicing your gloves.

Shredded Beef Sandwiches

PREP: 20 min.
COOK: 8 hours

- 1 boneless beef chuck roast (about 4 pounds)
- 1 large onion, thinly sliced
- 1 cup ketchup
- 1/4 cup lemon juice
- 3 tablespoons Worcestershire sauce
- 2 tablespoons brown sugar
- 2 tablespoons cider vinegar
- 1 teaspoon salt
- 1/4 teaspoon pepper
- 1/2 teaspoon Liquid Smoke, optional
- 24 kaiser rolls *or* hamburger buns, split

■ Cut the roast in half; place in a 5-qt. slow cooker. Top with the onion. Combine the next eight ingredients; pour over roast. Cover and cook on low for 8-9 hours or until meat is tender.

■ Remove roast and cool slightly; shred meat with two forks. Skim fat from cooking liquid. Return meat to slow cooker; heat through. Using a slotted spoon, place 1/3 cup of the meat mixture on each roll.

Yield: 24 servings.

JoLynn Hill
ROOSEVELT, UTAH

Whatever group you're cooking for, they'll love these flavor-packed sandwiches. The beef is slow cooked until tender, and the light, tangy barbecue sauce is mouthwatering. A side of creamy, crunchy coleslaw is delicious with this entree.

Spicy Turkey Bean Soup

Gary Fenski
HURON, SOUTH DAKOTA

I originally called this recipe "Turkey Dump Soup" because all you have to do is dump all the ingredients into the slow cooker and let them cook!

Spicy Turkey Bean Soup

PREP: 20 min. ■ COOK: 5 hours

2 cans (15 ounces *each*) white kidney *or* cannellini beans, rinsed and drained

2 cups cubed cooked turkey

1 can (14-1/2 ounces) chicken broth

1 can (10 ounces) diced tomatoes and green chilies, undrained

1 cup salsa

1/2 teaspoon ground cumin

1/4 teaspoon curry powder

1/4 teaspoon ground ginger

1/4 teaspoon paprika

■ In a 3- or 4-qt. slow cooker, combine all ingredients. Cover and cook on low for 5-6 hours or until heated through.

Yield: 4 servings.

Wintertime Meatball Soup

Eunice Justice
CODY, WYOMING

This recipe is versatile. If you like, you can vary the vegetables that are added to the soup. In my version, I add a bit of chopped jalapeno pepper for some heat and serve the robust soup with corn bread or garlic bread.

PREP: 20 min.
COOK: 9 hours

2 cans (16 ounces *each*) chili beans, undrained

2 cans (14-1/2 ounces *each*) beef broth

1 jar (26 ounces) spaghetti sauce

1/4 cup chopped onion

3 garlic cloves, minced

1 tablespoon Worcestershire sauce

1 teaspoon Italian seasoning

1 package (32 ounces) frozen fully cooked Italian meatballs

1 package (16 ounces) frozen mixed vegetables

4 cups chopped cabbage

■ In a 6-qt. slow cooker, combine beans, broth, spaghetti sauce, onion, garlic, Worcestershire sauce and Italian seasoning. Stir in the meatballs, mixed vegetables and cabbage. Cover and cook on low for 9-10 hours or until vegetables are tender.

Yield: 15 servings (3-3/4 quarts).

Jean Glacken
ELKTON, MARYLAND

This is one of those recipes you always count on. The sauce and mildly spiced meatballs make a great filling or pasta topping.

Italian Meatball Subs

Italian Meatball Subs

PREP: 25 min. ■ **COOK:** 4 hours

2 eggs, lightly beaten	1 small onion, chopped
1/4 cup milk	1/2 cup chopped green pepper
1/2 cup dry bread crumbs	1/2 cup dry red wine *or* beef broth
2 tablespoons grated Parmesan cheese	1/3 cup water
1 teaspoon salt	2 garlic cloves, minced
1/4 teaspoon pepper	1 teaspoon dried oregano
1/8 teaspoon garlic powder	1 teaspoon salt
1 pound ground beef	1/2 teaspoon sugar
1/2 pound bulk Italian sausage	1/2 teaspoon pepper
SAUCE:	6 to 7 Italian rolls, split
1 can (15 ounces) tomato sauce	Shredded Parmesan cheese, optional
1 can (6 ounces) tomato paste	

■ In a large bowl, combine the eggs and milk; add the bread crumbs, cheese, salt, pepper and garlic powder. Add beef and sausage; mix well. Shape into 1-in. balls. Broil 4 in. from the heat for 4 minutes; turn and broil 3 minutes longer.

■ Transfer to a 5-qt. slow cooker. Combine the tomato sauce and paste, onion, green pepper, wine or broth, water and seasonings; pour over the meatballs. Cover and cook on low for 4-5 hours. Serve on rolls. Sprinkle with shredded cheese if desired.

Yield: 6-7 servings.

No-Fuss Potato Soup*

Dotty Egge
PELICAN RAPIDS, MINNESOTA

My family loves to have a tasty bowl of this soup, along with fresh bread from our bread machine.

PREP: 15 min.
COOK: 7-1/2 hours

6 cups cubed peeled potatoes
5 cups water
2 cups chopped onion
1/2 cup chopped celery
1/2 cup thinly sliced carrots
1/4 cup butter, cubed
4 teaspoons chicken bouillon granules *or* 2 vegetable bouillon cubes
2 teaspoons salt
1/4 teaspoon pepper
1 can (12 ounces) evaporated milk
3 tablespoons minced fresh parsley
Minced chives, optional

■ In a 5-qt. slow cooker, combine the first nine ingredients. Cover and cook on high for 7-8 hours or until vegetables are tender.

■ Add milk and parsley. Cover and cook 30-60 minutes or until heated through. Garnish with chives if desired.

Yield: 8-10 servings (about 3 quarts).

*Nutrition Facts: 1 cup serving (prepared with margarine) equals 190 calories, 827 mg sodium, 12 mg cholesterol, 26 gm carbohydrate, 5 gm protein, 7 gm fat. **Diabetic Exchanges:** 1 vegetable, 1-1/2 starch, 1-1/2 fat.

Victoria1 Zmarzley-Hahn
NORTHHAMPTON, PENNSYLVANIA

Lots of wonderful vegetables are showcased in this chunky soup. It's a great way to use up summer's excess produce.

Summer's Bounty Soup

Summer's Bounty Soup*

PREP: 5 min. ■ **COOK:** 7 hours

4 medium tomatoes, chopped

2 medium potatoes, peeled and cubed

2 cups halved fresh green beans

2 small zucchini, cubed

1 medium yellow summer squash, cubed

4 small carrots, thinly sliced

2 celery ribs, thinly sliced

1 cup cubed peeled eggplant

1 cup sliced fresh mushrooms

1 small onion, chopped

1 tablespoon minced fresh parsley

1 tablespoon salt-free garlic and herb seasoning

4 cups V8 juice

■ In a 5-qt. slow cooker, combine all the ingredients. Cover and cook on low for 7-8 hours or until the vegetables are tender.

Yield: 12-14 servings (about 3-1/2 quarts).

✳Nutrition Facts: 1 cup serving (prepared with low-sodium V8) equals 60 calories, 59 mg sodium, 0 cholesterol, 13 g carbohydrate, 2 g protein, trace fat. **Diabetic Exchange:** 2 vegetable.

Summer squash have edible thin skins and soft seeds. Zucchini, pattypan and crookneck are the most common varieties. Choose firm summer squash with brightly colored skin that's free from spots and bruises. Smaller squash are more tender.

Savory Cheese Soup

Ann Huseby
LAKEVILLE, MINNESOTA

Let guests serve themselves and choose from toppings such as popcorn, croutons and bacon bits.

PREP: 15 min.
COOK: 8 hours

3 cans (14-1/2 ounces *each*) chicken broth

1 small onion, chopped

1 large carrot, chopped

1 celery rib, chopped

1/4 cup chopped sweet red pepper

2 tablespoons butter

1 teaspoon salt

1/2 teaspoon pepper

1/3 cup all-purpose flour

1/3 cup cold water

1 package (8 ounces) cream cheese, cubed and softened

2 cups (8 ounces) shredded cheddar cheese

1 can (12 ounces) beer, optional

Optional toppings: croutons, popcorn, crumbled cooked bacon, sliced green onions

■ In a 3-qt. slow cooker, combine the first eight ingredients. Cover and cook on low for 7-8 hours.

■ Combine flour and water until smooth; stir into soup. Cover and cook on high 30 minutes longer or until soup is thickened.

■ Stir in the cream cheese and cheddar cheese until blended. Stir in beer if desired. Cover and cook on low until heated through. Serve with desired toppings.

Yield: 6-8 servings.

Pork Sandwiches with Root Beer Barbecue Sauce

Karen Currie
KIRKWOOD, MISSOURI

This tasty recipe is sure to please a crowd! I love the subtle kick and hint of sweetness in this dish. Try serving these sandwiches with coleslaw and pickles.

Pork Sandwiches with Root Beer Barbecue Sauce

PREP: 30 min. ■ COOK: 9-1/2 hours

1 boneless pork sirloin roast (2 pounds)	3 cups root beer, *divided*
1 medium onion, sliced	1 bottle (12 ounces) chili sauce
2 tablespoons dried minced garlic	1/8 teaspoon hot pepper sauce
	8 kaiser rolls, split

■ Place roast in a 3-qt. slow cooker. Add the onion, garlic and 1 cup root beer. Cover and cook on low for 9-10 hours or until meat is tender.

■ In a small saucepan, combine the chili sauce, hot pepper sauce and remaining root beer. Bring to a boil. Reduce heat; simmer, uncovered, for 20-25 minutes or until thickened.

■ Remove meat from slow cooker; cool slightly. Discard cooking juices. Shred pork and return to slow cooker. Stir in barbecue sauce. Cover and cook on low for 30 minutes or until heated through. Serve on rolls.

Yield: 8 servings.

Vegetable Beef Soup

Earnest Riggs
NILES, MICHIGAN

I'm currently retired and an Assistant Scout Master of a troop. This is a nice recipe for teaching basic cooking skills to the boys. The soup cooks all day, leaving you free to do other things.

PREP: 35 min.
COOK: 8 hours

2 pounds beef stew meat, cut into 1/2-inch pieces
2 tablespoons canola oil
2 cans (one 28 ounces, one 14-1/2 ounces) diced tomatoes
3 cups tomato juice
1 can (14-1/2 ounces) beef broth
4 medium red potatoes, cut into 1/2-inch pieces
3 medium carrots, halved and thinly sliced
2 celery ribs, chopped
1 medium onion, finely chopped
2-1/2 cups chopped cabbage
1-1/2 cups frozen corn
1-1/4 cups frozen baby lima beans
4 teaspoons beef bouillon granules
1 teaspoon salt
3/4 teaspoon pepper

■ In a large skillet, brown the beef in oil; drain. Transfer to a 6-qt. slow cooker. Stir in remaining ingredients. Cover and cook on low for 8-10 hours or until meat and vegetables are tender.

Yield: 12 servings
(about 4-1/2 quarts).

Lisa DiPrima
MILFORD, NEW HAMPSHIRE

If you're looking for a great seafood recipe for your slow cooker, this classic fish stew is just the ticket. It's full to the brim with clams, crab, fish and shrimp, and is fancy enough to be an elegant meal. Serve the soup with toasted baguette slices or artisan bread for a special touch.

Seafood Cioppino*

PREP: 20 min. ■ COOK: 4-1/2 hours

- 1 can (28 ounces) diced tomatoes, undrained
- 2 medium onions, chopped
- 3 celery ribs, chopped
- 1 bottle (8 ounces) clam juice
- 1 can (6 ounces) tomato paste
- 1/2 cup white wine *or* vegetable broth
- 5 garlic cloves, minced
- 1 tablespoon red wine vinegar
- 1 tablespoon olive oil
- 1 to 2 teaspoons Italian seasoning
- 1/2 teaspoon sugar
- 1 bay leaf
- 1 pound haddock fillets, cut into 1-inch pieces
- 1 pound uncooked small shrimp, peeled, deveined and tails removed
- 1 can (6 ounces) lump crabmeat, drained
- 1 can (6 ounces) chopped clams
- 2 tablespoons minced fresh parsley *or* 2 teaspoons dried parsley flakes

■ In a 4- or 5-qt. slow cooker, combine the first twelve ingredients. Cover and cook on low for 4-5 hours. Stir in the haddock, shrimp, crabmeat and clams. Cover and cook for 30 minutes longer or until heated through. Stir in parsley. Discard bay leaf.

Yield: 8 servings (2-1/2 quarts).

✱ **Nutrition Facts:** 1-1/4 cups equals 205 calories, 3 g fat (1 g saturated fat), 125 mg cholesterol, 483 mg sodium, 15 g carbohydrate, 3 g fiber, 29 g protein. **Diabetic Exchanges:** 3 lean meat, 2 vegetable.

Italian seasoning might contain marjoram, thyme, rosemary, savory, sage, oregano and basil. If you're out of Italian seasoning, you can mix up your own. Try substituting 1/4 teaspoon each of basil, thyme, rosemary and oregano for each teaspoon of Italian seasoning called for in a recipe. If you don't have all the ingredients on your spice shelf, you can blend just a few of them with good results.

Italian Sausage Hoagies

Craig Wachs
RACINE, WISCONSIN

Germans and Italians who immigrated to Southeastern Wisconsin influenced the cuisine. When preparing this recipe, I usually substitute German bratwurst for the Italian sausage, blending the two influences with delicious results.

PREP: 15 min.
COOK: 4 hours

- 10 Italian sausage links
- 2 tablespoons olive oil
- 1 jar (26 ounces) meatless spaghetti sauce
- 1/2 medium green pepper, julienned
- 1/2 medium sweet red pepper, julienned
- 1/2 cup water
- 1/4 cup grated Romano cheese
- 2 tablespoons dried oregano
- 2 tablespoons dried basil
- 2 loaves French bread (20 inches)

■ In a large skillet over medium-high heat, brown sausage in oil; drain. Transfer to a 5-qt. slow cooker. Add spaghetti sauce, peppers, water, cheese, oregano and basil. Cover and cook on low for 4 hours or until sausage is no longer pink.

■ Slice French bread lengthwise but not all of the way through; cut each loaf widthwise into five pieces. Fill each piece with sausage, peppers and sauce.

Yield: 10 servings.

Jennifer Bauer
LANSING, MICHIGAN

A boneless beef roast simmers for hours in a slightly sweet sauce before it's shredded and tucked into rolls to make hearty sandwiches. This is a family favorite.

Texas Beef Barbecue

Texas Beef Barbecue*

PREP: 15 min. ■ COOK: 8 hours

1 beef sirloin tip roast (4 pounds)	1/2 cup packed brown sugar
1 can (5-1/2 ounces) spicy hot V8 juice	1 teaspoon salt
1/2 cup water	1 teaspoon ground mustard
1/4 cup white vinegar	1 teaspoon paprika
1/4 cup ketchup	1/4 teaspoon chili powder
2 tablespoons Worcestershire sauce	1/8 teaspoon pepper
	16 kaiser rolls, split

■ Cut roast in half; place in a 5-qt. slow cooker. Combine the V8 juice, water, vinegar, ketchup, Worcestershire sauce, brown sugar and seasonings; pour over roast. Cover and cook on low for 8-10 hours or until meat is tender.

■ Remove meat and shred with two forks; return to slow cooker and heat through. Spoon 1/2 cup meat mixture onto each roll.

Yield: 16 servings.

*Nutrition Facts: 1 sandwich equals 339 calories, 8 g fat (2 g saturated fat), 60 mg cholesterol, 606 mg sodium, 39 g carbohydrate, 1 g fiber, 27 g protein. **Diabetic Exchanges:** 3 lean meat, 2-1/2 starch.

Slow-Cooked Corn Chowder

PREP: 10 min.
COOK: 6 hours

2-1/2 cups 2% milk
    1 can (14-3/4 ounces) cream-style corn
    1 can (10-3/4 ounces) condensed cream of mushroom soup, undiluted
1-3/4 cups frozen corn
    1 cup frozen shredded hash brown potatoes
    1 cup cubed fully cooked ham
    1 large onion, chopped
    2 teaspoons dried parsley flakes
    2 tablespoons butter
Salt and pepper to taste

■ In a 3-qt. slow cooker, combine all ingredients. Cover and cook on low for 6 hours.

Yield: 8 servings (2 quarts).

Dress up soup

with a sprinkle of nuts, chopped fresh herbs, sliced green onions, slivers of fresh vegetables, croutons, shredded cheese or crumbled bacon.

Mary Hogue
ROCHESTER, PENNSYLVANIA

I combine and refrigerate the ingredients for this easy chowder the night before. In the morning, I pour the mixture into the slow cooker and turn it on before I leave for work. When I come home, a hot tasty meal awaits.

Hearty Italian Sandwiches

Hearty Chili With a Twist

Louise Jacino
EAST MORICHES, NEW YORK
Italian sausage adds new flavor to this chili. I serve it with rice, crushed crackers and cheese.

PREP: 30 min.
COOK: 6 hours

- 1 pound ground beef
- 1 pound bulk Italian sausage
- 2 large onions, chopped
- 4 garlic cloves, minced
- 2 cans (16 ounces *each*) kidney beans, rinsed and drained
- 2 cans (14-1/2 ounces *each*) Italian diced tomatoes, undrained
- 2 cans (10-3/4 ounces *each*) condensed tomato soup, undiluted
- 2 cans (6 ounces *each*) Italian tomato paste
- 1 can (8-1/2 ounces) peas, drained
- 2 tablespoons chili powder
- 2 teaspoons ground cumin
- 2 teaspoons dried oregano
- 1 teaspoon hot pepper sauce
- 3/4 teaspoon salt
- 1/2 teaspoon pepper

- ■ In a large skillet, cook the beef, sausage, onions and garlic over medium heat until the meat is no longer pink; drain.

- ■ Transfer to a 5-qt. slow cooker. Stir in the beans, tomatoes, soup, tomato paste, peas, chili powder, cumin, oregano, pepper sauce, salt and pepper. Cover and cook on low for 6-7 hours or until heated through.

Yield: 12 servings (3 quarts).

Elaine Krupsky
LAS VEGAS, NEVADA
I've been making this sweet and spicy sandwich filling for many years. The Italian-flavored meat mixture smells just as good as it tastes.

Hearty Italian Sandwiches

PREP: 20 min. ■ **COOK:** 6 hours

- 1-1/2 pounds lean ground beef (90% lean)
- 1-1/2 pounds bulk Italian sausage
- 2 large onions, sliced
- 2 large green peppers, sliced
- 2 large sweet red peppers, sliced
- 1 teaspoon salt
- 1 teaspoon pepper
- 1/4 teaspoon crushed red pepper flakes
- 8 sandwich rolls, split
- Shredded Monterey Jack cheese, optional

- ■ In a Dutch oven, cook beef and sausage over medium heat until no longer pink; drain. Place a third of the onions and peppers in a 5-qt. slow cooker; top with half of the meat mixture. Repeat layers; top with remaining vegetables. Sprinkle with salt, pepper and pepper flakes.

- ■ Cover and cook on low for 6 hours or until vegetables are tender. With a slotted spoon, serve about 1 cup of meat and vegetables on each roll. Top with cheese if desired. Use pan juices for dipping if desired.

Yield: 8 servings.

Chili Sandwiches

Kerry Haglund
WYOMING, MINNESOTA

No one will be able to resist these special sandwiches stuffed with spicy chili. Of course, the chili also makes a wonderfully filling meal by itself.

PREP: 30 min. + standing ■ COOK: 3 hours

1 pound dried navy beans	1 cup barbecue sauce
2 pounds beef stew meat	1 cup chili sauce
2 cups water	1/2 cup honey
1 pound sliced bacon, diced	1/4 cup hot pepper sauce
1 cup chopped onion	1 tablespoon chili powder
1 cup shredded carrots	1 tablespoon baking cocoa
1 cup chopped celery	1 tablespoon Dijon mustard
1/3 cup chopped green pepper	1 tablespoon Worcestershire sauce
1/3 cup chopped sweet red pepper	1 bay leaf
4 garlic cloves, minced	4 teaspoons beef bouillon granules
3 cans (14-1/2 ounces *each*) diced tomatoes, undrained	30 hamburger buns, split

■ Sort beans and rinse with cold water. Place beans in a Dutch oven; add water to cover by 2 in. Bring to a boil; boil for 2 minutes. Remove from the heat; cover and let soak for 1 to 4 hours or until beans are softened. Drain and rinse beans, discarding liquid.

■ Return beans to Dutch oven; add beef and water. Bring to a boil. Reduce heat; cover and simmer for 2 hours or until beef and beans are almost tender. Drain. Shred beef with two forks; place beef and beans in a 5-qt. slow cooker.

■ In a large skillet, cook bacon over medium heat until crisp. Using a slotted spoon, remove the bacon to slow cooker. Discard all but 3 tablespoons drippings. Saute the onion, carrots, celery and peppers in drippings until tender. Add garlic; cook 1 minute longer.

■ Transfer to the slow cooker. Add all the remaining ingredients except buns. Cover and cook on high for 3-4 hours, stirring often. Discard bay leaf. Spoon 1/2 cup onto each bun.

Yield: 30 servings.

A good way to keep shredded carrots on hand is to shred a lot of carrots at once and freeze them in plastic bags in 1-cup portions. When a recipe calls for shredded carrots, just pull a bag out of the freezer.

Curried Lentil Soup*

Christina Till
SOUTH HAVEN, MICHIGAN

Curry gives a different taste sensation to this soup. It's delicious with a dollop of sour cream. My family welcomes it with open arms.

PREP: 15 min.
COOK: 8 hours

4 cups hot water
1 can (28 ounces) crushed tomatoes
3 medium potatoes, peeled and diced
3 medium carrots, thinly sliced
1 large onion, chopped
1 celery rib, chopped
1 cup dried lentils, rinsed
2 garlic cloves, minced
2 bay leaves
4 teaspoons curry powder
1-1/2 teaspoons salt, optional

■ In a 3-qt. slow cooker, combine all the ingredients. Cover and cook on low for 8 hours or until the vegetables and lentils are tender. Discard bay leaves.

Yield: 10 servings
(2-1/2 quarts).

*Nutrition Facts: 1 cup (prepared without salt) equals 169 calories, 150 mg sodium, 0 cholesterol, 34 gm carbohydrate, 9 gm protein, 1 gm fat. **Diabetic Exchanges:** 2 starch, 1 vegetable.

Yvette Massey
LA LUZ, NEW MEXICO

This is an easy and tasty dish. When I fix it for company, I prepare the meat ahead so I can focus on side dishes and spending time with my friends.

Fiesta Pork Sandwiches

Fiesta Pork Sandwiches

PREP: 20 min. + marinating ■ COOK: 8 hours

- 1 boneless pork shoulder roast (3 to 4 pounds)
- 2/3 cup lime juice
- 1/4 cup water
- 1/4 cup grapefruit juice
- 2 bay leaves
- 12 garlic cloves, minced
- 1 teaspoon salt
- 1 teaspoon dried oregano
- 1 teaspoon chili powder
- 2 tablespoons olive oil
- 1 large onion, thinly sliced
- 12 to 14 sandwich rolls, split

■ Cut roast in half; pierce several times with a fork.

■ In a large bowl, combine next eight ingredients. Pour half of the marinade into a large resealable plastic bag; add the pork. Seal the bag and turn to coat; refrigerate overnight, turning occasionally. Cover and refrigerate remaining marinade.

■ Drain and discard marinade. In a Dutch oven over medium heat, brown roast in oil on all sides. Place the onion, roast and the reserved marinade in a 5-qt. slow cooker.

■ Cover and cook on high for 2 hours. Reduce the heat to low; cook 6-8 hours longer or until the meat is tender. Remove roast; shred or thinly slice. Discard the bay leaves. Skim fat from cooking juices and serve the pork on rolls with juices as a dipping sauce.

Yield: 12-14 servings.

Rich French Onion Soup

Linda Adolph
EDMONTON, ALBERTA

When entertaining guests, I bring out this savory soup while we're waiting for the main course. It's simple to make—just saute the onions early in the day and let the soup simmer until dinnertime. In winter, big bowls of it make a warming supper with a salad and buttered biscuits.

PREP: 10 min.
COOK: 5 hours

- 6 large onions, chopped
- 1/2 cup butter
- 6 cans (10-1/2 ounces *each*) condensed beef broth, undiluted
- 1-1/2 teaspoons Worcestershire sauce
- 3 bay leaves
- 10 slices French bread, toasted

Shredded Parmesan and shredded part-skim mozzarella cheese

■ In a large skillet, saute onions in butter until crisp-tender. Transfer to an ungreased 3-qt. slow cooker. Add the broth, Worcestershire and bay leaves.

■ Cover and cook on low for 5-7 hours or until the onions are tender. Discard bay leaves. Top each serving with French bread and cheeses.

Yield: 10 servings.

Butternut Squash Soup

Simply Delicious Roast Beef Sandwiches*

Scott Powell
PHILLIPSBURG, NEW JERSEY

Mushrooms add a different touch to these comforting roast beef sandwiches. I like to pile the shredded beef high on kaiser rolls.

PREP: 15 min.
COOK: 8 hours

- 1 beef rump roast *or* bottom round roast (3 to 4 pounds)
- 1 can (10-3/4 ounces) condensed cream of mushroom soup, undiluted
- 1 envelope onion soup mix
- 2 celery ribs, finely chopped
- 1 jar (6 ounces) sliced mushrooms, drained
- 15 kaiser rolls, split

■ Cut roast in half; transfer to a 5-qt. slow cooker. Combine soup and soup mix; stir in the celery. Pour over meat. Cover and cook on low for 8-10 hours or until the meat is tender, adding the mushrooms during the last hour of cooking.

■ Remove meat from slow cooker. Skim fat from cooking juices. When cool enough to handle, shred meat with two forks and return to slow cooker; heat through. Spoon 1/2 cup onto each roll.

Yield: 15 servings.

✱**Nutrition Facts**: 1 sandwich equals 307 calories, 8 g fat (2 g saturated fat), 55 mg cholesterol, 699 mg sodium, 33 g carbohydrate, 2 g fiber, 24 g protein. **Diabetic Exchanges:** 2 medium-fat meat, 2 starch.

Jackie Campbell
STANHOPE, NEW JERSEY

The golden color, smooth and creamy texture and wonderful taste of this soup is a welcome addition on a chilly fall day. It has a slightly tangy flavor from the cream cheese.

Butternut Squash Soup

PREP: 30 min. ■ **COOK:** 6-1/4 hours

- 1 medium onion, chopped
- 2 tablespoons butter
- 1 medium butternut squash (about 4 pounds), peeled and cubed
- 3 cans (14-1/2 ounces *each*) vegetable broth
- 1 tablespoon brown sugar
- 1 tablespoon minced fresh gingerroot
- 1 garlic clove, minced
- 1 cinnamon stick (3 inches)
- 1 package (8 ounces) cream cheese, softened and cubed

■ In a small skillet, saute onion in butter until tender. Transfer to a 5- or 6-quart slow cooker; add squash. Combine the broth, brown sugar, ginger, garlic and cinnamon; pour over squash. Cover and cook on low for 6-8 hours or until squash is tender.

■ Cool slightly. Discard cinnamon stick. In a blender, process soup in batches until smooth. Return all to slow cooker. Whisk in cream cheese; cover and cook 15 minutes longer or until cheese is melted.

Yield: 14 servings (2-1/2 quarts).

Beef & Ground Beef

28

34

30

To bring out the deep, full-bodied flavor of beef, nothing works better than a slow cooker. The robust and family-pleasing recipes in this chapter effortlessly put dinner on the table, placing smiles on the faces of those with hearty appetites.

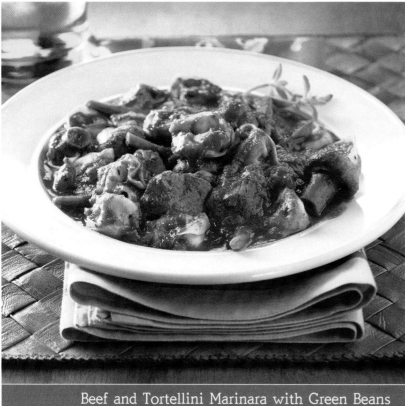

Beef and Tortellini Marinara with Green Beans

- In a large skillet, brown the beef in oil until beef is no longer pink. Add garlic; cook 1 minute longer. Transfer to a 5- or 6-qt. slow cooker.

- Stir in the marinara sauce, wine, green beans, tomatoes, mushrooms, sauce mix, parsley, onion, rosemary, pepper and salt. Cover and cook on low for 6-8 hours or until meat is tender.

- Stir in the tortellini. Cover; cook on high 30 minutes longer or until the tortellini are heated through.

Yield: 11 servings.

Joyce Frey
MACKSVILLE, KANSAS

This hearty Italian pasta stew is a tradition with my family. It's great served with crusty Italian bread and a nice big green salad. I like to have a glass of red wine with this meal-in-one.

Beef and Tortellini Marinara with Green Beans

PREP: 30 min. ■ **COOK:** 6-1/2 hours

1 pound beef stew meat	2 envelopes thick and zesty spaghetti sauce mix
2 tablespoons olive oil	
2 garlic cloves, minced	2 tablespoons minced fresh parsley
1 jar (26 ounces) marinara *or* spaghetti sauce	1 tablespoon dried minced onion
2 cups dry red wine *or* beef broth	2 teaspoons minced fresh rosemary
1 pound fresh green beans, trimmed	1 teaspoon coarsely ground pepper
1 can (14-1/2 ounces) Italian diced tomatoes, undrained	1/4 teaspoon salt
1/2 pound small fresh mushrooms	1 package (9 ounces) refrigerated cheese tortellini

When using red wine in recipes, consider wine that you enjoy drinking. For the Beef and Tortellini Marinara with Green Beans, some dry reds you can use include Chianti, Pinot Noir, Merlot or Cabernet Sauvignon.

Flank Steak Fajitas

- Place the beef in a 3-qt. slow cooker. In a small bowl, combine the tomatoes, garlic, jalapeno, cilantro, chili powder, cumin and salt; pour over beef. Cover and cook on low for 7-8 hours.

- Stir in red and green peppers. Cook 1 hour longer or until the meat and peppers are tender. Thicken juices if desired.

- Using a slotted spoon, place about 1/2 cup beef mixture down the center of each tortilla; fold sides over filling. Serve with the sour cream, salsa and cheese if desired.

Yield: 8-10 servings.

Editor's Note: When cutting hot peppers, disposable gloves are recommended. Avoid touching your face.

For a cooling and sweet dessert, have scoops of vanilla ice cream with Tex-Mex chocolate sauce. Just add a touch of ground cinnamon and cayenne pepper to bottled chocolate sauce to spice it up. Top with toasted pecans for crunch.

Twila Burkholder
MIDDLEBURG, PENNSYLVANIA

Our family loves Mexican food, and this is one of our favorites. The slow cooker tenderizes the flank steak for these filling fajitas, which have just the right amount of spice.

Flank Steak Fajitas

PREP: 10 min. ■ **COOK:** 8 hours

1-1/2 to 2 pounds beef flank steak, cut into thin strips

1 can (10 ounces) diced tomatoes and green chilies, undrained

2 garlic cloves, minced

1 jalapeno pepper, seeded and chopped

1 tablespoon minced fresh cilantro *or* parsley

1 teaspoon chili powder

1/2 teaspoon ground cumin

1/4 teaspoon salt

1 medium sweet red pepper, julienned

1 medium green pepper, julienned

8 to 10 flour tortillas (7 to 8 inches)

Sour cream, salsa and shredded cheddar cheese, optional

Rosemary Jarvis
SPARTA, TENNESSEE

I've worked full-time for more than 30 years, and this recipe has been a lifesaver. It smells heavenly when I walk in the door in the evening.

Slow-Cooked Cabbage Rolls

Slow-Cooked Cabbage Rolls

PREP: 20 min. ■ **COOK:** 6 hours

1 large head cabbage	1 ounce onion soup mix
1 can (8 ounces) tomato sauce	1-1/2 pounds lean ground beef (90% lean)
3/4 cup quick-cooking rice	1 can (46 ounces) V8 juice
1/2 cup chopped green pepper	Salt to taste
1/2 cup crushed saltines (about 15 crackers)	Grated Parmesan cheese, optional
1 egg, lightly beaten	

■ Cook cabbage in boiling water just until leaves fall off head. Set aside 12 large leaves for rolls; drain well. (Refrigerate remaining cabbage for another use.) Cut out the thick vein from the bottom of each reserved leaf, making a V-shaped cut; set aside.

■ In a large bowl, combine the tomato sauce, rice, green pepper, cracker crumbs, egg and soup mix. Crumble beef over mixture and mix well.

■ Place about 1/3 cup meat mixture on each cabbage leaf; overlap cut ends of leaf. Fold in sides, beginning from cut end. Roll up completely to enclose filling. Secure with toothpicks if desired.

■ Place cabbage rolls in a 3-qt. slow cooker. Pour V8 juice over rolls. Cover and cook on low for 6-7 hours or until filling reaches 160°. Just before serving, sprinkle with salt and cheese if desired.

Yield: 6 servings.

Slow Cooker Pizza Casserole

Virginia Krites
CRIDERSVILLE, OHIO

A comforting casserole with mass appeal is just what you need when cooking for a crowd. For added convenience, this one stays warm in a slow cooker.

PREP: 20 min.
COOK: 2 hours

- 1 package (16 ounces) rigatoni *or* large tube pasta
- 1-1/2 pounds ground beef
- 1 small onion, chopped
- 4 cups (16 ounces) shredded part-skim mozzarella cheese
- 2 cans (15 ounces *each*) pizza sauce
- 1 can (10-3/4 ounces) condensed cream of mushroom soup, undiluted
- 1 package (8 ounces) sliced pepperoni

■ Cook the pasta according to package directions. Meanwhile, in a skillet, cook beef and onion over medium heat until meat is no longer pink; drain.

■ Drain pasta; place in a 5-qt. slow cooker. Stir in the beef mixture, cheese, pizza sauce, soup and pepperoni. Cover and cook on low for 2-3 hours or until heated through and the cheese is melted.

Yield: 12-14 servings.

Marilyn Wolfe
DES MOINES, IOWA

I've long relied on this hearty dish, chock-full of veggies, to fill my family's hefty appetite. My friend gave me the recipe two decades ago, and all I added was a little more meat, the celery and mushrooms.

Asian-Style Round Steak

Asian-Style Round Steak

PREP: 20 min. ■ COOK: 7 hours

2 pounds beef top round steak, cut into 3-inch strips	1 can (15 ounces) tomato sauce
2 tablespoons canola oil	1 can (14 ounces) bean sprouts, rinsed and drained
1 cup chopped onion	1 can (8 ounces) sliced water chestnuts, drained
3 celery ribs, chopped	1 jar (4-1/2 ounces) sliced mushrooms, drained
1/4 cup soy sauce	1 tablespoon cornstarch
1 teaspoon sugar	1/2 cup cold water
1/2 teaspoon salt	Hot cooked rice
1/2 teaspoon minced garlic	
1/4 teaspoon ground ginger	
1/4 teaspoon pepper	
2 medium green peppers, julienned	

■ In a large skillet, brown meat in oil on all sides. Transfer the meat and drippings to a 5-qt. slow cooker. Combine the onion, celery, soy sauce, sugar, salt, garlic, ginger and pepper; pour over meat.

■ Cover and cook on low for 5-1/2 to 6 hours or until meat is tender.

■ Add the green peppers, tomato sauce, bean sprouts, water chestnuts and mushrooms; cover and cook on low 1 hour longer.

■ In a small bowl, combine cornstarch and water until smooth; stir into beef mixture. Cover and cook on high for 30 minutes or until gravy is thickened. Serve with rice.

Yield: 8 servings.

Southwest Beef Stew*

PREP: 30 min.
COOK: 7 hours

1-1/2 pounds lean ground beef (90% lean)
  1 large onion, chopped
  2 cans (14-1/2 ounces *each*) diced tomatoes, undrained
  1 package (16 ounces) frozen corn
  1 can (15 ounces) black beans, rinsed and drained
  1 can (14-1/2 ounces) chicken broth
  1 can (10 ounces) diced tomatoes and green chilies
  1 teaspoon garlic powder
1-1/2 teaspoons salt-free Southwest chipotle seasoning blend
1-1/2 cups cooked rice
 1/4 cup shredded cheddar cheese

■ In a large skillet, cook the beef and onion over medium heat until the meat is no longer pink; drain.

■ Transfer to a 5-qt. slow cooker. Stir in the tomatoes, corn, black beans, broth, tomatoes with chilies, garlic powder and seasoning blend. Cover and cook on low for 7-8 hours or until heated through.

■ Stir in rice and heat through. Sprinkle servings with cheese.

Yield: 11 servings (2-3/4 quarts).

✱**Nutrition Facts:** 1 cup equals 228 calories, 6 g fat (3 g saturated fat), 42 mg cholesterol, 482 mg sodium, 26 g carbohydrate, 4 g fiber, 17 g protein. **Diabetic Exchanges:** 2 lean meat, 1-1/2 starch, 1 vegetable.

Anita Roberson
WILLIAMSTON, NORTH CAROLINA

Our ladies group at church has a soup and sandwich supper, and before I went to work that morning, I prepared this soup in my slow cooker. It was ready when I got home. It was such a big hit, many asked for the recipe!

Spinach Alfredo Lasagna

- In a large skillet, cook the beef, onion and garlic over medium heat until meat is no longer pink; drain. Stir in spaghetti sauce.

- Spread 1 cup of the meat sauce in an ungreased 5- or 6-qt. slow cooker. Arrange four noodles over sauce, breaking noodles to fit if necessary. In a small bowl, combine the ricotta cheese, Parmesan cheese, parsley and pepper; spread half over the noodles. Layer with 2 cups mozzarella cheese and 1 cup meat sauce.

- Top with four noodles, spinach, Alfredo sauce, 2 cups mozzarella cheese, four noodles and remaining ricotta mixture. Layer with 2 cups mozzarella cheese, 1 cup meat mixture and remaining noodles, meat sauce and mozzarella cheese.

- Cover; cook on low for 4-5 hours or until noodles are tender.

Yield: 8 servings.

Deborah Bruno
MIRA LOMA, CALIFORNIA
With Alfredo and spaghetti sauce, plus ground beef, spinach and three kinds of cheeses, this main dish is super hearty and a true crowd-pleaser.

Spinach Alfredo Lasagna

PREP: 20 min. ■ COOK: 4 hours

- 1 pound ground beef
- 1 medium onion, chopped
- 2 garlic cloves, minced
- 1 jar (24 ounces) spaghetti sauce
- 1 package (8 ounces) no-cook lasagna noodles
- 1 carton (15 ounces) ricotta cheese
- 1/2 cup grated Parmesan cheese
- 2 tablespoons minced fresh parsley
- 1/2 teaspoon pepper
- 8 cups (32 ounces) shredded part-skim mozzarella cheese
- 1 package (10 ounces) frozen chopped spinach, thawed and squeezed dry
- 1 jar (15 ounces) Alfredo sauce

When serving the Spinach Alfredo Lasagna, be sure that you scoop all the way down the ceramic insert of the slow cooker. You want to be sure that you cut through all the layers.

Susan Kain
WOODBINE, MARYLAND

As the owner of a fitness center, I rely on a slow cooker many days to create a wonderful meal for my family. This robust stew is full of herbs and spices.

Hungarian Stew

Hungarian Stew

PREP: 30 min. ■ COOK: 8 hours

4 medium potatoes, cut into 1-inch cubes
2 medium onions, chopped
1 pound beef stew meat, cut into 1-inch cubes
2 tablespoons canola oil
1-1/2 cups hot water
3 teaspoons paprika
1 teaspoon salt
1 teaspoon caraway seeds
1 teaspoon tomato paste
1 garlic clove, minced
2 medium green peppers, cut into 1-inch pieces
2 medium tomatoes, peeled, seeded and chopped
3 tablespoons all-purpose flour
3 tablespoons cold water
1/2 cup sour cream

■ Place the potatoes and onions in a 3-qt. slow cooker. In a large skillet, brown meat in oil on all sides. Place over potato mixture.

■ Pour off excess fat from skillet. Add hot water to the drippings, stirring to loosen browned bits from pan. Stir in the paprika, salt, caraway seeds, tomato paste and garlic. Pour into the slow cooker. Cover and cook on low for 7 hours.

■ Add green peppers and tomatoes. Cover; cook 1 hour or until the meat and vegetables are tender. With a slotted spoon, transfer the meat and vegetables to a large serving bowl; cover and keep warm.

■ Pour cooking juices into a small saucepan. Combine the flour and cold water until smooth; gradually whisk into the pan. Bring to a boil; cook and stir for 2 minutes or until thickened. Remove from heat; whisk in sour cream. Stir into meat mixture.

Yield: 6 servings.

Slow-Cooked Taco Meat Loaf

Lacey Kirsch
THORNTON, COLORADO

This meat loaf is a hit with my gang. It's topped with a sweet, tangy sauce.

PREP: 20 min.
COOK: 3 hours + standing

2 cups crushed tortilla chips
1 cup (4 ounces) shredded cheddar cheese
1 cup salsa
1/2 cup egg substitute
1/4 cup sliced ripe olives
1 envelope taco seasoning
2 pounds lean ground beef (90% lean)
1/2 cup ketchup
1/4 cup packed brown sugar
2 tablespoons Louisiana-style hot sauce

■ Cut three 20-in. x 3-in. strips of heavy-duty aluminum foil; crisscross so they resemble spokes of a wheel. Place strips on the bottom and up the sides of a 3-qt. slow cooker. Coat strips with cooking spray.

■ Combine the first six ingredients. Crumble beef over mixture and mix well. Shape into a round loaf. Place meat loaf in the center of the strips. Cover and cook on low for 3-4 hours or until a meat thermometer reads 160° and juices run clear.

■ Combine ketchup, brown sugar and hot sauce; pour over meat loaf during last hour of cooking. Let stand for 10 minutes. Using foil strips as handles, remove meat loaf to a platter. Remove and discard foil.

Yield: 8 servings.

Deborah Dailey
VANCOUVER,
WASHINGTON

My family loves this tangy, slow-cooked beef roast with gravy. We always hope for leftovers that I turn into tasty sandwiches.

Pot Roast with Gravy

Pot Roast with Gravy

PREP: 30 min. ■ COOK: 7-1/2 hours

- 1 beef rump roast *or* bottom round roast (5 pounds)
- 6 tablespoons balsamic vinegar, *divided*
- 1 teaspoon salt
- 1/2 teaspoon garlic powder
- 1/4 teaspoon pepper
- 2 tablespoons canola oil
- 3 garlic cloves, minced
- 4 bay leaves
- 1 large onion, thinly sliced
- 3 teaspoons beef bouillon granules
- 1/2 cup boiling water
- 1 can (10-3/4 ounces) condensed cream of mushroom soup, undiluted
- 4 to 5 tablespoons cornstarch
- 1/4 cup cold water

■ Cut roast in half; rub with 2 tablespoons vinegar. Combine the salt, garlic powder and pepper; rub over meat. In a large skillet, brown roast in oil on all sides. Transfer to a 5-qt. slow cooker.

■ Place the garlic, bay leaves and onion on roast. In a small bowl, dissolve bouillon in boiling water; stir in soup and remaining vinegar. Slowly pour over roast. Cover and cook on low for 7-8 hours or until meat is tender.

■ Remove roast; keep warm. Discard bay leaves. Whisk cornstarch and cold water until smooth; stir into cooking juices.

■ Cover and cook on high for 30 minutes or until gravy is thickened. Slice roast; return to slow cooker and heat through.

Yield: 10 servings.

Old-World Corned Beef And Vegetables

PREP: 25 min.
COOK: 8 hours

- 2-1/2 pounds red potatoes, quartered
- 2 cups fresh baby carrots
- 1 package (10 ounces) frozen pearl onions
- 1 corned beef brisket with spice packet (3 to 3-1/2 pounds)
- 1/2 cup water
- 1 tablespoon marinade for chicken
- 1/8 teaspoon pepper
- 3 tablespoons cornstarch
- 1/4 cup cold water

■ In a 5-qt. slow cooker, combine potatoes, carrots and onions. Add beef; discard spice packet from corned beef or save for another use. Combine the water, Worcestershire sauce and pepper; pour over the meat. Cover and cook on low for 8-10 hours or until meat and vegetables are tender.

■ Remove meat and vegetables to a serving platter; keep warm. Skim fat from cooking juices; transfer to a small saucepan. Bring liquid to a boil. Combine cornstarch and water until smooth. Gradually stir into the pan. Bring to a boil; cook and stir for 1-2 minutes or until thickened. Serve with meat and vegetables.

Yield: 8 servings.

Editor's Note: This recipe was tested with Lea & Perrins Marinade for Chicken.

Ruth Burrus
ZIONSVILLE, INDIANA

This traditional corned beef dinner is a winner with my husband, family and friends. The potatoes, baby carrots and pearl onions cook together with the corned beef for a convenient and easy meal-in-one. It's great for special celebrations, like St. Patrick's Day.

Sandra Dudley
BEMIDJI, MINNESOTA

Because this healthy dish is slow cooked, you can use less-expensive roasts with results that are just as mouthwatering as the more costly cuts. I enjoy the variety of vegetables in this dish, but go ahead and change up the veggies to suit your tastes!

Beef Roast Dinner

PREP: 20 min. ■ COOK: 8 hours

1	pound red potatoes (about 4 medium), cubed
1/4	pound small fresh mushrooms
1-1/2	cups fresh baby carrots
1	medium green pepper, chopped
1	medium parsnip, chopped
1	small red onion, chopped
1	beef rump roast or bottom round roast (3 pounds)
1	can (14-1/2 ounces) beef broth
3/4	teaspoon salt
3/4	teaspoon dried oregano
1/4	teaspoon pepper
3	tablespoons cornstarch
1/4	cup cold water

■ Place vegetables in a 5-qt. slow cooker. Cut roast in half; place in slow cooker. Combine the broth, salt, oregano and pepper; pour over meat. Cover and cook on low for 8 hours or until meat is tender.

■ Remove meat and vegetables to a serving platter; keep warm. Skim the fat from the cooking juices; transfer juices to a small saucepan. Bring the liquid to a boil.

■ Combine cornstarch and water until smooth. Gradually stir into the pan. Bring to a boil; cook and stir for 2 minutes or until thickened. Serve with the meat and vegetables.

Yield: 10 servings.

Italian Chuck Roast

Jenny Bloomquist
HELENA, MONTANA
Moist, flavorful and a cinch to throw together, this roast creates a rich, glossy gravy that tastes wonderful over noodles or potatoes. The beef is also delicious when it's shredded for sandwiches.

PREP: 10 min. ■ COOK: 8 hours

1	boneless beef chuck roast (4 pounds)
1	package Italian salad dressing mix
1	envelope au jus gravy mix
1	envelope brown gravy mix
1/2	cup water, *divided*

■ Cut roast in half. Transfer to a 4- or 5-qt. slow cooker. Combine the salad dressing mix, au jus mix and gravy mix with 1/4 cup water; rub over the roast. Pour the remaining water around the roast.

■ Cover and cook on low for 8-10 hours or until the meat is tender. Serve with the gravy.

Yield: 10 servings.

Egg Noodle Lasagna

Mary Oberlin
SELINSGROVE, PENNSYLVANIA
I was lucky enough to receive this recipe from one of my friends. The perfect take-along for charity events and church potlucks, the comforting entree satisfies everyone who tries it.

PREP: 15 min.
COOK: 4 hours

6-1/2	cups uncooked wide egg noodles
3	tablespoons butter
1-1/2	pounds ground beef
2-1/4	cups spaghetti sauce
6	ounces process cheese (Velveeta), cubed
3	cups (12 ounces) shredded part-skim mozzarella cheese

■ Cook the noodles according to package directions; drain. Add butter; toss to coat.

■ In a large skillet, cook beef over medium heat until no longer pink; drain. Spread a fourth of the spaghetti sauce into an ungreased 5-qt. slow cooker. Layer with a third of the noodles, a third of the beef, a third of the remaining sauce and a third of the cheeses. Repeat layers twice.

■ Cover; cook on low for 4 hours or until cheese is melted and lasagna is heated through.

Yield: 12-16 servings.

Deanne Stephens
MCMINNVILLE, OREGON

My mom used to make this wonderful dish, and it's always been one that I love. I especially like how the thick gravy drapes both the meat and the potatoes.

Round Steak Italiano

Round Steak Italiano*

PREP: 15 min. ■ COOK: 7 hours 15 min.

- 2 pounds beef top round steak
- 1 can (8 ounces) tomato sauce
- 2 tablespoons onion soup mix
- 2 tablespoons canola oil
- 2 tablespoons red wine vinegar
- 1 teaspoon ground oregano
- 1/2 teaspoon garlic powder
- 1/4 teaspoon pepper
- 8 medium potatoes (7 to 8 ounces *each*)
- 1 tablespoon cornstarch
- 1 tablespoon cold water

■ Cut steak into serving-size pieces; place in a 5-qt. slow cooker. In a large bowl, combine the tomato sauce, soup mix, oil, vinegar, oregano, garlic powder and pepper; pour over meat. Scrub and pierce potatoes; place over meat. Cover and cook on low for 7 to 7-1/2 hours or until meat and potatoes are tender.

■ Remove meat and potatoes; keep warm. For gravy, pour cooking juices into a small saucepan; skim fat.

■ Combine cornstarch and water until smooth; gradually stir into juices. Bring to a boil; cook and stir for 2 minutes or until thickened. Serve with meat and potatoes.

Yield: 8 servings.

*Nutrition Facts: 3 ounces cooked beef with 1 potato and 3 tablespoons gravy equals 357 calories, 7 g fat (2 g saturated fat), 64 mg cholesterol, 329 mg sodium, 42 g carbohydrate, 4 g fiber, 31 g protein. Diabetic Exchanges: 3 lean meat, 2-1/2 starch, 1/2 fat.

Hawaiian Meatballs

Julie Schiefer
NAPPANEE, INDIANA

My mother-in-law gave me a close version of this recipe, which is one of my husband's favorites. My oldest daughter asked for this entree for her graduation party. One of her teachers raved about it!

PREP: 30 min.
COOK: 6 hours

- 1 can (20 ounces) unsweetened pineapple chunks, undrained
- 1/2 cup packed brown sugar
- 1/4 cup cornstarch
- 1/2 cup cider vinegar
- 1 package (32 ounces) frozen fully cooked home-style meatballs
- 2 medium green peppers, cut into 1-inch pieces
- 1 jar (10 ounces) maraschino cherries, drained

Hot cooked rice, optional

■ Drain pineapple, reserving juice, in a 2-cup measuring cup; add enough water to measure 2 cups. In a small saucepan, combine brown sugar and cornstarch. Gradually stir in juice mixture until smooth. Stir in vinegar. Bring to a boil; cook and stir for 2 minutes or until thickened.

■ In a 3-qt. slow cooker, combine the meatballs, peppers and pineapple chunks. Stir in pineapple juice mixture. Cover and cook pineapple on low for 6-8 hours or until heated through and peppers are tender, adding cherries during the last 30 minutes of cooking. Serve with rice if desired.

Yield: 8 servings.

Barbecue Beef Brisket

Braised Beef Short Ribs

Cheryl Martinetto
GRAND RAPIDS, MINNESOTA

The chili sauce and seasonings add a wonderful flavor to these beef short ribs. After slow cooking for a good time, they come out juicy every time. I like to serve them over rich mashed potatoes for a super, robust meal.

PREP: 15 min.
COOK: 6 hours

4	pounds bone-in beef short ribs
2	tablespoons canola oil
2-1/2	cups sliced onions
1-1/2	cups beef broth
1-1/2	cups chili sauce
2/3	cup cider vinegar
1	tablespoon brown sugar
2	teaspoons paprika
1-1/2	teaspoons curry powder
1	teaspoon minced garlic
1	teaspoon salt
1/2	teaspoon ground mustard
1/2	teaspoon pepper

■ In a large skillet, brown the beef short ribs in the oil in batches. Transfer to a 5-qt. slow cooker and add the onions. Combine the remaining ingredients; pour over the ribs. Cover and cook on low for 6-7 hours or until the meat is tender.

Yield: 8 servings.

Taste of Home Test Kitchen
This is such a simple dish, but oh boy, is it delicious. The meat comes out moist and tender and tastes great with rice or potatoes.

Barbecue Beef Brisket

PREP: 20 min. ■ **COOK:** 6 hours

1	fresh beef brisket (3 pounds)	1	teaspoon salt
1	cup barbecue sauce	1/2	teaspoon pepper
1/2	cup finely chopped onion	3	tablespoons cornstarch
2	tablespoons Worcestershire sauce	1/4	cup cold water
1	tablespoon prepared horseradish		

■ Cut the brisket in half; place in a 5-qt. slow cooker. Combine the barbecue sauce, onion, Worcestershire sauce, horseradish, salt and pepper; pour over beef. Cover and cook on low for 6-7 hours or until meat is tender.

■ Remove the beef and keep warm. Transfer cooking juices to a large saucepan; bring to a boil. Combine the cornstarch and water until smooth. Gradually stir into the pan. Bring to a boil; cook and stir for 2 minutes or until thickened. Slice meat across grain; serve with gravy.

Yield: 6 servings.

Editor's Note: This is a fresh beef brisket, not corned beef.

Brisket 'n' Bean Burritos

Ruth Weatherford
HUNTINGTON BEACH, CALIFORNIA
Smoky bacon and moist beef make this easy recipe a real winner. You can also add your choice of toppings to the filling, such as shredded lettuce, sour cream or diced avocado.

Brisket 'n' Bean Burritos

PREP: 20 min. ■ COOK: 4-1/2 hours

1 fresh beef brisket (2 pounds)	1/2 cup salsa
1 cup chopped onion	1 can (4 ounces) chopped green chilies
3 bacon strips, diced	1-1/2 cups (6 ounces) shredded Monterey Jack cheese
1 can (8 ounces) tomato sauce	
3/4 teaspoon pepper	10 flour tortillas (10 inches), warmed
1/4 teaspoon salt	
1 can (16 ounces) refried beans	

■ Place brisket in a 5-qt. slow cooker; top with onion and bacon. Combine the tomato sauce, pepper and salt; pour over meat. Cover and cook on low for 4-1/2 to 5 hours or until meat is tender.

■ In a microwave-safe bowl, combine the refried beans, salsa and chilies. Cover and microwave on high for 2-3 minutes or until heated through. Remove meat from slow cooker; shred with two forks.

■ Layer the bean mixture, meat and cheese off-center on each tortilla. Fold sides and ends over filling and roll up.

Yield: 10 servings.

Editor's Note: This is a fresh beef brisket, not corned beef.

Barbecued Beef Short Ribs

Erin Glass
WHITE HALL, MARYLAND
These tender, slow-cooked ribs with a tangy sauce are a cinch to make. They're great for picnics and parties.

PREP: 25 min.
COOK: 5 hours

4 pounds bone-in beef short ribs, trimmed
2 tablespoons canola oil
1 large sweet onion, halved and sliced
1 bottle (12 ounces) chili sauce
3/4 cup plum preserves *or* preserves of your choice
2 tablespoons brown sugar
2 tablespoons red wine vinegar
2 tablespoons Worcestershire sauce
2 tablespoons Dijon mustard
1/4 teaspoon ground cloves

■ In a large skillet, brown the ribs in oil in batches. Place the onion in a 5-qt. slow cooker; add ribs. Cover and cook on low for 4-1/2 to 5 hours or until meat is tender.

■ In a small saucepan, combine the remaining ingredients. Cook and stir over medium heat for 4-6 minutes or until heated through.

■ Remove ribs from slow cooker. Skim fat from cooking juices. Return ribs to slow cooker; pour sauce over ribs. Cover and cook on high for 25-30 minutes or until sauce is thickened.

Yield: 8 servings.

Annette
Mosbarger
PEYTON, COLORADO

This easy recipe came from my sister and has been a family favorite for years. Pineapple and peppers add color and taste.

Polynesian Roast Beef

Polynesian Roast Beef

PREP: 15 min. ■ COOK: 8 hours

1 beef top round roast (3-1/4 pounds)
2 tablespoons browning sauce, optional
1/4 cup all-purpose flour
1 teaspoon salt
1/4 teaspoon pepper
1 medium onion, sliced
1 can (8 ounces) unsweetened sliced pineapple
1/4 cup packed brown sugar
2 tablespoons cornstarch
1/4 teaspoon ground ginger
1/2 cup beef broth
1/4 cup soy sauce
1/2 teaspoon minced garlic
1 medium green pepper, sliced

■ Cut roast in half; brush with browning sauce if desired. Combine the flour, salt and pepper; rub over meat. Place onion in a 3-qt. slow cooker; top with roast.

■ Drain pineapple, reserving juice; refrigerate the pineapple. In a small bowl, combine the brown sugar, cornstarch and ginger; whisk in the broth, soy sauce, garlic and reserved pineapple juice until smooth. Pour over meat. Cover and cook on low for 7-8 hours.

■ Add pineapple and green pepper. Cook 1 hour longer or until meat and green pepper are tender.

Yield: 10-11 servings.

Moroccan Braised Beef

Taste of Home Test Kitchen

Curry powder is a blend of up to 20 spices, herbs and seeds. In this Moroccan stew, begin by adding 2 teaspoons curry, then adjust to your taste.

PREP: 20 min.
COOK: 7 hours

1/3 cup all-purpose flour
2 pounds boneless beef chuck roast, cut into 1-inch cubes
3 tablespoons olive oil
2 cans (14-1/2 ounces *each*) beef broth
2 cups chopped onions
1 can (14-1/2 ounces) diced tomatoes, undrained
1 cup dry red wine
1 tablespoon curry powder
1 tablespoon paprika
1 teaspoon salt
1 teaspoon ground cumin
1 teaspoon ground coriander
1/2 teaspoon cayenne pepper
1-1/2 cups golden raisins
Hot cooked couscous, optional

■ Place flour in a large resealable plastic bag; add beef and toss to coat. In a large skillet, brown beef in oil. Transfer to a 5-qt. slow cooker. Stir in the broth, onions, tomatoes, wine and seasonings. Cover and cook on low for 7-8 hours or until the meat is tender.

■ During the last 30 minutes of cooking, stir in the raisins. Serve with couscous if desired.

Yield: 6 servings.

Poultry

46

52

49

With the delicious chicken and turkey entrees in this chapter, you just might find a new favorite slow cooker recipe. There's a world of flavor in the wonderful variety of dishes offered here.

Creole Chicken Thighs

Turkey with Cranberry Sauce

Marie Ramsden
FAIRGROVE, MICHIGAN

This is a very tasty and simple way to cook a turkey breast in the slow cooker. Ideal for holiday potlucks, the sweet cranberry sauce complements the turkey nicely.

PREP: 15 min.
BAKE: 4 hours

  2 boneless skinless turkey breast halves (4 pounds *each*)
  1 can (14 ounces) jellied cranberry sauce
1/2 cup plus 2 tablespoons water, *divided*
  1 envelope onion soup mix
  2 tablespoons cornstarch

■ Cut each turkey breast in half; place in two 5-qt. slow cookers. In a large bowl, combine the cranberry sauce, 1/2 cup water and soup mix. Pour half over each turkey. Cover and cook on low for 4-6 hours or until the turkey is no longer pink and meat thermometer reads 170°. Remove turkey and keep warm.

■ Transfer both of the cranberry mixtures to a large saucepan. Combine the cornstarch and remaining water until smooth. Bring the cranberry mixture to a boil; gradually stir in the cornstarch mixture until smooth. Cook and stir for 2 minutes or until thickened. Slice turkey; serve with the cranberry sauce. May be frozen up to 3 months.

Yield: 20-25 servings.

Matthew Laman
HUMMELSTOWN, PENNSYLVANIA

Cajun seasoning adds loads of flavor and spice to this easy-to-assemble meal. The slow cooker does the work so you don't have to!

Creole Chicken Thighs

PREP: 30 min. ■ **COOK:** 7 hours

    8 bone-in chicken thighs (about 2-1/2 pounds), skin removed
    3 tablespoons Cajun seasoning, *divided*
    1 tablespoon canola oil
3-1/2 cups chicken broth
    1 can (16 ounces) red beans, rinsed and drained
1-1/2 cups uncooked converted rice
    2 medium tomatoes, finely chopped
    1 medium green pepper, chopped
    2 tablespoons minced fresh parsley

■ Sprinkle the chicken with 1 tablespoon Cajun seasoning. In a large skillet, brown the chicken in oil.

■ In a 5-qt. slow cooker, combine the broth, beans, rice, tomatoes, green pepper, parsley and the remaining Cajun seasoning. Top with chicken. Cover and cook on low for 7-8 hours or until chicken is tender.

Yield: 8 servings.

Mandarin Chicken

Aney Chatterson
SODA SPRINGS, IDAHO
Oranges and olives are elegantly paired in this unique but delicious dish. The chicken is marinated, then cooked slowly in a flavorful sauce, so it stays moist.

Mandarin Chicken

PREP: 10 min. + marinating ■ COOK: 7-1/2 hours

2 cups water
1 cup ketchup
1/4 cup packed brown sugar
1/4 cup soy sauce
1/4 cup orange juice concentrate
2 teaspoons salt
2 teaspoons ground mustard
1 teaspoon garlic salt
1 teaspoon ground ginger
1 teaspoon pepper

1 broiler/fryer chicken (3 to 3-1/2 pounds), cut up and skin removed
3 tablespoons cornstarch
1/2 cup cold water
1 can (11 ounces) mandarin oranges, drained
1/2 cup whole pitted ripe olives
2 tablespoons chopped green pepper
Hot cooked rice

■ In a large bowl, combine water, ketchup, brown sugar, soy sauce, orange juice concentrate, salt, mustard, garlic salt, ginger and pepper. Pour half into a large resealable plastic bag; add the chicken. Seal bag and turn to coat; refrigerate for 8 hours or overnight. Cover and refrigerate remaining marinade.

■ Drain and discard marinade from chicken. Place chicken in a 5-qt. slow cooker; add the reserved marinade. Cover and cook on low for 7-8 hours or until chicken juices run clear.

■ Combine cornstarch and cold water until smooth; gradually stir into chicken mixture. Add the oranges, olives and green pepper. Cover and cook on high for 30-45 minutes or until thickened. Serve with rice.

Yield: 4-6 servings.

A broiler/fryer

chicken is one that has been cut into two breast halves, two thighs, two drumsticks and two wings. It may or may not have the back.

Jenny Cook
EAU CLAIRE, WISCONSIN

I don't know where this recipe originally came from, but my mother used to make it for us when I was little. Now I love to make it. A sweet and tangy sauce nicely coats chicken that's ready in a few hours.

Lemonade Chicken

Lemonade Chicken*

PREP: 10 min. ■ **COOK:** 3 hours

 6 boneless skinless chicken breast halves (4 ounces each)
 3/4 cup thawed lemonade concentrate
 3 tablespoons ketchup
 2 tablespoons brown sugar
 1 tablespoon cider vinegar
 2 tablespoons cornstarch
 2 tablespoons cold water

■ Place chicken in a 5-qt. slow cooker. In a small bowl, combine the lemonade concentrate, ketchup, brown sugar and vinegar; pour over the chicken. Cover and cook on low for 2-1/2 hours or until the chicken is tender.

■ Remove chicken and keep warm. For gravy, combine cornstarch and water until smooth; gradually stir into cooking juices. Cover and cook on high for 30 minutes or until thickened. Return chicken to the slow cooker; heat through.

Yield: 6 servings.

✱Nutrition Facts: 1 chicken breast half with 1/4 cup sauce equals 208 calories, 3 g fat (1 g saturated fat), 63 mg cholesterol, 147 mg sodium, 22 g carbohydrate, trace fiber, 23 g protein. **Diabetic Exchanges:** 3 very lean meat, 1-1/2 fruit.

Herbed Chicken And Veggies

Dorothy Pritchett
WILLS POINT, TEXAS

This subtly seasoned chicken and vegetable combination is a snap to prepare on a hectic workday. A dessert is all that's needed to complete this satisfying supper.

PREP: 20 min.
COOK: 7-3/4 hours

 1 broiler/fryer chicken (3 to 4 pounds), cut up and skin removed
 2 medium tomatoes, chopped
 1 medium onion, chopped
 2 garlic cloves, minced
 1/2 cup chicken broth
 2 tablespoons white wine *or* additional chicken broth
 1 bay leaf
 1-1/2 teaspoons salt
 1 teaspoon dried thyme
 1/4 teaspoon pepper
 2 cups fresh broccoli florets
Hot cooked rice

■ Place chicken in a 3-qt. slow cooker. Top with the tomatoes, onion and garlic. Combine the broth, wine, bay leaf, salt, thyme and pepper; pour over chicken. Cover and cook on low for 7-8 hours.

■ Add the broccoli; cook 45-60 minutes longer or until chicken juices run clear and broccoli is tender. Discard the bay leaf. Thicken pan juices if desired. Serve with rice.

Yield: 4-6 servings.

Nancy Wit
FREMONT, NEBRASKA

I created this recipe to prepare a dish lower in calories and fat. Everyone likes the taste, including my grandchildren. A hint of orange adds yummy flavor. This favorite dish travels well, and I often take it to potlucks.

Slow-Cooked Orange Chicken

Slow-Cooked Orange Chicken*

PREP: 10 min. ■ **COOK:** 4-1/2 hours

1 broiler/fryer chicken (3 pounds), cut up and skin removed	1 tablespoon minced fresh parsley *or* 1 teaspoon dried parsley flakes
3 cups orange juice	1/2 teaspoon salt, optional
1 cup chopped celery	1/4 teaspoon pepper
1 cup chopped green pepper	3 tablespoons cornstarch
1 can (4 ounces) mushroom stems and pieces, drained	3 tablespoons cold water
4 teaspoons dried minced onion	Hot cooked rice, optional
	Additional minced fresh parsley, optional

■ In a 3-qt. slow cooker, combine the first nine ingredients. Cover and cook on low for 4-5 hours or until chicken juices run clear.

■ Combine the cornstarch and water until smooth; gradually stir into the cooking liquid. Cover; cook on high for 30-45 minutes or until thickened. Serve with the rice and sprinkle with the parsley if desired.

Yield: 4 servings.

✱Nutrition Facts: 1 serving (prepared without salt; calculated without rice) equals 306 calories, 10 g fat (0 saturated fat), 70 mg cholesterol, 189 mg sodium, 31 g carbohydrate, 0 fiber, 23 g protein. **Diabetic Exchanges:** 3 lean meat, 1 starch, 1 fruit.

Creamy Herbed Chicken

PREP: 5 min.
COOK: 4 hours

- 4 boneless skinless chicken breast halves (4 ounces *each*)
- 1 can (10-3/4 ounces) condensed cream of chicken soup, undiluted
- 1 cup milk
- 1 envelope garlic and herb pasta sauce mix
- 1 teaspoon dried thyme
- 1 teaspoon dried parsley flakes

Hot cooked fettuccine

■ Place the chicken in a 3-qt. slow cooker. Combine the soup, milk, sauce mix, thyme and parsley; pour over chicken. Cover and cook on low for 4-5 hours or until chicken is tender. Serve with fettuccine.

Yield: 4 servings.

Editor's Note: This recipe was tested with Knorr Garlic Herb Pasta Sauce Mix.

Mary Humeniuk-Smith
PERRY HALL, MARYLAND

I'm a nurse and work nights, so when I get home in the morning, I put this chicken in the slow cooker so it's ready at suppertime for my family. At the end of the day, the chicken is moist and tender, and the rich sauce seasoned with garlic and thyme is delicious.

Roxanne Chan
ALBANY, CALIFORNIA

If you enjoy Indian food, you'll love this dish. An array of spices and dried fruit slow cook with boneless chicken thighs for an aromatic and satisfying dinner. To make it a complete meal, I like to serve it over Jasmine or Basmati rice.

Casablanca Chutney Chicken

PREP: 25 min. ■ COOK: 7 hours

- 1 pound boneless skinless chicken thighs, cut into 3/4-inch pieces
- 1 can (14-1/2 ounces) chicken broth
- 1/3 cup finely chopped onion
- 1/3 cup chopped sweet red pepper
- 1/3 cup chopped carrot
- 1/3 cup chopped dried apricots
- 1/3 cup chopped dried figs
- 1/3 cup golden raisins
- 2 tablespoons orange marmalade
- 1 tablespoon mustard seed
- 2 garlic cloves, minced
- 1/2 teaspoon curry powder
- 1/4 teaspoon crushed red pepper flakes
- 1/4 teaspoon ground cumin
- 1/4 teaspoon ground cinnamon
- 1/4 teaspoon ground cloves
- 2 tablespoons minced fresh parsley
- 2 tablespoons minced fresh mint
- 1 tablespoon lemon juice
- 4 tablespoons chopped pistachios

■ In a 3-qt. slow cooker, combine the first 16 ingredients. Cover and cook on low for 7-8 hours or until chicken is tender. Stir in the parsley, mint and lemon juice; heat through. Sprinkle each serving with pistachios.

Yield: 4 servings.

Slow-Cooked Asian Chicken

Ruth Seitz
COLUMBUS JUNCTION, IOWA

Tender chicken is smothered in a dark, flavorful sauce in this easy and elegant entree. This is a dish I proudly serve to family or guests.

PREP: 20 min. ■ COOK: 5 hours

- 1 broiler/fryer chicken (3-1/2 to 4 pounds), cut up
- 2 tablespoons canola oil
- 1/3 cup soy sauce
- 2 tablespoons brown sugar
- 2 tablespoons water
- 1 garlic clove, minced
- 1 teaspoon ground ginger
- 1/4 cup slivered almonds

■ In a large skillet over medium heat, brown the chicken in oil on both sides. Transfer to a 5-qt. slow cooker. In a small bowl, combine the soy sauce, brown sugar, water, garlic and ginger; pour over chicken.

■ Cover and cook on low for 5-6 hours or until chicken juices run clear. Remove chicken to a serving platter and sprinkle with almonds.

Yield: 4-6 servings.

Turkey Thigh Supper

Betty Gingrich
OXFORD, ARKANSAS

This family-pleasing meal-in-one has it all—tender turkey thighs, tasty vegetables and a home-made sauce. You can substitute chicken breasts for the turkey or honey-flavored barbecue sauce for the soup mixture.

PREP: 10 min.
COOK: 7 hours

- 3 medium red potatoes, cut into chunks
- 1/2 pound fresh baby carrots
- 2 medium onions, cut into chunks
- 4 turkey thighs, skin removed
- 1 can (10-3/4 ounces) condensed tomato soup, undiluted
- 1/3 cup water
- 1 teaspoon minced garlic
- 1 teaspoon Italian seasoning
- 1/2 to 1 teaspoon salt

■ In a 5-qt. slow cooker, layer the potatoes, carrots and onions. Top with turkey. Combine soup, water, garlic, Italian seasoning and salt; pour over the turkey. Cover and cook on high for 7-8 hours or until a meat thermometer reads 180° and vegetables are tender.

Yield: 4 servings.

Ginny Stuby
ALTOONA,
PENNSYLVANIA

This easy meal-in-a-pot is both healthy and delicious. It's wonderful served with a slice of Italian or hot garlic bread. I found the recipe in a magazine and made just a few adjustments to suit myself. Enjoy!

Italian Sausage and Vegetables

Italian Sausage and Vegetables

PREP: 20 min. ■ COOK: 5-1/2 hours

1-1/4 pounds sweet *or* hot Italian turkey sausage links

1 can (28 ounces) diced tomatoes, undrained

2 medium potatoes, cut into 1-inch pieces

4 small zucchini, cut into 1-inch slices

1 medium onion, cut into wedges

1/2 teaspoon garlic powder

1/4 teaspoon crushed red pepper flakes

1/4 teaspoon dried oregano

1/4 teaspoon dried basil

1 tablespoon dry bread crumbs

3/4 cup shredded pepper Jack cheese

■ In a nonstick skillet, cook the sausages over medium heat until sausages are no longer pink; drain. Place in a 5-qt. slow cooker. Add vegetables and seasonings. Cover and cook on low for 5-1/2 to 6-1/2 hours or until vegetables are tender.

■ Remove the sausages and cut into 1-in. pieces; return to slow cooker. Stir in bread crumbs. Serve in bowls; sprinkle with the cheese.

Yield: 6 servings.

No-Fuss Chicken

Mark Twiest
ALLENDALE, MICHIGAN

My mother-in-law devised this recipe when her children were growing up and schedules were hectic. It was a favorite Sunday dish because it could be cooking while the family was at church. When they came home, it didn't take long to finish the preparations and put dinner on the table.

PREP: 20 min.
COOK: 2 hours

1-1/3 cups all-purpose flour

2 teaspoons dried sage leaves

2 teaspoons dried basil

2 teaspoons seasoned salt

1 broiler/fryer chicken (2-1/2 to 3 pounds), cut up

1/4 cup butter

2 cups chicken broth

■ In a large resealable plastic bag, combine flour, sage, basil and seasoned salt, reserving 1/4 cup. Add chicken, a few pieces at a time, and shake to coat. In a large skillet, brown chicken in butter on all sides.

■ Transfer chicken to a 5-qt. slow cooker. Add the reserved flour mixture to the skillet; stir until smooth. When mixture begins to bubble, stir in the chicken broth and bring to a boil; boil for 1 minute. Pour over chicken. Cover and cook on high for 2 to 2-1/2 hours or until chicken juices run clear.

Yield: 4 servings.

Chicken with Mushroom Gravy

Creamy Chicken Fettuccine

Melissa Cowser
GREENVILLE, TEXAS
This creamy pasta is loaded with delicious chunks of chicken.

PREP: 15 min.
COOK: 3 hours

1-1/2 pounds boneless skinless chicken breasts, cut into cubes

  1/2 teaspoon garlic powder

  1/2 teaspoon onion powder

  1/8 teaspoon pepper

    1 can (10-3/4 ounces) condensed cream of chicken soup, undiluted

    1 can (10-3/4 ounces) condensed cream of celery soup, undiluted

    4 ounces process cheese (Velveeta), cubed

    1 can (2-1/4 ounces) sliced ripe olives, drained

    1 jar (2 ounces) diced pimientos, drained, optional

    1 package (16 ounces) fettuccine *or* spaghetti

Thin breadsticks, optional

■ Place chicken in a 3-qt. slow cooker; sprinkle with the garlic powder, onion powder and pepper. Top with soups. Cover and cook on high for 3-4 hours or until chicken is no longer pink.

■ Stir in the cheese, olives and pimientos if desired. Cover and cook until cheese is melted. Meanwhile, cook the fettuccine according to package directions; drain. Serve with chicken and breadsticks if desired.

Yield: 6 servings.

Darolyn Jones
FISHERS, INDIANA
This moist chicken is a longtime favorite with family and friends. A friend shared the recipe years ago, and I added a few new ingredients. I serve it over mashed potatoes or rice.

Chicken with Mushroom Gravy

PREP: 10 min. ■ **COOK:** 4-1/4 hours

    4 boneless skinless chicken breast halves (6 ounces *each*)

    1 can (12 ounces) mushroom gravy

    1 cup 2% milk

    1 can (8 ounces) mushroom stems and pieces, drained

    1 can (4 ounces) chopped green chilies

    1 envelope Italian salad dressing mix

    1 package (8 ounces) cream cheese, cubed

■ In a 3-qt. slow cooker, combine the chicken, gravy, milk, mushrooms, chilies and dressing mix. Cover and cook on low for 4 to 4-1/2 hours or until chicken is tender.

■ Stir in the cream cheese; cover and cook 15 minutes longer or until cheese is melted.

Yield: 4 servings.

Turkey Sloppy Joes

Nichole Jones
PLEASANT GROVE, UTAH

The chili sauce and ground turkey that are used to make these sloppy joes create a deliciously unique flavor. The avocado adds a special taste to the sandwiches.

Turkey Sloppy Joes

PREP: 35 min. ■ **COOK:** 4 hours

1-1/2 pounds lean ground turkey	1 teaspoon ground cumin
2 medium onions, finely chopped	1 teaspoon paprika
4 garlic cloves, minced	1/2 teaspoon salt
1 jar (12 ounces) chili sauce	1/2 teaspoon pepper
1 jalapeno pepper, seeded and chopped	2 cups (8 ounces) shredded Monterey Jack cheese
1 tablespoon Worcestershire sauce	8 onion rolls, split
2 teaspoons dried oregano	2 medium ripe avocados, peeled and thinly sliced

■ In a large skillet coated with cooking spray, cook the turkey, onions and garlic over medium heat until meat is no longer pink; drain.

■ Transfer to a 1-1/2-qt. slow cooker. Stir in the chili sauce, jalapeno, Worcestershire sauce, oregano, cumin, paprika, salt and pepper. Cover and cook on low for 4-5 hours or until heated through. Just before serving, stir in cheese. Serve on rolls topped with avocado.

Yield: 8 servings.

Editor's Note: When cutting hot peppers, disposable gloves are recommended. Avoid touching your face.

Chicken with Vegetables

Norlene Razak
KYLE, TEXAS

This tender chicken entree comes together surprisingly easy.

PREP: 25 min.
COOK: 5 hours

1 cup sliced fresh mushrooms
4 chicken drumsticks, skin removed
4 bone-in chicken thighs (about 1-1/2 pounds), skin removed
4 celery ribs, sliced
1 cup sliced zucchini
1 cup sliced carrots
1 medium onion, sliced
1 cup tomato juice
1/2 cup chicken broth
1 garlic clove, minced
1/4 teaspoon paprika
Pepper to taste
3 tablespoons cornstarch
3 tablespoons cold water
Hot cooked rice

■ Place mushrooms and chicken in a 3-qt. slow cooker. Add the vegetables, tomato juice, broth, garlic, paprika and pepper. Cover and cook on low for 5 hours or until chicken is tender.

■ Remove chicken and veggies to a platter; keep warm. Skim fat from cooking juices; transfer to a small pot. Bring liquid to a boil. Mix the cornstarch and water until smooth; slowly stir into pan. Bring to a boil; cook and stir for 2 minutes or until thickened. Serve with chicken and vegetables. Serve with rice.

Yield: 4 servings.

Chicken with Cream Cheese Sauce

Julie Quail
ORION, MICHIGAN

Cream cheese adds richness and wonderful flavor to the sauce in this recipe. The almonds sprinkled over the finished dish are a nice touch.

PREP: 20 min. ■ COOK: 4 hours

- 4 bone-in chicken breast halves (12 ounces *each*), skin removed
- 2 tablespoons butter, melted
- 1 envelope Italian salad dressing mix
- 1/4 teaspoon salt
- 1/4 teaspoon pepper
- 3/4 cup chicken broth, *divided*
- 1 medium onion, chopped
- 1 tablespoon butter
- 1 can (10-3/4 ounces) condensed cream of chicken soup, undiluted
- 2 garlic cloves, minced
- 6 ounces cream cheese, cubed

Hot cooked rice

- 1/4 cup slivered almonds, toasted

■ Brush chicken with butter; sprinkle with dressing mix, salt and pepper. Pour 1/4 cup broth into a 5-qt. slow cooker; add chicken. Cover and cook on low for 4-5 hours or until a meat thermometer reads 170°. Remove to a serving platter and keep warm. Reserve 3/4 cup cooking juices; set aside.

■ In a large saucepan, cook onion in butter over medium heat until tender. Stir in the soup, cooking juices, garlic and remaining broth; heat through. Add cream cheese; cook and stir until cheese is melted. Serve with chicken and rice; sprinkle with almonds.

Yield: 4 servings.

Toasting nuts before using them in a recipe intensifies their flavor. For slivered almonds, spread the nuts on a baking sheet and bake at 350° for 3 to 6 minutes or until lightly toasted. Be sure to watch them carefully so they don't burn.

Tarragon Mushroom Chicken

Mary Kretschmer
MIAMI, FLORIDA

Round out this saucy seasoned chicken with some rice or pasta. I often make this dish when my children and grandchildren visit. Using the slow cooker leaves me more time to enjoy their company.

PREP: 20 min.
COOK: 4 hours

- 6 boneless skinless chicken breast halves (4 ounces *each*)
- 1 can (10-3/4 ounces) condensed cream of chicken soup, undiluted
- 1 jar (4-1/2 ounces) sliced mushrooms, drained
- 1/2 cup sherry *or* chicken broth
- 2 tablespoons butter, melted
- 1 teaspoon dried tarragon
- 1 teaspoon Worcestershire sauce
- 1/4 teaspoon garlic powder
- 1/4 cup all-purpose flour

■ Place chicken in a 5-qt. slow cooker. Combine the soup, mushrooms, sherry, butter, tarragon, Worcestershire sauce and garlic powder; pour over chicken. Cover and cook on low for 4-5 hours or until chicken is tender.

■ Remove the chicken and keep warm. Place the flour in a small saucepan; gradually whisk in cooking liquid until blended. Bring to a boil; cook and stir for 2 minutes or until thickened. Serve with chicken.

Yield: 6 servings.

Tangy Tender Chicken

Milton Schutz
PANDORA, OHIO

Brown sugar, garlic and ginger provide the traditional sweet-sour flavor in this chicken medley. The aroma is heavenly after working outside all day.

PREP: 15 min. ■ COOK: 8-1/2 hours

1 pound baby carrots	1 tablespoon soy sauce
1 medium green pepper, cut into 1/2-inch strips	2 teaspoons chicken bouillon granules
1 medium onion, cut into wedges	1/2 teaspoon salt
6 boneless skinless chicken breast halves (4 ounces *each*)	1/2 teaspoon ground ginger
	1/4 teaspoon garlic powder
1 can (20 ounces) pineapple chunks	3 tablespoons cornstarch
	1/4 cup cold water
1/3 cup packed brown sugar	Hot cooked rice

■ In a 5-qt. slow cooker, layer the carrots, green pepper and onion. Top with chicken. Drain pineapple, reserving juice. Place pineapple over chicken. Add brown sugar, soy sauce, bouillon, salt, ginger and garlic powder to pineapple juice; pour over pineapple. Cover and cook on low for 8-9 hours or until chicken is tender.

■ Combine cornstarch and water until smooth; gradually stir into cooking juices. Cook 30 minutes longer or until sauce is thickened, stirring once. Serve with rice.

Yield: 4-6 servings.

Both light and dark brown sugar are a mixture of granulated sugars and molasses, with dark brown sugar containing more molasses than light brown sugar. Light brown sugar has a delicate flavor while dark brown sugar has a stronger more intense molasses flavor. They can be used interchangeably depending on your personal preference.

Cranberry Turkey Breast With Gravy*

PREP: 15 min.
COOK: 5 hours

- 1 bone-in turkey breast (5 to 6 pounds)
- 1 can (14 ounces) whole-berry cranberry sauce
- 1/4 cup orange juice
- 1 envelope onion soup mix
- 1/4 teaspoon salt
- 1/4 teaspoon pepper
- 3 to 4 teaspoons cornstarch
- 1 tablespoon water

■ Place the turkey in a 5-qt. slow cooker. Combine the cranberry sauce, orange juice, onion soup mix, salt and pepper; pour over turkey. Cover and cook on low for 5-6 hours or until tender.

■ Remove turkey to a serving platter; keep warm. Skim fat from cooking juices; transfer to a small saucepan. Bring the liquid to a boil. In a small bowl, combine the cornstarch and water until smooth. Slowly stir into pan. Bring to a boil; cook and stir for 2 minutes or until thickened. Serve with turkey.

Yield: 12 servings (3 cups gravy).

✱Nutrition Facts: 5 ounces cooked turkey with 1/4 cup gravy equals 318 calories, 10 g fat (3 g saturated fat), 102 mg cholesterol, 346 mg sodium, 15 g carbohydrate, 1 g fiber, 40 g protein. **Diabetic Exchanges:** 5 lean meat, 1 starch.

Shirley Welch
TULSA, OKLAHOMA

This is wonderful served for a celebration, because it's so convenient and takes the stress out of holiday meal-making. The turkey turns out tender and moist. You can use extra slow cookers to prepare side dishes such as homemade stuffing.

Turkey Enchiladas

Stella Schams
TEMPE, ARIZONA

I discovered a different way to serve economical turkey thighs.

PREP: 10 min.
COOK: 6 hours 10 min.

- 2 pounds turkey thighs *or* drumsticks
- 1 can (8 ounces) tomato sauce
- 1 can (4 ounces) chopped green chilies
- 1/3 cup chopped onion
- 2 tablespoons Worcestershire sauce
- 1 to 2 tablespoons chili powder
- 1/4 teaspoon garlic powder
- 8 flour tortillas (6 inches), warmed

Optional toppings: chopped green onions, sliced ripe olives, chopped tomatoes, shredded cheddar cheese, sour cream *and/or* shredded lettuce

- Remove skin from turkey. Place in a 5-qt. slow cooker. Combine the tomato sauce, chilies, onion, Worcestershire sauce, chili powder and garlic powder; pour over turkey. Cover and cook on low for 6-8 hours or until turkey is tender.

- Remove turkey; shred meat with a fork and return to the slow cooker. Heat through.

- Spoon about 1/2 cup of turkey mixture down the center of each tortilla. Fold the bottom of the tortilla over filling and roll up. Add the toppings of your choice.

Yield: 4 servings.

Cranberry Chicken

Edith Holliday
FLUSHING, MICHIGAN

I've been married for 42 years, have 3 children and 2 grandchildren, and cook often. This recipe is delicious, simple and good served with rice and a side vegetable.

Cranberry Chicken

PREP: 10 min. ■ **COOK:** 5 hours

- 1 broiler/fryer chicken (3 to 4 pounds), cut up
- 1 can (14 ounces) whole-berry cranberry sauce
- 1 cup barbecue sauce
- 1 small onion, finely chopped
- 1 celery rib, finely chopped
- 1/2 teaspoon salt
- 1/4 teaspoon pepper
- Hot cooked rice

- Place the chicken in a 3-qt. slow cooker. In a small bowl, combine the cranberry sauce, barbecue sauce, onion, celery, salt and pepper; pour over chicken.

- Cover and cook on low for 5-6 hours or until the chicken is tender. Serve with rice.

Yield: 6 servings.

Mary Zawlocki
GIG HARBOR,
WASHINGTON

Spicy barbecue sauce blends with sweet pineapple in this quick-to-fix chicken dish. It's tasty enough for a company dinner...just add a salad and rolls.

Sweet and Tangy Chicken

Sweet and Tangy Chicken

PREP: 10 min ■ COOK: 8 hours

8 boneless skinless chicken breast halves (4 ounces *each*)
2 bottles (18 ounces *each*) barbecue sauce
1 can (20 ounces) pineapple chunks, undrained
1 medium green pepper, chopped
1 medium onion, chopped
2 garlic cloves, minced
Hot cooked rice

■ Place four chicken breasts in a 5-qt. slow cooker. Combine barbecue sauce, pineapple, green pepper, onion and garlic; pour half over chicken. Top with the remaining chicken and sauce.

■ Cover and cook on low for 8-9 hours or until chicken is tender. Thicken sauce if desired. Serve chicken and sauce with rice.

Yield: 8 servings.

To make your own Creole seasoning, for every teaspoon needed, combine 1/4 teaspoon each of salt, garlic powder and paprika, plus a pinch each of dried thyme, ground cumin and cayenne pepper.

Chicken With Noodles And Gravy

Glenda Prince
GRAVETTE, ARKANSAS

When this homey chicken entree comes out of the slow cooker, the golden, creamy sauce coats the noodles, and the tender chicken easily falls off the bone.

PREP: 15 min.
COOK: 6 hours

4 chicken leg quarters (8 ounces *each*)
2 cans (10-3/4 ounces *each*) condensed cream of chicken soup, undiluted
2 envelopes chicken gravy mix
2 teaspoons dried celery flakes
1-3/4 teaspoons Creole seasoning
1 teaspoon dried minced onion
1/4 teaspoon pepper
3 cups uncooked egg noodles

■ With a sharp knife, cut the leg quarters at the joints if desired. Place in a 4- or 5-qt. slow cooker. Combine soup, gravy mix and seasonings; pour over chicken.

■ Cover and cook on low for 6-8 hours or until chicken is tender. Meanwhile, cook the noodles according to package directions; serve with chicken and sauce.

Yield: 4 servings.

Other Entrees

65

60

69

Check out all the new and delicious meals you can create with this chapter, such as pork ribs, lamb chops, bratwursts, meatless stuffed peppers, smoked ham and hearty brunch dishes. Regardless of your taste preferences, you won't be disappointed!

Cantonese Sweet and Sour Pork

Wayne Tews
ANTIGO, WISCONSIN
This Asian-inspired dish is similar to sweet-and-sour pork. The tender vegetables, juicy pork and flavorful sauce are delicious over rice.

Cantonese Sweet and Sour Pork

PREP: 20 min. ■ **COOK:** 7-1/2 hours

1 can (15 ounces) tomato sauce	2 teaspoons steak sauce
1 medium onion, halved and sliced	1 teaspoon salt
1 medium green pepper, cut into strips	1-1/2 pounds pork tenderloin, cut into 1-inch cubes
1 can (4-1/2 ounces) sliced mushrooms, drained	1 tablespoon olive oil
3 tablespoons brown sugar	1 can (8 ounces) unsweetened pineapple chunks, drained
4-1/2 teaspoons white vinegar	Hot cooked rice

■ In a large bowl, combine the first eight ingredients; set aside.

■ In a large skillet, brown pork in oil; drain. Transfer to a 3- or 4-qt. slow cooker. Pour tomato sauce mixture over pork. Cover and cook on low for 7-8 hours or until meat is tender.

■ Add pineapple to slow cooker; cover and cook 30 minutes longer or until heated through. Serve with rice.

Yield: 6 servings.

Pork Ribs with Apple-Mustard Glaze

Gilda Lester
MILLSBORO, DELAWARE
Broiling the baby back ribs first gives them some lovely color.

PREP: 30 min.
COOK: 6 hours

- 2 racks pork baby back ribs (about 4-1/2 pounds)
- 1 teaspoon salt
- 1/2 teaspoon pepper
- 1 large onion, chopped
- 1 cup picante sauce
- 3/4 cup thawed apple juice concentrate
- 1/2 cup ketchup
- 1/3 cup packed brown sugar
- 2 tablespoons Dijon mustard
- 1 tablespoon soy sauce
- 2 teaspoons hot pepper sauce

■ Cut the ribs into serving-size pieces; sprinkle with salt and pepper. Place the ribs, meat side up, on a broiler pan. Broil 4 in. from heat for 5-7 minutes or until browned.

■ Place onion in a 5- or 6-qt. slow cooker; top with ribs. Combine the remaining ingredients and pour over the ribs. Cover; cook on low for 6-8 hours or until the meat is tender.

■ Remove meat to a platter; keep warm. Skim fat from cooking juices; transfer to a small saucepan. Bring to a boil; cook until liquid is reduced by half. Serve with ribs.

Yield: 5 servings.

- In a large skillet, cook bacon over medium heat until crisp. Drain on paper towels; reserve. Cut the roast in half. Brown meat in drippings on all sides. Transfer to a 5-qt. slow cooker; reserve 1 tablespoon drippings.

- Brown onion in drippings. Add garlic; cook 1 minute. Add the jalapeno, chili powder, salt and pepper. Slowly stir in 1/2 cup chicken broth, orange juice and bacon; pour over roast. Cover and cook on low for 4-1/2 to 5 hours or until meat is tender.

- Remove the pork and onion to a serving platter; keep warm. Pour cooking juices into a small saucepan and skim fat. Bring liquid to a boil. Combine the flour and remaining broth until smooth; stir into cooking juices. Bring to a boil; cook and stir for 2 minutes or until thickened. Serve with pork and mashed potatoes if desired.

Yield: 8 servings.

Editor's Note: When cutting hot peppers, disposable gloves are recommended. Avoid touching your face.

Pork Roast with Twist of Orange

Janie Canals
WEST JORDAN, UTAH

The citrus flavor sets this dish apart. It's my family's favorite! With a nice and easy gravy, the pork is perfect served with rice or mashed potatoes.

Pork Roast with Twist of Orange

PREP: 25 min. ■ COOK: 4-1/2 hours

4 bacon strips, diced	4-1/2 teaspoons chili powder
1 boneless pork shoulder roast (3 to 4 pounds), trimmed	1 teaspoon salt
	1 teaspoon pepper
1 large onion, thinly sliced	1 cup chicken broth, *divided*
1-1/2 teaspoons minced garlic	2/3 cup orange juice
1 jalapeno pepper, seeded and finely chopped	1/4 cup all-purpose flour
	Hot mashed potatoes, optional

For easy mashed

potatoes, peel and cube 2 pounds of russet potatoes. Place in a pot and cover with water. Cover and boil for 20 to 25 minutes or until tender. Drain. Add 1/2 cup warm milk, 1/4 cup butter, 3/4 teaspoon salt and a dash of pepper. Mash until light and fluffy. Makes 6 servings.

Slow-Cooked Lamb Chops

Sandra McKenzie
BRAHAM, MINNESOTA

This is my favorite recipe for lamb chops. It's great for people who are trying lamb for the first time, since the meat turns out extra tender and tasty.

PREP: 10 min. ■ **COOK:** 5-1/2 hours

4 bacon strips	1/4 teaspoon pepper
4 lamb shoulder blade chops, trimmed	1/4 cup chopped onion
2-1/4 cups thinly sliced peeled potatoes	2 garlic cloves, minced
1 cup thinly sliced carrots	1 can (10-3/4 ounces) condensed cream of mushroom soup, undiluted
1/2 teaspoon dried rosemary, crushed	1/3 cup 2% milk
1/4 teaspoon garlic powder	1 jar (4-1/2 ounces) sliced mushrooms, drained
1/4 teaspoon salt	

■ Wrap bacon around lamb chops; secure with toothpicks. Place in a 3-qt. slow cooker. Cover and cook on high for 1-1/2 hours.

■ Remove chops; discard toothpicks and bacon. Drain liquid from slow cooker. Add potatoes and carrots; top with lamb chops. Sprinkle with rosemary, garlic powder, salt, pepper, onion and garlic.

■ Combine soup and milk; add mushrooms. Pour over chops. Cover and cook on low for 4-6 hours or until the meat and vegetables are tender.

Yield: 4 servings.

Chinese Pork Ribs

June Ross
BELMONT, NORTH CAROLINA

Add an Asian flair to an all-American dish like ribs. These have wonderful flavor, with the saltiness of soy sauce and the sweetness of marmalade.

PREP: 10 min. ■ **COOK:** 6 hours

1/4 cup reduced-sodium soy sauce	3 tablespoons ketchup
1/3 cup reduced-sugar orange marmalade	2 garlic cloves, minced
	3 to 4 pounds bone-in country-style pork ribs

■ Combine soy sauce, marmalade, ketchup and garlic. Pour half into a 5-qt. slow cooker. Top with ribs; drizzle with remaining sauce. Cover and cook on low for 6 hours or until tender. Thicken cooking juices if desired.

Yield: 6 servings.

Roasted Red Pepper Sauce

Mrs. Timothy Tosh
LUMBERTON, NEW JERSEY

I often use Greek olives with the artichoke hearts to add some zing to this pasta sauce. Roast the peppers yourself if you have time.

PREP: 15 min.
COOK: 4 hours

4 pounds plum tomatoes (about 17), coarsely chopped

1 large sweet onion, chopped

1 can (29 ounces) tomato puree

3 jars (7 ounces *each*) roasted sweet red peppers, drained and chopped

2 jars (6-1/2 ounces *each*) marinated artichoke hearts, drained and chopped

1/2 pound fresh mushrooms, quartered

2 cans (2-1/4 ounces *each*) sliced ripe olives, drained

1/4 cup sugar

1/4 cup balsamic vinegar

1/4 cup olive oil

3 garlic cloves, minced

1 tablespoon dried basil

1 tablespoon dried oregano

1 teaspoon salt

Hot cooked pasta

■ In a 5-qt. slow cooker, combine the first 14 ingredients. Cover and cook on high for 4 hours or until flavors are blended. Serve with pasta.

Yield: about 15 cups.

Country Cassoulet

Suzanne McKinley
LYONS, GEORGIA

This bean stew goes great with fresh dinner rolls and your favorite green salad. It's a hearty meal that's perfect after a long day in the garden.

PREP: 15 min. + standing ■ **COOK:** 5 hours

- 1 pound (2 cups) dried great northern beans
- 2 fresh garlic sausage links
- 3 bacon strips, diced
- 1-1/2 pounds boneless pork, cut into 1-inch cubes
- 1 pound boneless lamb, cut into 1-inch cubes
- 1-1/2 cups chopped onion
- 3 garlic cloves, minced
- 2 teaspoons salt
- 1 teaspoon dried thyme
- 4 whole cloves
- 2 bay leaves
- 2-1/2 cups chicken broth
- 1 can (8 ounces) tomato sauce

■ Sort beans and rinse with cold water. Place beans in a Dutch oven; add water to cover by 2 in. Bring to a boil; boil for 2 minutes. Remove from the heat; cover and let stand for 1 to 4 hours or until beans are softened. Drain and rinse beans, discarding liquid.

■ In a large skillet over medium-high heat, brown sausage; remove with a slotted spoon to a 5-qt. slow cooker. Add bacon to skillet; cook until crisp. Remove with a slotted spoon to slow cooker.

■ In bacon drippings, cook the pork and lamb until browned on all sides. Remove pork and lamb with a slotted spoon to slow cooker. Stir in beans and remaining ingredients.

■ Cover and cook on high for 2 hours. Reduce the heat to low and cook 3-4 hours longer. Discard cloves and bay leaves. Remove sausage and slice into 1/4-in. pieces; return to slow cooker and stir gently.

Yield: 8-10 servings.

Store uncooked dried beans tightly covered in a cool, dry area. It is best to use dried beans within 12 months, because the older the bean, the longer it takes to cook. One pound of packaged, uncooked dried beans makes about 6 cups of cooked beans.

Slow Cooker Pork Chops

PREP: 20 min.
COOK: 5 hours

- 6 bone-in pork loin chops (8 ounces *each*)
- 1 tablespoon canola oil
- 1 large onion, sliced
- 1 medium sweet red pepper, cut into rings
- 1 can (4 ounces) mushroom stems and pieces, drained
- 1 can (28 ounces) diced tomatoes, undrained
- 1 tablespoon brown sugar
- 1 tablespoon balsamic vinegar
- 2 teaspoons Worcestershire sauce
- 1/4 teaspoon salt
- 1/4 teaspoon pepper

Hot cooked rice

■ In a large skillet, brown chops in oil in batches; drain. Transfer to a 5-qt. slow cooker. Layer with the onion, red pepper and mushrooms. Combine the tomatoes, brown sugar, vinegar, Worcestershire sauce, salt and pepper; pour over vegetables.

■ Cover and cook on low for 5-6 hours or until meat is tender. Serve with rice.

Yield: 6 servings.

Lea Ann Schalk
GARFIELD, ARIZONA

These scrumptious chops turn out nice and tender, and fall apart easily after being slow cooked. The tomatoey sauce, made with onion, sweet red peppers and mushrooms, is sweet and tangy, and tastes wonderfully over cooked rice.

Kelly Graham
ST. THOMAS, ONTARIO

When I have leftover ham to use up, this is the most requested recipe in the house! I love it because I can make it with items that I already have in the house. The dish comes together in a snap and has a yummy flavor that is irresistible.

Mom's Scalloped Potatoes and Ham

PREP: 20 min. ■ COOK: 8 hours

- 10 medium potatoes, peeled and thinly sliced
- 3 cups cubed fully cooked ham
- 2 large onions, thinly sliced
- 2 cups (8 ounces) shredded cheddar cheese
- 1 can (10-3/4 ounces) condensed cream of mushroom soup, undiluted
- 1/2 teaspoon paprika
- 1/4 teaspoon pepper

■ In a greased 6-qt. slow cooker, layer half of the potatoes, ham, onions and cheese. Repeat layers. Pour soup over top. Sprinkle with paprika and pepper.

■ Cover and cook on low for 8-10 hours or until potatoes are tender.

Yield: 9 servings.

Hot Dogs 'n' Beans

June Formanek
BELLE PLAINE, IOWA

You'll please kids of all ages with this tasty combination that works well for casual get-togethers. I frequently fix this when my whole family is home. It's so easy to throw together because the simple recipe uses only five ingredients that I already have on hand.

PREP: 10 min. ■ COOK: 7 hours

- 3 cans (28 ounces *each*) plus 1 can (15-3/4 ounces) pork and beans
- 1 package (1 pound) hot dogs, halved lengthwise and cut into 1-inch pieces
- 1 large onion, chopped
- 1/2 cup packed brown sugar
- 3 tablespoons prepared mustard
- 4 bacon strips, cooked and crumbled

■ In a 5-qt. slow cooker, combine all ingredients. Cover and cook on low for 7-8 hours.

Yield: 10 servings.

Pork Chops & Acorn Squash*

Mary Johnson
COLOMA, WISCONSIN

My husband and I can never get enough fresh buttery squash from our garden. These chops cook up sweet and tender in the slow cooker, and the classic, comfort-food flavor doesn't take up my whole day to prepare.

PREP: 15 min.
COOK: 4 hours

- 6 boneless pork loin chops (4 ounces *each*)
- 2 medium acorn squash, peeled and cubed
- 1/2 cup packed brown sugar
- 2 tablespoons butter, melted
- 1 tablespoon orange juice
- 3/4 teaspoon salt
- 1/2 teaspoon grated orange peel
- 3/4 teaspoon browning sauce, optional

■ Place the pork chops in a 5-qt. slow cooker; add the squash. Combine brown sugar, butter, orange juice, salt, orange peel and browning sauce if desired; pour over squash. Cover and cook on low for 4 hours or until meat is tender.

Yield: 6 servings.

*Nutrition Facts: 1 pork chop with 2/3 cup squash (calculated without browning sauce) equals 317 calories, 10 g fat (5 g saturated fat), 65 mg cholesterol, 365 mg sodium, 34 g carbohydrate, 2 g fiber, 23 g protein. **Diabetic Exchanges:** 3 lean meat, 2 starch, 1 fat.

Melissa McCabe
LONG BEACH,
CALIFORNIA

These peppers are an updated version of my mom's stuffed peppers, which were a favorite when I was growing up in upstate New York.

Vegetarian Stuffed Peppers

Vegetarian Stuffed Peppers

PREP: 30 min. ■ COOK: 3-1/2 hours

6 large sweet peppers
2 cups cooked brown rice
3 small tomatoes, chopped
1 cup frozen corn, thawed
1 small sweet onion, chopped
1/3 cup canned red beans, rinsed and drained
1/3 cup canned black beans, rinsed and drained
3/4 cup cubed Monterey Jack cheese
1 can (4-1/4 ounces) chopped ripe olives
4 fresh basil leaves, thinly sliced
3 garlic cloves, minced
1 teaspoon salt
1/2 teaspoon pepper
3/4 cup meatless spaghetti sauce
1/2 cup water
4 tablespoons grated Parmesan cheese, *divided*

■ Cut tops off peppers and remove the seeds; set aside. In a large bowl, combine the rice, tomatoes, corn, onion and beans. Stir in the Monterey Jack cheese, olives, basil, garlic, salt and pepper. Spoon into peppers.

■ Combine spaghetti sauce and water; pour half into an oval 5-qt. slow cooker. Add the stuffed peppers. Top with remaining sauce. Sprinkle with 2 tablespoons Parmesan cheese.

■ Cover and cook on low for 3-1/2 to 4 hours or until peppers are tender and filling is heated through. Sprinkle with remaining Parmesan cheese.

Yield: 6 servings.

Cider-Glazed Ham

Jennifer Foos-Furer
MARYSVILLE, OHIO

We raise our own pork so I'm always looking for new ways to serve it that'll warm up everyone at the end of a long day. This recipe wins the hearts of all.

PREP: 15 min.
COOK: 4 hours

1 boneless fully cooked ham (3 pounds)
1-3/4 cups apple cider *or* juice
1/4 cup packed brown sugar
1/4 cup Dijon mustard
1/4 cup honey
2 tablespoons cornstarch
2 tablespoons cold water

■ Place the ham in a 5-qt. slow cooker. In a small bowl, combine the cider, brown sugar, mustard and honey; pour over the ham. Cover and cook on low for 4-5 hours or until heated through. Remove ham and keep warm.

■ Pour cooking juices into a small saucepan. Combine cornstarch and water until smooth; stir into cooking juices. Bring to a boil; cook and stir for 2 minutes or until thickened. Serve with the ham.

Yield: 8 servings.

Slow-Cooked Ham 'n' Broccoli

Jill Pennington
JACKSONVILLE, FLORIDA

This sensational dish is so wonderful to come home to, especially on a cool fall or winter day. It's a delicious way to use up leftover holiday ham, too.

PREP: 10 min.
COOK: 2 hours + standing

 3 cups cubed fully cooked ham
 3 cups frozen chopped broccoli, thawed
 1 can (10-3/4 ounces) condensed cream of mushroom soup, undiluted
 1 jar (8 ounces) process cheese sauce
 1 can (8 ounces) sliced water chestnuts, drained
1-1/4 cups uncooked instant rice
 1 cup 2% milk
 1 celery rib, chopped
 1 medium onion, chopped
 1/8 to 1/4 teaspoon pepper
 1/2 teaspoon paprika

■ In a 3-qt. slow cooker, combine the first 10 ingredients. Cover and cook on high for 2-3 hours or until the rice is tender. Let stand for 10 minutes before serving. Sprinkle with paprika.

Yield: 6-8 servings.

Saucy Pork Chops

Jennifer Ruberg
TWO HARBORS, MINNESOTA

I don't always have time to fix the home-cooked meals my family loves, so I've come to rely on my slow cooker. These tangy chops are so tender you can cut them with a fork.

Saucy Pork Chops

PREP: 15 min. ■ **COOK:** 4-1/4 hours

 4 bone-in pork loin chops (8 ounces *each*)
 1 teaspoon garlic powder
 1/2 teaspoon salt
 1/4 teaspoon pepper

 2 tablespoons canola oil
 2 cups ketchup
 1/2 cup packed brown sugar
 1 teaspoon Liquid Smoke, optional

■ Sprinkle the pork chops with garlic powder, salt and pepper. In a large skillet, brown the chops in oil on both sides; drain.

■ In a small bowl, combine the ketchup, brown sugar and Liquid Smoke if desired. Pour half of the sauce into a 3-qt. slow cooker. Top with pork chops and remaining sauce. Cover and cook on low for 4-1/4 to 5-1/4 hours or until meat is tender.

Yield: 4 servings.

Jessica Philleo
CARMEL, INDIANA

The colorful cranberry sauce in this recipe has a sweet-tart flavor that pairs wonderfully with the juicy pork. It's a great meal for a special occasion, such as a holiday dinner, but it's also perfect for an easy weeknight dinner. There is plenty of sauce for each serving of pork.

Cranberry Pork Roast*

PREP: 25 min. ■ COOK: 8 hours

1 package (12 ounces) fresh *or* frozen cranberries, thawed	1 large apple, peeled and sliced
1 package (12 ounces) frozen pitted dark sweet cherries, thawed	1 boneless whole pork loin roast (4 pounds)
1/4 cup packed brown sugar	1 teaspoon minced fresh rosemary *or* 1/4 teaspoon dried rosemary, crushed
1/4 cup marsala wine *or* unsweetened apple juice	1 teaspoon coarsely ground pepper
1/3 cup raspberry vinaigrette	2 teaspoons cornstarch
1 large red onion, sliced	2 teaspoons water

■ In a large saucepan, combine the cranberries, cherries, brown sugar and wine. Cook over medium heat until the cranberries pop, about 15 minutes. Stir in the vinaigrette.

■ Place half of the onion and apple in a 4- or 5-qt. slow cooker. Cut roast in half; add to slow cooker. Top with remaining onion and apple. Pour cranberry mixture over top. Sprinkle with rosemary and pepper. Cover and cook on low for 8-10 hours or until meat is tender.

■ Remove the meat to a serving platter; keep warm. Skim the fat from the cooking juices and transfer to a small saucepan. Bring liquid to a boil. Combine cornstarch and water until smooth. Gradually stir into pan. Bring to a boil; cook and stir for 2 minutes or until thickened. Serve with meat.

Yield: 10 servings (5 cups sauce).

＊Nutrition Facts: 5 ounces cooked pork with 1/2 cup sauce equals 294 calories, 11 g fat (3 g saturated fat), 68 mg cholesterol, 110 mg sodium, 21 g carbohydrate, 3 g fiber, 27 g protein. **Diabetic Exchanges:** 4 lean meat, 1/2 starch, 1 fat, 1 fruit.

Fresh cranberries are in season from early fall through December. When buying, look for packages with shiny, bright red (light or dark) berries. Avoid berries that are bruised, shriveled or have brown spots.

Slow-Cooked Pork and Beans

Patricia Hager
NICHOLASVILLE, KENTUCKY

I like to get this dish started before leaving for work in the morning. When I get home, my supper's ready! It's a hearty slow cooker meal that is also good for a potluck. A generous helping of tender pork and beans is perfect with a slice of warm corn bread.

PREP: 15 min.
COOK: 6 hours

1	boneless whole pork loin roast (3 pounds)
1	medium onion, sliced
3	cans (15 ounces *each*) pork and beans
1-1/2	cups barbecue sauce
1/4	cup packed brown sugar
1	teaspoon garlic powder

■ Cut roast in half; place in a 5-qt. slow cooker. Top with onion.

■ Combine the beans, barbecue sauce, brown sugar and garlic powder; pour over meat. Cover and cook on low for 6 hours or until meat is tender.

■ Remove roast; shred with two forks. Return meat to the slow cooker; heat through.

Yield: 12 servings.

Diana Seeger
NEW SPRINGFIELD, OHIO

Guests will think you stayed home all day when you serve these tender stuffed chops. I often share this recipe with new brides because I know it will become one of their favorites.

Herb Stuffed Chops

Herb Stuffed Chops

PREP: 25 min. ■ COOK: 8 hours

3/4 cup chopped onion	1-1/2 teaspoons salt, *divided*
1/4 cup chopped celery	1/2 teaspoon pepper, *divided*
2 tablespoons butter	6 bone-in pork rib *or* loin chops (8 ounces *each*)
2 cups day-old bread cubes	
1/2 cup minced fresh parsley	1 tablespoon canola oil
1/3 cup evaporated milk	3/4 cup white wine *or* chicken broth
1 teaspoon fennel seed, crushed	

■ In a small skillet, saute onion and celery in butter until tender. Add the bread cubes, parsley, milk, fennel, 1/4 teaspoon salt and 1/8 teaspoon pepper; toss to coat.

■ Cut a pocket in each chop by slicing from the fat side almost to the bone. Spoon about 1/4 cup stuffing into each pocket. Combine the remaining salt and pepper; rub over chops.

■ In a large skillet, brown chops in oil; transfer to a 3-qt. slow cooker. Pour wine over top. Cover and cook on low for 8-9 hours or until a meat thermometer reads 160°.

Yield: 6 servings.

Thai-Style Peanut Pork

Dawn Schmidt
DURHAM, NORTH CAROLINA

My husband and I both work long hours. This slow cooker recipe is large enough that the two of us can eat as much yummy pork as we like and still have leftovers!

PREP: 20 min.
COOK: 8 hours

2	medium sweet red peppers, julienned
1	boneless pork shoulder roast (3 pounds)
1/3	cup reduced-sodium teriyaki sauce
3	tablespoons rice vinegar
2	garlic cloves, minced
1/2	teaspoon crushed red pepper flakes
1/4	cup creamy peanut butter
4	cups hot cooked rice
1/2	cup chopped unsalted peanuts
4	green onions, sliced

■ Place peppers in a 3-qt. slow cooker. Cut roast in half; place on top of peppers. Combine the teriyaki sauce, rice vinegar and garlic; pour over the roast. Sprinkle with pepper flakes. Cover; cook on low for 8-9 hours or until meat is tender.

■ Remove the meat from slow cooker; when cool enough to handle, shred with two forks. Reserve 2 cups cooking juices; skim fat. Stir the peanut butter into reserved juices. Return pork and cooking juices to slow cooker; heat through. Serve with cooked rice; sprinkle with peanuts and green onions.

Yield: 8 servings.

Hash Brown Egg Breakfast

Creamy Ham And Potatoes

Peggy Key
GRANT, ALABAMA

The creamy mixture of robust ham and moist potatoes in this stick-to-your-ribs dish is brimming with homemade flavor.

PREP: 20 min.
COOK: 8 hours

- 4 medium red potatoes, thinly sliced
- 2 medium onions, finely chopped
- 1-1/2 cups cubed fully cooked ham
- 2 tablespoons butter
- 2 tablespoons all-purpose flour
- 1 teaspoon ground mustard
- 1/2 teaspoon salt
- 1/2 teaspoon pepper
- 1 can (10-3/4 ounces) condensed cream of celery soup, undiluted
- 1-1/3 cups water
- 1 cup (4 ounces) shredded cheddar cheese, optional

- ■ In a 3-qt. slow cooker, layer the potatoes, onions and ham.

- ■ In a large saucepan, melt the butter. Stir in flour, mustard, salt and pepper until smooth. Combine the soup and water; gradually stir into flour mixture. Bring to a boil; cook and stir for 2 minutes or until thickened and bubbly. Pour over ham. Cover and cook on low for 8-9 hours or until the potatoes are tender. If desired, sprinkle with cheese before serving.

Yield: 4 servings.

Nancy Marion
FROSTPROOF, FLORIDA

I love this hearty slow cooker breakfast dish because it has all kinds of wonderful ingredients in it. It's great for potlucks because it travels well and is always popular.

Hash Brown Egg Breakfast

PREP: 15 min. ■ **COOK:** 3-1/2 hours

- 1 package (32 ounces) frozen cubed hash brown potatoes, thawed
- 2 cups cubed fully cooked ham
- 1-1/2 cups (6 ounces) shredded cheddar cheese
- 1 large green pepper, chopped
- 1 medium onion, chopped
- 12 eggs, beaten
- 1 cup 2% milk
- 1 teaspoon salt
- 1 teaspoon pepper

- ■ Layer a third of the potatoes, ham, cheese, green pepper and onion in a 6-qt. slow cooker coated with cooking spray. Repeat layers twice. In a large bowl, whisk the eggs, milk, salt and pepper; pour over top.

- ■ Cover and cook on low for 3-1/2 to 4 hours or until a thermometer reads 160°.

Yield: 12 servings (1-1/3 cup each).

Judy Armstrong
PRAIRIEVILLE, LOUISIANA
This festive and spicy main dish is wonderful served for either weeknight meals or for entertaining. The cranberry and ginger make an excellent flavor combination.

Cranberry-Ginger Pork Ribs

PREP: 20 min. ■ **COOK:** 5 hours

1	can (14 ounces) whole-berry cranberry sauce	2-1/2	pounds boneless country-style pork ribs
2	habanero peppers, seeded and minced	1/2	teaspoon salt
		1/2	teaspoon cayenne pepper
4-1/2	teaspoons minced grated gingerroot	1/2	teaspoon pepper
3	garlic cloves, minced	2	tablespoons olive oil
			Hot cooked rice

■ Combine cranberry sauce, habaneros, ginger and garlic. Sprinkle the ribs with salt and peppers. In a large skillet, brown the ribs in oil on all sides and drain.

■ Transfer meat to a 3-qt. slow cooker; pour cranberry mixture over ribs. Cover and cook on low high for 5-6 hours or until meat is tender. Skim fat from cooking juices. Serve with pork and rice.

Yield: 8 servings.

Editor's Note: When cutting hot peppers, disposable gloves are recommended. Avoid touching your face.

German Potato Salad with Sausage

Teresa McGill
TROTWOOD, OHIO
Hearty and saucy, this potato salad is an old family recipe.

PREP: 30 min.
COOK: 6 hours

8	bacon strips, diced
1	large onion, chopped
1	pound smoked kielbasa *or* Polish sausage, halved and cut into 1/2-inch slices
2	pounds medium red potatoes, cut into chunks
1	can (10-3/4 ounces) condensed cream of potato soup, undiluted
1	cup sauerkraut, rinsed and well drained
1/2	cup water
1/4	cup cider vinegar
1	tablespoon sugar
1/2	teaspoon salt
1/2	teaspoon coarsely ground pepper

■ In a large skillet, cook bacon over medium heat until crisp. Remove to paper towels with a slotted spoon to drain. Saute onion in drippings for 1 minute. Add sausage; cook until lightly browned. Add potatoes; cook 2 minutes longer. Drain.

■ Transfer the sausage mixture to a 3-qt. slow cooker. In a small bowl, combine soup, sauerkraut, water, vinegar, sugar, salt and pepper. Pour over the sausage mixture. Sprinkle with bacon. Cover and cook on low for 6-7 hours or until potatoes are tender.

Yield: 8 servings.

Kathleen Wolf
NAPERVILLE, ILLINOIS

Sometimes I use Bibb lettuce leaves instead of tortillas to make crunchy lettuce wraps. The leftovers are great for burritos.

Slow-Cooked Pork Tacos

Slow-Cooked Pork Tacos*

PREP: 20 min. ■ COOK: 4 hours

1 boneless pork sirloin roast (2 pounds), cut into 1-inch pieces
1-1/2 cups salsa verde
1 medium sweet red pepper, chopped
1 medium onion, chopped
1/4 cup chopped dried apricots
2 tablespoons lime juice
2 garlic cloves, minced

1 teaspoon ground cumin
1/2 teaspoon salt
1/4 teaspoon white pepper
Dash hot pepper sauce
10 flour tortillas (8 inches), warmed
Reduced-fat sour cream, thinly sliced green onions, cubed avocado, shredded reduced-fat cheddar cheese and chopped tomato, optional

■ In a 3-qt. slow cooker, combine the first 11 ingredients. Cover and cook on high for 4-5 hours or until meat is very tender.

■ Shred the pork with two forks. Place about 1/2 cup pork mixture down center of each tortilla. Serve with toppings if desired.

Yield: 10 tacos.

*Nutrition Facts: 1 taco (calculated without optional toppings) equals 301 calories, 8 g fat (2 g saturated fat), 54 mg cholesterol, 616 mg sodium, 32 g carbohydrate, 1 g fiber, 24 g protein. **Diabetic Exchanges:** 3 lean meat, 2 starch.

Crock O' Brats

Maryellen Boettcher
FAIRCHILD, WISCONSIN

I've taken this robust dish to countless events, and it's popular every time. Slices of bratwurst take center stage with potatoes, sauerkraut, apple and onion.

PREP: 10 min.
COOK: 4 hours

5 uncooked bratwurst links (1-1/4 pounds), cut into 1/2-inch pieces
5 medium potatoes, peeled and cubed
1 can (27 ounces) sauerkraut, rinsed and well drained
1 medium tart apple, chopped
1 small onion, chopped
1/4 cup packed brown sugar
1/2 teaspoon salt, optional

■ In a large skillet, brown the bratwurst on all sides. In a 5-qt. slow cooker, combine the remaining ingredients. Stir in bratwurst and pan drippings. Cover and cook on high for 4-6 hours or until potatoes and apple are tender.

Yield: 6 servings.

Side Dishes

76

84

80

Let a slow cooker do the work for you when you need a delicious side dish for your weeknight dinner, potluck, family get-together or church supper. You have a variety of recipes to choose from, such as turkey dressing, applesauce, scalloped potatoes and more!

Cheesy Spinach

Pineapple Sweet Potatoes

Bette Fulcher
LEXINGTON, TEXAS

Pineapple and pecans make a pretty topping for this no-fuss fall side dish. It's light, tasty and not too sweet. Making it in the slow cooker leaves extra space in the oven when preparing a holiday turkey and other dishes.

PREP: 10 min.
COOK: 4 hours

      4 eggs
      1 cup milk
  1/2 cup butter, softened
      6 to 6-1/2 cups mashed sweet potatoes (without added milk *or* butter)
      1 teaspoon vanilla extract
      1 teaspoon salt
      1 teaspoon ground cinnamon
  1/2 teaspoon ground nutmeg
  1/2 teaspoon lemon extract
      1 can (8 ounces) sliced pineapple, drained
  1/4 cup chopped pecans

■ In a large bowl, combine the first nine ingredients. Transfer to a 3-qt. slow cooker. Top with pineapple slices and pecans. Cover and cook on low for 4-5 hours or until a thermometer reads 160°.

Yield: 12-14 servings.

Frances Moore
DECATUR, ILLINOIS

My daughter often serves this cheese and spinach blend at church suppers. Even people who don't usually eat spinach enjoy this flavorful treat once they try it. There is never any left.

Cheesy Spinach

PREP: 10 min. ■ **COOK:** 5 hours

      2 packages (10 ounces *each*) frozen chopped spinach, thawed and well drained
      2 cups (16 ounces) 4% cottage cheese
  1-1/2 cups cubed process cheese (Velveeta)

      3 eggs, lightly beaten
  1/4 cup butter, cubed
  1/4 cup all-purpose flour
      1 teaspoon salt

■ In a large bowl, combine all the ingredients. Pour into a greased 3-qt. slow cooker. Cover and cook on high for 1 hour. Reduce heat to low; cook 4-5 hours longer or until a knife inserted near center comes out clean.

Yield: 6-8 servings.

Cheesy Creamed Corn

Mary Ann Truitt
WICHITA, KANSAS

Even those who usually don't eat much corn will ask for a second helping of this creamy, cheesy side dish. Folks love the flavor, but I love how easy it is to make with ingredients already on hand.

PREP: 5 min. ■ **COOK:** 4 hours

3 packages (16 ounces *each*) frozen corn

2 packages (one 8 ounces, one 3 ounces) cream cheese, cubed

1/4 cup butter, cubed

3 tablespoons water

3 tablespoons milk

2 tablespoons sugar

6 slices process American cheese, cut into small pieces

■ In a 3-qt. slow cooker, combine all the ingredients. Cover and cook on low for 4 hours or until heated through and the cheese is melted. Stir well before serving.

Yield: 12 servings.

Slow-Cooked Applesauce

Susanne Wasson
MONTGOMERY, NEW YORK

This chunky, sweet applesauce is perfect alongside main entrees. Because it's prepared in a slow cooker, you can set it and forget it before you and the family head out for some winter fun.

PREP: 20 min. ■ **COOK:** 6 hours

6 pounds medium apples (about 18 medium), peeled and sliced

1 cup sugar

1 cup water

1 teaspoon salt

1 teaspoon ground cinnamon

1/4 cup butter, cubed

2 teaspoons vanilla extract

■ In a 5-qt. slow cooker, combine apples, sugar, water, salt and cinnamon. Cover and cook on low for 6-8 hours or until tender.

■ Turn off heat; stir in butter and vanilla. Mash if desired. Serve warm or cold.

Yield: 12 cups.

Italian Mushrooms

PREP: 10 min.
COOK: 4 hours

1 pound medium fresh mushrooms

1 large onion, sliced

1/2 cup butter, melted

1 package Italian salad dressing mix

■ In a 3-qt. slow cooker, layer the mushrooms and onion. Combine the butter and salad dressing mix; pour over the vegetables. Cover and cook on low for 4-5 hours or until the vegetables are tender. Serve with a slotted spoon.

Yield: 6 servings.

When preparing

side dishes for company, variety is important. Offer vegetables along with grains and pasta, and for kids and older guests, provide at least one lightly seasoned side dish. The entree and side dishes should complement one another. If an entree has lots of garlic, onion or nuts, avoid a side dish that's loaded with any of those same ingredients.

Kim Reichert
ST. PAUL, MINNESOTA

Only four items create a rich and flavorful side dish that goes great with a tender steak and mashed potatoes. It's nice to have a slow cooker do the work so I can spend time with my family or doing other tasks.

Julie Butsch
HARTLAND, WISCONSIN

The ground beef and beans in this filling dish are perfectly flavored. It's a tradition at the table when my girlfriends and I go up North for a "girl's weekend." The husbands and kids are left at home, but the slow cooker comes with us!

Cowboy Calico Beans

PREP: 30 min. ■ COOK: 4 hours

- 1 pound lean ground beef (90% lean)
- 1 large sweet onion, chopped
- 1/2 cup packed brown sugar
- 1/4 cup ketchup
- 3 tablespoons cider vinegar
- 2 tablespoons yellow mustard
- 1 can (16 ounces) butter beans, drained
- 1 can (16 ounces) kidney beans, rinsed and drained
- 1 can (15 ounces) pork and beans
- 1 can (15-1/4 ounces) lima beans, rinsed and drained

■ In a large skillet, cook beef and onion over medium heat until meat is no longer pink; drain.

■ Transfer to a 3-qt. slow cooker. Combine brown sugar, ketchup, vinegar and mustard; add to meat mixture. Stir in the beans. Cover and cook on low for 4-5 hours or until heated through.

Yield: 8 servings.

Scalloped Taters

Lucinda Wolker
SOMERSET, PENNSYLVANIA

This creamy and comforting side dish tastes great with almost any entree and is a snap to assemble with convenient frozen hash browns. This is a good way to make potatoes when your oven is busy with other dishes.

PREP: 10 min. ■ COOK: 4-1/2 hours

- 1 package (2 pounds) frozen cubed hash brown potatoes
- 1 can (10-3/4 ounces) condensed cream of chicken soup, undiluted
- 1-1/2 cups milk
- 1 cup (4 ounces) shredded cheddar cheese
- 1/2 cup plus 1 tablespoon butter, melted, *divided*
- 1/4 cup dried minced onion
- 1/2 teaspoon salt
- 1/8 teaspoon pepper
- 3/4 cup crushed cornflakes

■ In a large bowl, combine the hash browns, soup, milk, cheese, 1/2 cup butter, onion, salt and pepper. Pour into a greased 5-qt. slow cooker. Cover and cook on low for 4-1/2 to 5 hours or until potatoes are tender.

■ Just before serving, combine cornflake crumbs and remaining butter in a pie plate. Bake at 350° for 4-6 minutes or until golden brown. Stir the potatoes; sprinkle with crumb topping.

Yield: 12 servings.

Creamy Red Potatoes

Shelia Schmitt
TOPEKA, KANSAS

It's simple to please a crowd with this rich, yummy side. It's easy to double, and I always receive compliments when I take it to potlucks.

PREP: 5 min.
COOK: 8 hours

- 2 pounds small red potatoes, quartered
- 1 package (8 ounces) cream cheese, softened
- 1 can (10-3/4 ounces) condensed cream of potato soup, undiluted
- 1 envelope ranch salad dressing mix

■ Place potatoes in a 3-qt. slow cooker. In a small bowl, beat cream cheese, soup and salad dressing mix until blended. Stir into potatoes. Cover and cook on low for 8 hours or until the potatoes are tender.

Yield: 4-6 servings.

When storing

potatoes, be sure to store them separately from onions, because onions can cause potatoes to spoil more quickly.

Green Beans with Bacon and Tomatoes*

Cathy Bell
JOPLIN, MISSOURI

If needed, my recipe can easily be doubled or tripled to serve larger crowds. Garlic salt can be substituted for the seasoned salt if you like.

PREP: 30 min. ■ BAKE: 4-1/2 hours

- 1 package (14 ounces) thick-sliced bacon strips, chopped
- 1 large red onion, chopped
- 2 packages (16 ounces *each*) frozen cut green beans
- 1 can (28 ounces) petite diced tomatoes, undrained
- 1/4 cup packed brown sugar
- 1 tablespoon seasoned pepper
- 1/2 teaspoon seasoned salt
- 1 can (16 ounces) red beans, rinsed and drained

■ In a small skillet, cook bacon over medium heat until partially cooked but not crisp. Remove to paper towels with a slotted spoon; drain, reserving 2 tablespoons drippings. Saute onion in drippings until tender.

■ In a 4- or 5-qt. slow cooker, combine the green beans, tomatoes, brown sugar, pepper, salt, bacon and onion. Cover and cook on low for 4 hours. Stir in red beans; cook 30 minutes longer or until heated through and green beans are tender.

Yield: 14 servings.

*Nutrition Facts: 3/4 cup equals 139 calories, 6 g fat (2 g saturated fat), 9 mg cholesterol, 507 mg sodium, 17 g carbohydrate, 4 g fiber, 6 g protein. **Diabetic Exchanges:** 2 vegetable, 1/2 starch, 1 fat.

Sweet Sausage And Beans

PREP: 10 min.
COOK: 4 hours

- 1/2 cup thinly sliced carrots
- 1/2 cup chopped onion
- 2 cups frozen lima beans, thawed
- 2 cups frozen cut green beans, thawed
- 1 pound smoked sausage, cut into 1/4-inch slices
- 1 can (16 ounces) baked beans
- 1/2 cup ketchup
- 1/3 cup packed brown sugar
- 1 tablespoon cider vinegar
- 1 teaspoon prepared mustard

■ In a 3-qt. slow cooker, layer the carrots, onion, lima beans, green beans, sausage and baked beans. In a small bowl, combine the ketchup, brown sugar, vinegar and mustard; pour over beans. Cover and cook on high for 4 hours or until vegetables are tender. Stir before serving.

Yield: 4-6 servings.

Salt is a flavor enhancer in most recipes. If you wish, eliminate salt from meat dishes, vegetable dishes, pasta, rice, soups, salad dressings, casseroles and more. To make up for the missing salt, add additional herbs.

Doris Heath
FRANKLIN, NORTH CAROLINA

This slow cooker version of a traditional French dish called cassoulet is sweet, saucy and chock-full of beans, smoked sausage and vegetables. It's a versatile recipe, because you can serve it as a hearty side dish or an entree.

Sherry Vink
LACOMBE, ALBERTA

Remember Grandma's delicious turkey dressing during Thanksgiving or Christmas? Well, you can taste it again, combined with flavorful herbs and aromatic veggies, in this family-favorite dressing. You'll love that you can make it in your slow cooker.

Old-Fashioned Dressing

PREP: 35 min. ■ COOK: 3 hours

2 celery ribs, chopped
1 medium onion, chopped
1 cup sliced fresh mushrooms
1/2 cup butter, cubed
1/2 cup minced fresh parsley
2 teaspoons rubbed sage
2 teaspoons dried marjoram
1 teaspoon dried thyme

1 teaspoon poultry seasoning
1/2 teaspoon pepper
1/4 teaspoon salt
6 cups cubed day-old white bread
6 cups cubed day-old whole wheat bread
1 can (14-1/2 ounces) chicken broth

■ In a large skillet, saute the celery, onion and mushrooms in butter until tender. Stir in the seasonings. Place bread cubes in a large bowl. Add vegetable mixture and toss to coat. Stir in broth.

■ Transfer to a 3-qt. slow cooker coated with cooking spray. Cover and cook on low for 3-4 hours or until heated through.

Yield: 8 servings.

Slow-Cooked Mac 'n' Cheese

Shelby Molina
WHITEWATER, WISCONSIN
This recipe is comfort food at its finest; it's rich, hearty and extra-cheesy. And because it's made in the slow cooker, it's also very easy.

PREP: 25 min. ■ COOK: 2-3/4 hours

2 cups uncooked elbow macaroni
1 can (12 ounces) evaporated milk
1-1/2 cups milk
1/2 cup egg substitute

1/4 cup butter, melted
1 teaspoon salt
2-1/2 cups (10 ounces) shredded cheddar cheese
2-1/2 cups (10 ounces) shredded sharp cheddar cheese, *divided*

■ Cook macaroni according to package directions; drain and rinse in cold water. In a large bowl, combine the evaporated milk, milk, egg substitute, butter and salt. Stir in the cheddar cheese, 2 cups sharp cheddar cheese and macaroni.

■ Transfer to a greased 3-qt. slow cooker. Cover and cook on low for 2-3/4 to 3 hours or until center is set, stirring once. Sprinkle with remaining sharp cheddar cheese.

Yield: 9 servings.

Green Beans In Bacon Cheese Sauce

Karen Lewis
PLEASANT GROVE, ALABAMA
I like to make this side dish for potlucks, because it's fast to assemble and is always popular.

PREP: 10 min.
COOK: 5 hours

2 packages (16 ounces *each*) frozen French-style green beans, thawed
1 can (10-3/4 ounces) condensed cream of mushroom soup, undiluted
1 can (10-3/4 ounces) condensed cheddar cheese soup, undiluted
3/4 cup chopped onion
3/4 cup bacon bits
1/2 cup shredded cheddar cheese
1 jar (4-1/2 ounces) sliced mushrooms, drained
1 jar (4 ounces) diced pimientos, drained
1/2 teaspoon pepper

■ In a 3- or 4-qt. slow cooker, combine all ingredients. Cover and cook on low for 5-6 hours or until beans are tender.

Yield: 10 servings.

Slow-Cooked Broccoli

Connie Slocum
ANTIOCH, TENNESSEE

My crumb-topped side dish is quick to assemble and full of flavor. It frees up my oven for other things. This is a great help when I'm preparing several items for a big meal at home.

Slow-Cooked Broccoli

PREP: 10 min. ■ COOK: 2-1/2 hours

6 cups frozen chopped broccoli, partially thawed

1 can (10-3/4 ounces) condensed cream of celery soup, undiluted

1-1/2 cups (6 ounces) shredded sharp cheddar cheese, *divided*

1/4 cup chopped onion

1/2 teaspoon Worcestershire sauce

1/4 teaspoon pepper

1 cup crushed butter-flavored crackers (about 25)

2 tablespoons butter

■ In a large bowl, combine the broccoli, soup, 1 cup cheese, onion, Worcestershire sauce and pepper. Pour mixture into a greased 3-qt. slow cooker. Sprinkle crackers on top; dot with butter.

■ Cover and cook on high for 2-1/2 to 3 hours. Sprinkle with remaining cheese. Cook 10 minutes longer or until cheese is melted.

Yield: 8-10 servings.

Barbecued Beans

PREP: 5 min. + standing
COOK: 10 hours

1 pound dried navy beans

1 pound sliced bacon, cooked and crumbled

1 bottle (32 ounces) tomato juice

1 can (8 ounces) tomato sauce

2 cups chopped onions

2/3 cup packed brown sugar

1 tablespoon soy sauce

2 teaspoons garlic salt

1 teaspoon ground mustard

1 teaspoon Worcestershire sauce

■ Place the beans in a large saucepan; add water to cover by 2 in. Bring to a boil; boil for 2 minutes. Remove from the heat; let stand for 1 hour. Drain beans and discard liquid.

■ In a 5-qt. slow cooker, combine remaining ingredients. Add the beans. Cover and cook on high for 2 hours. Reduce heat to low and cook 8-10 hours longer or until beans are tender.

Yield: 12-15 servings.

Diane Hixon
NICEVILLE, FLORIDA

Most members of my family would agree that no picnic is complete until these delicious beans have made their appearance. And even better, preparing them in a slow cooker makes them easy to transport to any gathering.

Creamy Hash Brown Potatoes

Maple Baked Beans

Nadine Brissey
JENKS, OKLAHOMA

This recipe was one of my mother's, and it was always a hit. The chopped jalapeno pepper spices it up a bit. It's an easy-to-remember recipe because most of the ingredients are 1/2 cup.

PREP: 15 min.
COOK: 6 hours

- 3 cans (15 ounces *each*) pork and beans
- 1/2 cup finely chopped onion
- 1/2 cup chopped green pepper
- 1/2 cup ketchup
- 1/2 cup maple syrup
- 2 tablespoons finely chopped seeded jalapeno pepper
- 1/2 cup crumbled cooked bacon

- In a 3-qt. slow cooker, combine the first six ingredients. Cover and cook on low for 6-7 hours or until vegetables are tender. Just before serving, stir in the bacon.

Yield: 8 servings.

Editor's Note: When cutting hot peppers, disposable gloves are recommended. Avoid touching your face.

Julianne Brown
SPRINGFIELD, ILLINOIS

I like to fix a batch of these cheesy potatoes for potlucks and big gatherings. Convenient frozen hash browns, canned soup and flavored cream cheese make this side a snap.

Creamy Hash Brown Potatoes

PREP: 5 min. ■ **COOK:** 3-1/2 hours

- 1 package (32 ounces) frozen cubed hash brown potatoes
- 1 can (10-3/4 ounces) condensed cream of potato soup, undiluted
- 2 cups (8 ounces) shredded Colby-Monterey Jack cheese
- 1 cup (8 ounces) sour cream
- 1/4 teaspoon pepper
- 1/8 teaspoon salt
- 1 carton (8 ounces) spreadable chive and onion cream cheese

- Place the potatoes in a lightly greased 3-qt. slow cooker. In a small bowl, combine the soup, cheese, sour cream, pepper and salt. Pour over the potatoes and mix well.

- Cover and cook on low for 3-1/2 to 4 hours or until potatoes are tender. Stir in cream cheese.

Yield: 12-14 servings.

Heidi Ferkovich
PARK FALLS, WISCONSIN

Our kids just love this. Sometimes I add cocktail sausages, sliced Polish sausage or cubed ham to the cheesy pasta for an all-in-one dinner.

Cheddar Spirals

Cheddar Spirals

PREP: 20 min. ■ **COOK:** 2-1/2 hours

1 package (16 ounces) spiral pasta

2 cups half-and-half cream

1 can (10-3/4 ounces) condensed cheddar cheese soup, undiluted

1/2 cup butter, melted

4 cups (16 ounces) shredded cheddar cheese

■ Cook pasta according to package directions; drain. In a 5-qt. slow cooker, combine the cream, soup and butter until smooth; stir in the cheese and pasta. Cover and cook on low for 2-1/2 hours or until the cheese is melted.

Yield: 12-15 servings.

Creamy Jalapeno Corn

Judy Carty
WICHITA, KANSAS

This comforting and creamy corn side dish is appealing to almost everyone. It gets its spicy kick from jalapeno peppers.

PREP: 15 min.
COOK: 4 hours

2 packages (16 ounces *each*) frozen corn

1 package (8 ounces) cream cheese, softened and cubed

4 jalapeno peppers, seeded and finely chopped

1/4 cup butter, cubed

2 tablespoons water

1/2 teaspoon salt

1/4 teaspoon pepper

■ In a 3-qt. slow cooker, combine all the ingredients. Cover and cook on low for 4-5 hours or until the corn is tender, stirring occasionally.

Yield: 8 servings.

Editor's Note: When cutting hot peppers, disposable gloves are recommended. Avoid touching your face.

It's simple to prevent shredded cheese from spoiling before you have the chance to use it all. Buy large bags of shredded cheddar, put measured amounts in resealable freezer bags and freeze individually. When you need the cheese for a recipe, just thaw a bag (or two).

Snacks & Sweets

92

98

94

Celebrating never tasted so sweet! Here are plenty of fun and delicious recipes to help you plan your next party. Your guests will rave after tasting the delectable dips, tantalizing appetizers, scrumptious desserts and warm, festive beverages in this chapter.

Green Olive Dip

Beth Dunahay
LIMA, OHIO

Olive fans will love this dip. It's cheesy and full of ground beef and refried beans. It's hearty and yummy enough that it could even be used to fill taco shells.

Green Olive Dip

PREP: 30 min. ■ COOK: 3 hours

- 1 pound ground beef
- 1 medium sweet red pepper, chopped
- 1 small onion, chopped
- 1 can (16 ounces) refried beans
- 1 jar (16 ounces) mild salsa
- 2 cups (8 ounces) shredded part-skim mozzarella cheese
- 2 cups (8 ounces) shredded cheddar cheese
- 1 jar (5-3/4 ounces) sliced green olives with pimientos, drained

Tortilla chips

■ In a large skillet, cook the beef, pepper and onion over medium heat until meat is no longer pink; drain. Transfer to a greased 3-qt. slow cooker. Add the beans, salsa, cheeses and olives.

■ Cover and cook on low for 3-4 hours or until cheese is melted, stirring occasionally. Serve with chips.

Yield: 8 cups.

Mulled Pomegranate Sipper*

Lisa Renshaw
KANSAS CITY, MISSOURI

This comforting beverage fills the entire house with a warm and wonderful aroma.

PREP: 10 min.
COOK: 1 hour

- 1 bottle (64 ounces) cranberry-apple juice
- 2 cups unsweetened apple juice
- 1 cup pomegranate juice
- 2/3 cup honey
- 1/2 cup orange juice
- 3 cinnamon sticks (3 inches)
- 10 whole cloves
- 2 tablespoons grated orange peel

■ In a 5-qt. slow cooker, combine the first five ingredients. Place the cinnamon sticks, cloves and orange peel on a double thickness of cheesecloth; bring up corners of cloth and tie with a string to form a bag. Add to slow cooker. Cover and cook on low for 1-2 hours. Discard spice bag before serving.

Yield: 16 servings (about 3 quarts).

✱ **Nutrition Facts:** 3/4 cup equals 131 calories, trace fat (trace saturated fat), 0 cholesterol, 21 mg sodium, 33 g carbohydrate, trace fiber, trace protein. **Diabetic Exchange:** 2 fruit.

Glazed Cinnamon Apples

Slow Cooker Chai*

PREP: 20 min.
COOK: 8 hours

3-1/2 ounces fresh gingerroot, peeled and thinly sliced
25 whole cloves
15 cardamom pods, crushed
3 cinnamon sticks (3 inches)
3 whole peppercorns
3-1/2 quarts water
8 individual black tea bags
1 can (14 ounces) sweetened condensed milk

■ Place the fresh ginger, cloves, cardamom, cinnamon sticks and peppercorns on a double thickness of cheesecloth; bring up corners of cloth and tie with string to form a bag. Add spice bag and water to a 5- or 6-qt. slow cooker. Cover and cook on low for 8 hours.

■ Add the tea bags; cover and steep for 3-5 minutes. Discard tea bags and spice bag. Stir in the milk and heat through. Serve warm.

Yield: 12 servings (3 quarts).

✱Nutrition Facts: 1 cup equals 114 calories, 3 g fat (2 g saturated fat), 11 mg cholesterol, 43 mg sodium, 19 g carbohydrate, trace fiber, 3 g protein. Diabetic Exchange: 1 starch.

Megan Maze
OAK CREEK, WISCONSIN
If you are seeking comfort food on the sweet side, this warm and yummy apple dessert, made with cinnamon and nutmeg, fits the bill.

Glazed Cinnamon Apples

PREP: 20 min. ■ COOK: 3 hours

6 large tart apples
2 tablespoons lemon juice
1/2 cup packed brown sugar
1/2 cup sugar
2 tablespoons all-purpose flour
1 teaspoon ground cinnamon
1/4 teaspoon ground nutmeg
6 tablespoons butter, melted
Vanilla ice cream

■ Peel, core and cut each apple into eight wedges; transfer to a 3-qt. slow cooker. Drizzle with lemon juice. Combine sugars, flour, cinnamon and nutmeg; sprinkle over apples. Drizzle with butter.

■ Cover and cook on low for 3-4 hours or until apples are tender. Serve in dessert dishes with ice cream.

Yield: 7 servings.

Crystal Jo Bruns
ILIFF, COLORADO

The word "chai" simply means "tea." In this case, the sweet and spicy aroma that wafts from the slow cooker as this pleasantly flavored tea cooks is wonderful. I love that I can make this at home, because normally I would go to an expensive coffeehouse to purchase hot tea like this.

Warm Fruit Compote

Burgundy Pears

Elizabeth Hanes,
PERALTA, NEW MEXICO

These spiced pears elevate slow cooking to a new level of elegance, yet they're incredibly easy to make. Your friends won't believe this fancy-looking dessert came from a slow cooker.

PREP: 10 min.
COOK: 3 hours

- 6 medium ripe pears
- 1/3 cup sugar
- 1/3 cup Burgundy wine *or* grape juice
- 3 tablespoons orange marmalade
- 1 tablespoon lemon juice
- 1/4 teaspoon ground cinnamon
- 1/4 teaspoon ground nutmeg

Dash salt

Whipped cream cheese

■ Peel the pears, leaving stems intact. Core from the bottom. Stand pears upright in a 5-qt. slow cooker. In a small bowl, combine the sugar, wine or grape juice, marmalade, lemon juice, cinnamon, nutmeg and salt. Carefully pour over pears.

■ Cover and cook on low for 3-4 hours or until tender. To serve, drizzle the pears with sauce and garnish with the whipped cream cheese.

Yield: 6 servings.

Mary Ann Jonns
MIDLOTHIAN, ILLINOIS

I rely on the convenience of canned goods to make this old-fashioned side dish. Full of peaches, pears, pineapple and apricots, it's a heartwarming medley for holiday menus.

Warm Fruit Compote

PREP: 10 min. ■ **COOK:** 2 hours

- 2 cans (29 ounces *each*) sliced peaches, drained
- 2 cans (29 ounces *each*) pear halves, drained and sliced
- 1 can (20 ounces) pineapple chunks, drained
- 1 can (15-1/4 ounces) apricot halves, drained and sliced
- 1 can (21 ounces) cherry pie filling

■ In a 5-qt. slow cooker, combine the peaches, pears, pineapple and apricots. Top with the pie filling. Cover; cook on high for 2 hours or until heated through. Serve with a slotted spoon.

Yield: 14-18 servings.

Hot Christmas Punch

Patricia Dick
ANDERSON, INDIANA

I originally got this recipe from a co-worker who brought it to work for our office Christmas party. The punch has a homey cinnamon flavor and a rosy red color that is pleasing to almost everyone.

PREP: 15 min. ■ **COOK:** 3 hours

- 1 quart brewed tea
- 1 quart unsweetened apple juice
- 1 quart orange juice
- 1 quart unsweetened pineapple juice
- 1 package (9 ounces) red-hot candies

■ In a 6-qt. slow cooker, combine all the ingredients. Cover and cook on low for 3-4 hours or until the candies are melted, stirring occasionally.

Yield: 22 servings (4 quarts).

Slow Cooker Bread Pudding

Edna Hoffman
HEBRON, INDIANA

I use my slow cooker to turn day-old cinnamon rolls into a comforting classic dessert. It tastes wonderful topped with whipped cream or even a homemade lemon or vanilla sauce.

PREP: 15 min. ■ **COOK:** 3 hours

- 8 cups cubed day-old unfrosted cinnamon rolls
- 4 eggs
- 2 cups milk
- 1/4 cup sugar
- 1/4 cup butter, melted
- 1/2 teaspoon vanilla extract
- 1/4 teaspoon ground nutmeg
- 1 cup raisins

■ Place cubed cinnamon rolls in a 3-qt. slow cooker. In a small bowl, whisk the eggs, milk, sugar, butter, vanilla and nutmeg. Stir in raisins. Pour over cinnamon rolls; stir gently. Cover and cook on low for 3 hours or until a knife inserted near the center comes out clean.

Yield: 6 servings.

Editor's Note: 8 slices of cinnamon or white bread, cut into 1-inch cubes, may be substituted for the cinnamon rolls.

Tropical Tea*

Irene Helen Zundel
CARMICHAELS, PENNSYLVANIA

I suggest brewing a batch of this fragrant, flavorful tea in a slow cooker for your next family gathering.

PREP: 15 min.
COOK: 2 hour

- 6 cups boiling water
- 6 individual tea bags
- 1-1/2 cups orange juice
- 1-1/2 cups unsweetened pineapple juice
- 1/3 cup sugar
- 1 medium navel orange, sliced and halved
- 2 tablespoons honey

■ In a 5-qt. slow cooker, combine the boiling water and tea bags. Cover; let stand for 5 minutes. Discard the tea bags. Stir in the remaining ingredients. Cover; cook on low for 2-4 hours or until heated through. Serve warm.

Yield: about 2-1/2 quarts.

✻Nutrition Facts: 1 cup equals 82 calories, trace fat (0 saturated fat), 0 cholesterol, 1 mg sodium, 21 g carbohydrate, trace fiber, trace protein. **Diabetic Exchange:** 1-1/2 fruit.

Parmesan Fondue

Gwynn Fleener
COEUR D'ALENE, IDAHO

This recipe was given to me many years ago at a New Year's potluck. Since then, it has been a tradition to serve it at our holiday open house. The creamy mixture is always a hit.

PREP/TOTAL TIME: 15 min.

1-1/2 to 2 cups milk
   2 packages (8 ounces *each*) cream cheese, cubed
1-1/2 cups grated Parmesan cheese
1/2 teaspoon garlic salt
   1 loaf (1 pound) French bread, cubed

■ In a large saucepan, cook and stir milk and cream cheese over low heat until cheese is melted. Stir in the Parmesan cheese and garlic salt; cook and stir until heated through. Keep warm. Serve with the bread cubes.

Yield: about 3-1/2 cups.

Slow Cooker Cheese Dip

Marion Bartone
CONNEAUT, OHIO

I brought this slightly spicy cheese dip to a gathering with friends, where it was a huge success.

PREP: 15 min. ■ **COOK:** 4 hours

   1 pound ground beef
1/2 pound bulk spicy pork sausage
   2 pounds process cheese (Velveeta), cubed
   2 cans (10 ounces *each*) diced tomatoes and green chilies
      Tortilla chips

■ In a large skillet, cook the beef and sausage over medium heat until no longer pink; drain. Transfer to a 5-qt. slow cooker. Stir in the cheese and tomatoes.

■ Cover and cook on low for 4 hours or until cheese is melted, stirring occasionally. Serve with tortilla chips.

Yield: 3 quarts.

Editor's Note: If you're planning on serving Slow Cooker Cheese Dip at a holiday party or family get-together, make it ahead and freeze it. Than all you need to do is thaw and reheat it.

Hot Spiced Wine

PREP: 15 min.
COOK: 4 hours

   2 cinnamon sticks (3 inches)
   3 whole cloves
   2 bottles (750 milliliters *each*) dry red wine
   3 medium tart apples, peeled and sliced
1/2 cup sugar
   1 teaspoon lemon juice

■ Place cinnamon sticks and cloves on a double thickness of cheesecloth; bring up corners of cloth and tie with string to form a bag.

■ In a 3-qt. slow cooker, combine the wine, apples, sugar and lemon juice. Add spice bag. Cover and cook on low for 4-5 hours or until the wine is heated through. Discard the spice bag. Serve warm.

Yield: 8 servings.

Whole bottles of
spices can be costly, so to save money, go to your local bulk food store and buy only what you need. You can also widen your assortment of spices, making it easy to try delicious new recipes.

Noel Lickenfelt
BOLIVAR, PENNSYLVANIA

My friends, family and I enjoy this festive spiced wine during cold-winter gatherings. It tastes great either with food or alone, and will warm your body to the toes. This ruby drink will be especially pleasing to those who enjoy dry red wines.

Nelda Cronbaugh
BELLE PLAINE, IOWA

This simple-to-make dessert comes together in a jiffy because it uses very few ingredients. If you like, you can substitute the blueberry pie filling with other flavors, such as apple or cherry. The vanilla ice cream adds a final touch that everyone enjoys.

Everyday Slow Cooker & One Dish Recipes

Blueberry Cobbler

PREP: 10 min. ■ COOK: 3 hours

- 1 can (21 ounces) blueberry pie filling
- 1 package (9 ounces) yellow cake mix
- 1/4 cup chopped pecans
- 1/4 cup butter, melted
- Vanilla ice cream, optional

■ Place pie filling in a 1-1/2-qt. slow cooker. Sprinkle with cake mix and pecans. Drizzle with butter. Cover and cook on high for 3 hours or until the topping is golden brown. Serve warm with ice cream if desired.

Yield: 6 servings.

Tangy Pork Meatballs

Katie Koziolek
HARTLAND, MINNESOTA

Buffet grazers stampede for these meatballs! The mouthwatering morsels go so fast, I often make several batches at once. Barbecue sauce adds a nice bite to the mildly seasoned ground pork.

PREP/TOTAL TIME: 30 min.

- 2 eggs, lightly beaten
- 2/3 cup dry bread crumbs
- 2 tablespoons dried minced onion
- 2 teaspoons seasoned salt
- 2 pounds ground pork

SAUCE:

1-1/2 cups ketchup
- 1 can (8 ounces) tomato sauce
- 3 tablespoons Worcestershire sauce
- 2 to 3 tablespoons cider vinegar
- 2 teaspoons Liquid Smoke, optional

■ In a large bowl, combine the eggs, bread crumbs, onion and salt. Crumble pork over mixture and mix well. Shape into 3/4-in. balls.

■ Place meatballs on a greased rack in a shallow baking pan. Bake at 400° for 15 minutes or until the meat is no longer pink; drain.

■ Meanwhile, in a large saucepan, combine sauce ingredients. Simmer, uncovered, for 10 minutes, stirring occasionally. Add meatballs. Serve in a 5-qt. slow cooker or chafing dish.

Yield: 7-1/2 dozen.

Slow-Cooked Salsa

Toni Menard
LOMPOC, CALIFORNIA

I love the garden-fresh taste of homemade salsa, but as a working mother, I have little time to make it. So I came up with this slow-cooked version that practically makes itself!

PREP: 15 min.
COOK: 2-1/2 hours + cooling

- 10 plum tomatoes
- 2 garlic cloves
- 1 small onion, cut into wedges
- 2 jalapeno peppers
- 1/4 cup cilantro leaves
- 1/2 teaspoon salt, optional

■ Core tomatoes. Cut a small slit in two tomatoes; insert a garlic clove into each slit. Place the tomatoes and onion in a 3-qt. slow cooker. Cut the stems off jalapenos; remove seeds if a milder salsa is desired. Place jalapenos in the slow cooker. Cover and cook on high for 2-1/2 to 3 hours or until the vegetables are softened (some may brown slightly); cool.

■ In a blender, combine tomato mixture, cilantro and salt if desired; cover and process until blended. Refrigerate leftovers.

Yield: about 2 cups.

Editor's Note: When cutting hot peppers, disposable gloves are recommended. Avoid touching your face.

Elaine Sweet
DALLAS, TEXAS

For a truly different chocolate cake, think outside of the box and inside the slow cooker! This easy dessert comes out warm, moist, fudgy and wonderful.

Cherry Cola Chocolate Cake

Cherry Cola Chocolate Cake

PREP: 30 min. + standing ■ **COOK:** 2 hours + standing

1/2 cup cola	2 teaspoons vanilla extract
1/2 cup dried tart cherries	TOPPING:
1-1/2 cups all-purpose flour	1-1/4 cups cola
1/2 cup sugar	1/2 cup sugar
2 ounces semisweet chocolate, chopped	1/2 cup packed brown sugar
2-1/2 teaspoons baking powder	2 ounces semisweet chocolate, chopped
1/2 teaspoon salt	1/4 cup dark rum
1 cup chocolate milk	Vanilla ice cream and maraschino cherries, optional
1/2 cup butter, melted	

■ In a small saucepan, bring the cola and dried cherries to a boil. Remove from heat; let stand for 30 minutes.

■ In a large bowl, combine the flour, sugar, chocolate, baking powder and salt. Combine the chocolate milk, butter and vanilla; stir into the dry ingredients just until moistened. Fold in the cherry mixture. Pour into a 3-qt. slow cooker coated with cooking spray.

■ For the topping, in a small saucepan, combine the cola, sugar and brown sugar. Cook and stir until the sugar is dissolved. Remove from the heat; stir in the chocolate and rum until smooth. Pour over the cherry mixture; do not stir.

■ Cover and cook on high for 2 to 2-1/2 hours or until set. Turn off heat; let stand, covered, for 30 minutes. Serve warm with ice cream and the maraschino cherries if desired.

Yield: 8 servings.

Editor's Note: This recipe does not use eggs.

Moist and Tender Wings

Sharon Morcilio
JOSHUA TREE, CALIFORNIA

These no-fuss wings are fall-off-the-bone tender. Chili sauce offers a bit of spice while molasses lends a hint of sweetness. They also make a great meal with a side dish of rice.

PREP: 15 min.
COOK: 8 hours

25	whole chicken wings (about 5 pounds)
1	bottle (12 ounces) chili sauce
1/4	cup lemon juice
1/4	cup molasses
2	tablespoons Worcestershire sauce
6	garlic cloves, minced
1	tablespoon chili powder
1	tablespoon salsa
1	teaspoon garlic salt
3	drops hot pepper sauce

■ Cut the chicken wings into three sections; discard the wing tips. Place the wings in a 5-qt. slow cooker. In a bowl, combine the remaining ingredients; pour over chicken. Stir to coat. Cover and cook on low for 8 hours or until chicken is tender.

Yield: about 4 dozen.

Editor's Note: Uncooked chicken wing sections (wingettes) may be substituted for whole chicken wings.

Granola Apple Crisp

Butterscotch Fondue

Taste of Home Test Kitchen
Folks of all ages will enjoy dipping into a warm pot filled with this yummy concoction.

PREP/TOTAL TIME: 30 min.

- 1/2 cup butter, cubed
- 2 cups packed brown sugar
- 1 can (14 ounces) sweetened condensed milk
- 1 cup light corn syrup
- 2 tablespoons water
- 1/4 cup English toffee bits *or* almond brickle chips
- 1 teaspoon vanilla extract
- Angel food cake cubes and fresh fruit

■ In a large saucepan, combine the butter, brown sugar, milk, corn syrup and water. Cook and stir over medium heat until smooth. Remove from the heat. Stir in toffee bits and vanilla. Keep warm. Serve with cake and fruit.

Yield: 4 cups.

Barbara Schindler
NAPOLEON, OHIO
Tasty apple slices are tucked beneath a sweet, crunchy topping in this comforting crisp. For something different, replace the apples with your favorite fruit.

Granola Apple Crisp

PREP: 20 min. ■ COOK: 5 hours

- 8 medium tart apples, peeled and sliced
- 1/4 cup lemon juice
- 1-1/2 teaspoons grated lemon peel
- 2-1/2 cups granola with fruit and nuts
- 1 cup sugar
- 1 teaspoon ground cinnamon
- 1/2 cup butter, melted

■ In a large bowl, toss the apples, lemon juice and peel. Transfer to a greased 3-qt. slow cooker. Combine the granola, sugar and cinnamon; sprinkle over the apples. Drizzle with butter.

■ Cover; cook on low for 5-6 hours or until the apples are tender. Serve warm.

Yield: 6-8 servings.

Be creative when picking dippers for sweet fondue. Try shortbread cookies, almond biscotti, marshmallows or pretzels. Other fruit options include dried apricots, cantaloupe squares, orange segments or fresh pineapple chunks.

Michelle Domm
ATLANTA, NEW YORK

This cheesy recipe has a nice combination of seafood flavors from crab and shrimp, and it clings nicely to slices of bread. I like to serve it at potlucks because the slow cooker keeps the dip warm. But it also works as an elegant starter when served already spread on bread slices.

Seafood Cheese Dip

PREP: 15 min. ■ COOK: 1-1/2 hours

- 1 package (32 ounces) process cheese (Velveeta), cubed
- 2 cans (6 ounces *each*) lump crabmeat, drained
- 1 can (10 ounces) diced tomatoes and green chilies, undrained
- 1 cup frozen cooked salad shrimp, thawed
- French bread baguettes sliced and toasted

■ In a greased 3-qt. slow cooker, combine the cheese, crab, tomatoes and shrimp. Cover and cook on low for 1-1/2 to 2 hours or until cheese is melted, stirring occasionally. Serve with baguette slices.

Yield: *5 cups.*

Gingerbread Pudding Cake

Barbara Cook
YUMA, ARIZONA

A handful of spices and a half cup of molasses give this delightful dessert a yummy, old-fashioned flavor. It's pretty, too, with a dollop of whipped cream and a mint sprig on top.

PREP: 20 min. ■ COOK: 2 hours + standing

- 1/4 cup butter, softened
- 1/4 cup sugar
- 1 egg white
- 1 teaspoon vanilla extract
- 1/2 cup molasses
- 1 cup water
- 1-1/4 cups all-purpose flour
- 3/4 teaspoon baking soda
- 1/2 teaspoon ground cinnamon
- 1/2 teaspoon ground ginger
- 1/4 teaspoon salt
- 1/4 teaspoon ground allspice
- 1/8 teaspoon ground nutmeg
- 1/2 cup chopped pecans

TOPPING:
- 6 tablespoons brown sugar
- 3/4 cup hot water
- 2/3 cup butter, melted

■ In a large bowl, cream butter and sugar until light and fluffy. Beat in the egg white and vanilla. Combine molasses and water. Combine the flour, baking soda, cinnamon, ginger, salt, allspice and nutmeg; gradually add to creamed mixture alternately with molasses mixture, beating well after each addition. Fold in pecans.

■ Pour into a greased 3-qt. slow cooker. For topping, sprinkle with brown sugar. Combine hot water and butter; pour over batter (do not stir).

■ Cover and cook on high for 2 to 2-1/2 hours or until a toothpick inserted near the center of cake comes out clean. Turn off the heat. Let stand for 15 minutes. Serve warm.

Yield: *6-8 servings.*

Pear-Blueberry Granola

Lisa Workman
BOONES MILL, VIRGINIA

Oatmeal fans will love this dish. Although the pears, blueberries and granola make a beautiful breakfast, the recipe also makes a delicious dessert when served with vanilla ice cream.

PREP: 15 min.
COOK: 3 hours

- 5 medium pears, thinly sliced and peeled
- 2 cups fresh *or* frozen unsweetened blueberries
- 1/2 cup packed brown sugar
- 1/3 cup apple cider *or* unsweetend apple juice
- 1 tablespoon all-purpose flour
- 1 tablespoon lemon juice
- 2 teaspoons ground cinnamon
- 2 tablespoons butter
- 3 cups granola without raisins

■ In a 4-qt. slow cooker, combine the first seven ingredients. Dot with butter. Sprinkle granola over top. Cover and cook on low for 3-4 hours or until fruit is tender.

Yield: *10 servings.*

Maxine Cenker
WEIRTON, WEST VIRGINIA

A tasty sweet-sour sauce glazes bite-size sausages in this recipe. Serve these effortless appetizers with toothpicks at parties or holiday get-togethers.

Simmered Smoked Links

Simmered Smoked Links

PREP: 5 min. ■ COOK: 4 hours

> 2 packages (16 ounces *each*) miniature smoked sausage links
>
> 1 cup packed brown sugar
>
> 1/2 cup ketchup
>
> 1/4 cup prepared horseradish

■ Place sausages in a 3-qt. slow cooker. Combine brown sugar, ketchup and horseradish; pour over sausages. Cover; cook on low for 4 hours.

Yield: 16-20 servings.

Mulled Dr. Pepper

Bernice Morris
MARSHFIELD, MISSOURI

When neighbors or friends visit us on a chilly evening, I'll serve this warm beverage with ham sandwiches and deviled eggs.

PREP: 10 min. ■ COOK: 2 hours

> 8 cups Dr. Pepper
>
> 1/4 cup packed brown sugar
>
> 1/4 cup lemon juice
>
> 1/2 teaspoon ground allspice
>
> 1/2 teaspoon whole cloves
>
> 1/4 teaspoon salt
>
> 1/4 teaspoon ground nutmeg
>
> 3 cinnamon sticks (3 inches)

■ In a 3-qt. slow cooker, combine all ingredients. Cover and cook on low for 2 hours or until desired temperature is reached.

■ Discard cloves and cinnamon sticks.

Yield: 8-10 servings.

Strawberry Rhubarb Sauce

Judith Wasman
HARKERS ISLAND, NORTH CAROLINA

I prepare a tart and tangy fruit sauce that's excellent over pound cake or ice cream. I've served this rosy-colored mixture many times and gotten rave reviews from friends and family.

PREP: 10 min.
COOK: 6 hours

> 6 cups chopped rhubarb (1/2-inch pieces)
>
> 1 cup sugar
>
> 1/2 teaspoon grated orange peel
>
> 1/2 teaspoon ground ginger
>
> 1 cinnamon stick (3 inches)
>
> 1/2 cup white grape juice
>
> 2 cups halved unsweetened strawberries
>
> Angel food cake, pound cake *or* vanilla ice cream

■ Place rhubarb in a 3-qt. slow cooker. Combine sugar, orange peel and ginger; sprinkle over rhubarb. Add cinnamon stick and grape juice. Cover and cook on low for 5-6 hours or until rhubarb is tender.

■ Stir in strawberries; cook 1 hour longer. Discard cinnamon stick. Serve with cake or ice cream.

Yield: 10 servings.

Hot Chili Dip

Nikki Rosati
FRANKSVILLE, WISCONSIN
I first made this zippy dip for my husband's birthday party. So many people asked for the recipe that I photocopied it to give to my guests.

Hot Chili Dip

PREP: 5 min. ■ **COOK:** 1 hour

1 jar (24 ounces) salsa	12 ounces process cheese (Velveeta), cubed
1 can (15 ounces) chili with beans	Tortilla chips
2 cans (2-1/4 ounces *each*) sliced ripe olives, drained	

■ In a 1-1/2-qt. slow cooker, combine the salsa, chili and olives. Stir in cheese. Cover and cook on low for 1-2 hours or until cheese is melted, stirring halfway through. Serve with chips.

Yield: about 2 cups.

Holiday Wassail Punch

Jennifer Stout
BLANDON, PENNSYLVANIA
This festive and fruity punch is made with five kinds of juices plus cinnamon and allspice for a unique, well-balanced flavor.

PREP: 10 min.
COOK: 4 hours

- 3 to 4 cinnamon sticks (3 inches)
- 8 whole allspice
- 4 cups unsweetened apple juice
- 4 cups orange juice
- 2 cups cranberry juice
- 1 can (11.3 ounces) pineapple nectar
- 1/2 cup sugar
- 2 teaspoons lemon juice
- 8 to 10 orange slices

■ Place the cinnamon sticks and allspice on a double thickness of cheesecloth; bring up the corners of cloth and tie with string to form a bag. In a 5- or 6-qt. slow cooker, combine the juices, pineapple nectar, sugar, lemon juice, orange slices and spice bag.

■ Cover and cook on low for 4-5 hours or until heated through. Discard oranges and spice bag. Serve warm.

Yield: 3 quarts.

STOVETOP SUPPERS

Beef & Ground Beef

114

116

108

There are plenty of hearty beef and ground beef dishes to choose from in this chapter. All made on the stovetop, these single-skillet suppers mean you spend less time in the kitchen, and more time with your family. In fact, you're sure to find a new favorite family recipe!

- In a small bowl, combine garlic powder, thyme and cayenne. Sprinkle over the beef.

- In a large saucepan coated with cooking spray, cook beef in oil until no longer pink; drain. Stir in celery and green pepper; cook 2 minutes longer or until vegetables are crisp-tender. Stir in the water and rice mix with contents of seasoning packet.

- Bring to a boil. Reduce heat; cover and simmer for 23-28 minutes or until rice is tender. Stir in tomato; heat through. Sprinkle with onion.

Yield: 4 servings.

*Nutrition Facts: 1 cup equals 327 calories, 10 g fat (2 g saturated fat), 63 mg cholesterol, 626 mg sodium, 33 g carbohydrate, 1 g fiber, 26 g protein. **Diabetic Exchanges:** 3 lean meat, 2 starch, 1/2 fat.

Beef and Wild Rice Medley

Janelle Christensen
BIG LAKE, MINNESOTA

A packaged rice mix speeds up preparation of this meal-in-one entree. Cayenne pepper gives the beef a little kick, and an assortment of veggies adds color and crunch.

Beef and Wild Rice Medley*

PREP: 5 min. ■ COOK: 40 min.

1/2 teaspoon garlic powder
1/2 teaspoon dried thyme
1/8 teaspoon cayenne pepper
1 pound beef top sirloin steak, cut into 3/4-inch cubes
1 tablespoon canola oil
1/4 cup sliced celery
1/4 cup julienned green pepper
2-1/4 cups water
1 package (6 ounces) long grain and wild rice mix
1 small tomato, chopped
2 tablespoons chopped green onion

For a refreshing accompaniment to Beef and Wild Rice Medley, try serving it with Lemony Iced Tea. In a large pitcher, combine 8 cups water, 3/4 cup sugar, 1/2 cup lemon juice, 1/2 cup white grape juice and 1/4 cup unsweetened lemon-flavored instant tea mix. Serve in chilled glasses over ice and garnish with lemon slices.

Joan Best
GARRISON, MONTANA
My husband goes deer hunting, so I have quite a few recipes for venison, and this is his favorite. Hope you enjoy it too!

Country-Style Pot Roast

Country-Style Pot Roast

PREP: 10 min. + marinating ■ **COOK:** 3-1/2 hours

- 2 cups water
- 2 cups cider vinegar
- 2 teaspoons salt
- 1 teaspoon Worcestershire sauce
- 1/2 teaspoon garlic powder
- 1/2 teaspoon pepper
- 1 boneless beef *or* venison rump *or* chuck roast (3-1/2 to 4 pounds)
- 6 medium onions, thinly sliced, *divided*
- 12 whole peppercorns, *divided*
- 4 bay leaves, *divided*
- 4 whole cloves, *divided*
- 2 tablespoons canola oil
- 10 medium carrots, cut into 1-inch chunks
- 5 to 7 tablespoons cornstarch
- 1/3 cup cold water

■ In a large bowl, combine first six ingredients. Pour half of the marinade into a large resealable plastic bag; add the beef and half of the onions, peppercorns, bay leaves and cloves. Seal the bag and turn to coat; refrigerate for 24 hours. To the remaining marinade, add the remaining onions, peppercorns, bay leaves and cloves. Cover and refrigerate.

■ Drain and discard marinade. In a Dutch oven, brown roast in oil; drain. Add carrots and reserved marinade; bring to a rolling boil. Reduce heat; cover and simmer for 3-1/2 to 4 hours or until meat is tender.

■ Remove roast and keep warm. Strain cooking juices; discard vegetables and spices. Return juices to pan. Combine cornstarch and cold water until smooth; gradually add to pan juices. Bring to a boil; cook and stir for 2 minutes or until thickened. Slice roast; serve with gravy.

Yield: *6-8 servings.*

Bow Tie Beef Skillet

PREP/TOTAL TIME: 25 min.

- 1 pound ground beef
- 1/2 teaspoon salt
- 1/8 teaspoon pepper
- 2 cups uncooked bow tie pasta
- 1 can (14-1/2 ounces) diced tomatoes, drained
- 1-1/3 cups beef broth
- 1 can (8 ounces) tomato sauce
- 1 tablespoon Worcestershire sauce
- 3 medium yellow summer squash, thinly sliced
- 3/4 cup chopped green pepper
- 1 cup (4 ounces) shredded Parmesan cheese, *divided*

■ In a large skillet, cook beef over medium heat until no longer pink; drain. Sprinkle with salt and pepper. Stir in the pasta, tomatoes, broth, tomato sauce and the Worcestershire sauce. Bring to a boil. Reduce the heat; cover and simmer for 10-12 minutes.

■ Add the squash and green pepper. Cook, uncovered, for 3-4 minutes or until the pasta and vegetables are tender, stirring occasionally. Add 1/2 cup cheese; cook 1-2 minutes longer or until the cheese is melted. Sprinkle with the remaining cheese.

Yield: *5 servings.*

Tammy Perrault
LANCASTER, OHIO

When I have a busy day, this is the dish I choose to make for dinner. It has all the ingredients for a well-rounded meal and comes together so quickly. I've come to rely on it for a real family-pleasing meal. It's always delicious.

- Cook the pasta according to package directions. Meanwhile, in a large skillet, cook the beef, onion, celery and green pepper over medium heat until meat is no longer pink. Add garlic; add 1 minute. Drain.

- Drain the pasta; add to the beef mixture. Stir in soup, parsley, oregano, salt and pepper. Bring to a boil. Reduce heat; simmer, uncovered, for 4-5 minutes or until heated through. Sprinkle with cheese.

Yield: 3 servings.

*Nutrition Facts: 1-1/3 cups equals 351 calories, 11 g fat (5 g saturated fat), 50 mg cholesterol, 758 mg sodium, 38 g carbohydrate, 3 g fiber, 24 g protein. Diabetic Exchanges: 3 lean meat, 2 starch, 1 vegetable, 1 fat.

Macaroni Scramble

Patricia Kile
NOKOMIS, FLORIDA

This quick-and-easy dinner has all the pasta, cheese, meat and sweet tomato sauce that make for a classic. Serve with a green salad and crusty French bread for a surefire hit.

Macaroni Scramble*

PREP/TOTAL TIME: 25 min.

- 1 cup uncooked cellentani (spiral pasta) *or* elbow macaroni
- 1/2 pound lean ground beef (90% lean)
- 1 small onion, chopped
- 1 celery rib, chopped
- 1 small green pepper, chopped
- 1 garlic clove, minced
- 1 can (10-3/4 ounces) reduced-sodium condensed tomato soup, undiluted
- 1 tablespoon minced fresh parsley *or* 1 teaspoon dried parsley flakes
- 1 teaspoon dried oregano
- 1/4 teaspoon salt
- 1/4 teaspoon pepper
- 1/2 cup shredded reduced-fat cheddar cheese

Freezing ground

beef, after it's been cooked and browned, is a good way to have it on hand. On a day when you have the time, crumble and brown several pounds of ground beef. Spread on a cookie sheet, cover and freeze until solid. Transfer in 1/2- or 1-pound amounts to freezer bags. Use them for any recipe that uses browned ground beef.

Lisa Williams
COMSTOCK PARK, MICHIGAN

Here's a hearty, one-dish meal that's lower in fat but very filling. The cabbage, ground beef and brown rice give it a comforting, down-home feel.

Inside-Out Cabbage Rolls

Inside-Out Cabbage Rolls*

PREP: 15 min. ■ **COOK:** 30 min.

1 pound lean ground beef (90% lean)	1 cup reduced-sodium beef broth
1 large onion, chopped	1 can (8 ounces) pizza sauce
1 large green pepper, chopped	1 cup cooked brown rice
1 small head cabbage, chopped	1/2 cup shredded reduced-fat cheddar cheese
1 can (10 ounces) diced tomatoes and green chilies	

■ In a Dutch oven, cook the beef, onion and green pepper over medium heat until meat is no longer pink; drain.

■ Stir in the cabbage, tomatoes, broth and pizza sauce. Bring to a boil. Reduce heat; cover and simmer for 20-25 minutes or until cabbage is tender, stirring occasionally.

■ Stir in rice; heat through. Remove from the heat. Sprinkle with cheese; cover and let stand until cheese is melted.

Yield: 6 servings.

✳Nutrition Facts: 1-1/3 cups equals 244 calories, 8 g fat (4 g saturated fat), 45 mg cholesterol, 502 mg sodium, 23 g carbohydrate, 5 g fiber, 21 g protein. **Diabetic Exchanges:** 2 lean meat, 1-1/2 starch, 1/2 fat.

Ravioli Skillet
Taste of Home Test Kitchen

To create this robust dish, we dressed up store-bought ravioli and made it really special by adding prosciutto and mozzarella.

PREP/TOTAL TIME: 30 min.

1	pound ground beef
3/4	cup chopped green pepper
1	ounce prosciutto *or* deli ham, chopped
3	cups spaghetti sauce
3/4	cup water
1	package (25 ounces) frozen cheese ravioli
1	cup (4 ounces) shredded part-skim mozzarella cheese

■ In a large skillet, cook the beef, green pepper and prosciutto over medium heat until meat is no longer pink; drain.

■ Stir in the spaghetti sauce and water; bring to a boil. Add the ravioli. Reduce heat; cover and simmer for 7-9 minutes or until ravioli is tender, stirring once. Sprinkle with cheese. Simmer, uncovered, 1-2 minutes longer or until cheese is melted.

Yield: 4 servings.

James Hayes,
RIDGECREST, CALIFORNIA

This delicious stew makes for a hearty supper with a lighter touch. The leaner cut of meat, herbs, seasonings and fresh vegetables make it so satisfying and flavorful, you'll want another bowl!

Jamaican-Style Beef Stew

Jamaican-Style Beef Stew

PREP: 25 min. ■ **COOK:** 1-1/2 hours

1 tablespoon canola oil	1/4 cup barbecue sauce
1 tablespoon sugar	1/4 cup reduced-sodium soy sauce
1-1/2 pounds beef top sirloin steak, cut into 3/4-inch cubes	2 tablespoons steak sauce
5 plum tomatoes, finely chopped	1 tablespoon garlic powder
	1 teaspoon dried thyme
3 large carrots, cut into 1/2-inch slices	1/4 teaspoon ground allspice
3 celery ribs, cut into 1/2-inch slices	1/4 teaspoon pepper
	1/8 teaspoon hot pepper sauce
4 green onions, chopped	1 tablespoon cornstarch
3/4 cup reduced-sodium beef broth	2 tablespoons cold water
	Hot cooked rice or mashed potatoes, optional

■ In a Dutch oven, heat the oil over medium-high heat. Add the sugar; cook and stir for 1 minute or until lightly browned. Add the beef and brown on all sides.

■ Stir in the vegetables, broth, barbecue sauce, soy sauce, steak sauce and seasonings. Bring to a boil. Reduce heat; cover and simmer for 1 to 1-1/4 hours or until meat and vegetables are tender.

■ Combine cornstarch and water until smooth; stir into stew. Bring to a boil; cook and stir for 2 minutes or until thickened. Serve with the rice or potatoes if desired.

Yield: 5 servings.

Cubed Steak Skillet Supper

Karen Rodgers
VERONA, VIRGINIA

I first made this delicious main dish in the '70s for a progressive dinner party. It was easy to prepare and came in handy while I was a working mom.

PREP/TOTAL TIME: 30 min.

1/4 cup all-purpose flour

1/4 teaspoon salt

Dash pepper

2 beef cubed steaks (6 ounces *each*)

1 to 2 tablespoons canola oil

1 small onion, sliced

1 can (15 ounces) sliced potatoes, drained

1 can (14-1/2 ounces) French-style green beans, drained

1 can (10-3/4 ounces) condensed golden mushroom soup, undiluted

Paprika

■ In a large resealable plastic bag, combine the flour, salt and pepper. Add steaks, one at a time, and shake to coat.

■ In a large skillet, brown steaks on both sides in oil until no longer pink. Set aside and keep warm. Add the onion, potatoes and beans to the skillet; stir in the soup.

■ Return steaks to skillet. Cover and simmer for 15 minutes or until meat is tender. Sprinkle with paprika.

Yield: 2 servings.

Hominy Taco Chili

- In a Dutch oven, cook beef and onion over medium heat until meat is no longer pink; drain. Stir in the next 11 ingredients. Bring to a boil. Reduce the heat; cover and simmer for 30 minutes.

- Serve half of chili with corn chips if desired. Freeze remaining chili in a freezer container for up to 3 months.

- **TO USE FROZEN CHILI:** Thaw in the refrigerator. Transfer to a large saucepan; heat through, adding water if desired.

**Yield: 2 batches
(5 servings each).**

Barbara Wheless
SHELDON, SOUTH CAROLINA
This robust chili is easy to create with canned items. It makes enough for dinner and leftovers to freeze. With beans, ground beef and seasonings, it always receives rave reviews.

Hominy Taco Chili

PREP: 15 min. ■ COOK: 30 min.

1 pound ground beef	1 can (15 ounces) black beans, rinsed and drained
1 large onion, chopped	1 cup water
2 cans (15-1/2 ounces *each*) hominy, drained	1 envelope taco seasoning
2 cans (14-1/2 ounces *each*) stewed tomatoes, undrained	1 envelope ranch salad dressing mix
1 can (15-1/4 ounces) whole kernel corn, drained	2 teaspoons ground cumin
1 can (15 ounces) pinto beans, rinsed and drained	1/2 teaspoon garlic salt
	1/2 teaspoon pepper
	Corn chips, optional

To add a touch

of fun, flavor and flair to Hominy Taco Chili, top servings with different garnishes. You might want to try dollops of sour cream, chopped green onions, guacamole, sliced avocados, chopped tomatoes or shredded cheddar cheese.

Meatballs with Pepper Sauce

Garden Skillet

GaleLynn Peterson
LONG BEACH, CALIFORNIA

As part of our final exam in a gourmet cooking class, we had to improve upon an existing recipe and serve it to the other students. This effortless dish was my class-approved creation.

PREP/TOTAL TIME: 30 min.

- 2 pounds ground beef
- 3 medium zucchini, julienned
- 4 medium carrots, julienned
- 1 can (15 ounces) canned bean sprouts, drained
- 1 medium onion, cut into thin wedges
- 3/4 cup julienned green pepper
- 1 medium tomato, cut into wedges
- 1 garlic clove, minced
- 1 teaspoon salt
- 1 teaspoon ground cumin

■ In a large skillet, cook beef over medium heat until no longer pink; drain. Add the zucchini, carrots, bean sprouts, onion and green pepper. Cook and stir for 3-4 minutes or until crisp-tender. Add the tomato, garlic, salt and cumin. Cook 2 minutes longer or until heated through.

Yield: 6-8 servings.

Editor's Note: To give the Garden Skillet a little more heat, toss in strips of jalapeno peppers and serve with taco sauce on the side.

Julie Neal
GREEN BAY, WISCONSIN

I've found these colorful meatballs keep well in a slow cooker for a no-fuss meal. We enjoy them served over pasta or rice. They also make great appetizers.

Meatballs with Pepper Sauce

PREP: 25 min. ■ BAKE: 1-1/4 hours

- 1 cup evaporated milk
- 1 tablespoon Worcestershire sauce
- 1 envelope onion soup mix
- 2 pounds ground beef

SAUCE:
- 1/2 pound sliced fresh mushrooms
- 1-1/2 cups ketchup
- 3/4 cup packed brown sugar
- 3/4 cup water
- 1/2 cup chopped green pepper
- 1/2 cup chopped sweet red pepper
- 2 tablespoons chopped onion
- 1 tablespoon Worcestershire sauce

■ In a large bowl, combine the milk, Worcestershire sauce and soup mix. Crumble beef over mixture and mix well. Shape into 1-in. balls.

■ Place meatballs on a rack in a shallow baking pan. Broil 4-6 in. from heat for 5-8 minutes or until browned. In a Dutch oven, combine sauce ingredients. Bring to a boil. Reduce the heat; add meatballs. Simmer, uncovered, for 1 hour or until the meat is no longer pink.

Yield: 60 meatballs.

Swiss Steak Supper*

Dorothy Collins
WINNSBORO, TEXAS

This recipe is a tasty, satisfying meal-in-one dish. It has everything a hungry family needs for a nutritional supper.

PREP: 20 min. ■ **COOK:** 1 hour 40 min.

1/4	cup all-purpose flour
1	teaspoon salt, optional
1/4	teaspoon pepper
1-1/2	pounds boneless beef top round steak (about 1/2 inch thick), cut into 1/2-inch pieces
1	tablespoon canola oil
1	can (28 ounces) diced tomatoes, undrained
1	medium onion, sliced
1	can (4 ounces) whole green chilies, drained
4	medium red potatoes (about 1 pound), peeled and quartered
4	carrots, cut into 2-inch chunks
2	tablespoons cornstarch
2	tablespoons water

■ In a large resealable plastic bag, combine the flour, salt if desired and pepper. Add steak and shake to coat. In a large skillet, brown beef on both sides in oil over medium heat until no longer pink; drain. Add the tomatoes, onion and chilies; bring to a boil. Reduce the heat; cover and simmer for 30 minutes.

■ Add potatoes and carrots. Cover and simmer for 70-80 minutes or until meat and vegetables are tender. Combine cornstarch and water until smooth; stir into skillet. Bring to a boil, cook and stir for 2 minutes or until thickened.

Yield: 6 servings.

❋Nutrition Facts: 1 serving (prepared without salt) equals 366 calories, 427 mg sodium, 70 mg cholesterol, 30 gm carbohydrate, 29 gm protein, 14 gm fat. **Diabetic Exchanges:** 3 lean meat, 1-1/2 starch, 2 vegetable, 1 fat.

To use cornstarch as a thickener, dissolve the cornstarch in a small amount of a cold liquid before slowly adding it to the hot mixture. Then, to produce a nicely thickened sauce, gravy or pudding, cook and stir a full 2 minutes after adding the cornstarch mixture.

Pepper Beef With Cashews

Sharon Wolf
CAMROSE, ALBERTA

The tantalizing bell peppers in this dish make it look so attractive and are a nice, sweet contrast to the peppery beef. Served over hot cooked rice or pasta, it's special enough for company yet quick enough for every day.

PREP/TOTAL TIME: 30 min.

1-1/2	pounds ground beef
1	small onion, chopped
2	teaspoons coarsely ground pepper
2	garlic cloves, minced
4	tablespoons beef broth, *divided*
1	*each* large sweet red, yellow and green pepper, chopped
2	tablespoons oyster sauce, optional
1	tablespoon soy sauce
2	teaspoons cornstarch
3/4	cup cashew halves

■ In a large skillet, cook the beef, onion and pepper over medium heat until no longer pink. Remove with a slotted spoon and keep warm. Add garlic to skillet; cook for 1 minute. Stir in 2 tablespoons broth. Add the peppers. Cover and steam for 1 minute.

■ Return the beef mixture to pan. Stir in oyster sauce if desired and soy sauce. Combine the cornstarch with the remaining broth until smooth; gradually add to skillet. Bring to a boil. Cook and stir for 2 minutes or until thickened. Stir in cashews.

Yield: 6 servings.

Elaine Selander
LITTLETON, COLORADO

I first made this elegant dish in the 1960s, and it's been a family hit since. It makes any meal special.

Steak and Rice Roll-Ups

Steak and Rice Roll-Ups

PREP: 25 min. ■ **COOK:** 1-1/4 hours

1 cup finely chopped fresh mushrooms	1/4 teaspoon dried thyme
2 green onions, finely chopped	1/4 teaspoon dried marjoram
1/4 cup finely chopped green pepper	2 pounds boneless beef top round steak (1/2 inch thick)
2 tablespoons butter	2 tablespoons canola oil
1-1/2 cups cooked long grain rice	2 tablespoons plus 1 teaspoon onion soup mix
2 tablespoons diced pimientos	1 cup water

■ In a large skillet, saute the mushrooms, onions and pepper in butter until tender. Transfer to a small bowl; stir in the rice, pimientos, thyme and marjoram.

■ Cut steak into six pieces; flatten to 1/2-in. thickness. Spread evenly with mushroom mixture; roll up and secure with toothpicks.

■ In the same skillet, brown roll-ups in oil on all sides. Add soup mix and water; cover and simmer for 1 to 1-1/4 hours or until meat is tender, occasionally spooning cooking liquid over roll-ups.

■ Thicken cooking juices if desired; serve with roll-ups. Discard toothpicks.

Yield: 6 servings.

German Pizza

PREP: 20 min.
COOK: 35 min.

1 pound ground beef
1/2 medium onion, chopped
1/2 green pepper, diced
1-1/2 teaspoons salt, *divided*
1/2 teaspoon pepper
2 tablespoons butter
6 medium potatoes (about 2-1/4 pounds), peeled and finely shredded
3 eggs, lightly beaten
1/3 cup milk
2 cups (8 ounces) shredded cheddar cheese *or* shredded part-skim mozzarella cheese

■ In a large skillet over medium heat, cook and stir beef, onion, green pepper, 1/2 teaspoon salt and pepper until meat is no longer pink; drain. Remove and keep warm.

■ Reduce heat to low; melt butter in pan. Spread potatoes over butter and sprinkle with the remaining salt. Top with beef mixture. Combine eggs and milk; pour over all.

■ Cover; cook about 30 minutes or until a meat thermometer reaches 160°. Sprinkle with cheese; cover and cook until the cheese is melted, about 5 minutes. Cut into wedges.

Yield: 4-6 servings.

Audrey Nolt
VERSAILLES, MISSOURI

Most of our extended family lives in Pennsylvania. They visit us often, and I like to serve this simple meal when they do. Even when it's just my husband, our son and me around the table, hearty-tasting German Pizza is always a favorite.

Vicki Raatz
WATERLOO, WISCONSIN
This good-for-you recipe proves you can still enjoy the flavor of beef Stroganoff even when you're watching your diet.

Mushroom Beef Skillet

Mushroom Beef Skillet*

PREP/TOTAL TIME: 30 min.

1 beef flank steak (1 pound)
2 cups reduced-sodium beef broth
1 pound sliced fresh mushrooms
1 large onion, chopped
2 tablespoons all-purpose flour

2 tablespoons cornstarch
1/4 cup cold water
1/2 cup fat-free plain yogurt
1 teaspoon paprika
1 teaspoon prepared mustard
1/2 teaspoon garlic powder
Hot cooked egg noodles, optional

■ Broil beef 4-6 in. from the heat for 6-9 minutes on each side or until meat reaches desired doneness (for medium-rare, a meat thermometer should read 145°; medium, 160°; well-done, 170°). Set aside and keep warm.

■ Meanwhile, in a large skillet, bring broth to a boil. Add mushrooms and onion; cover and simmer until tender, about 5 minutes. In a small bowl, whisk the flour, cornstarch and water until smooth. Whisk into broth. Bring to a boil. Cook and stir for 2 minutes or until thickened and bubbly. Remove from the heat.

■ In another small bowl, combine the yogurt, paprika, mustard and garlic powder; stir into broth mixture until smooth. Cut beef diagonally into thin strips; add to broth mixture. Cook and stir over low heat until heated through. Serve with noodles if desired.

Yield: 4 servings.

✱Nutrition Facts: 1 serving (calculated without noodles) equals 264 calories, 9 g fat (4 g saturated fat), 57 mg cholesterol, 325 mg sodium, 18 g carbohydrate, 2 g fiber, 28 g protein. **Diabetic Exchanges:** 3 lean meat, 1 starch, 1 vegetable.

Pizza Pasta Dinner

Claudia Malone
LOUISVILLE, KENTUCKY
The flavors found in this delicious dish are always welcome in my house. Packed with pasta, three kinds of meats, veggies and cheese, it makes a hearty and filling meal.

PREP/TOTAL TIME: 25 min.

2 cups uncooked spiral pasta
1/2 pound ground beef
1/2 pound bulk Italian sausage
1 small green pepper, chopped
1 small onion, chopped
3 ounces sliced pepperoni
1 can (14-1/2 ounces) diced tomatoes, undrained
1 jar (14 ounces) spaghetti sauce
1 jar (4-1/2 ounces) sliced mushrooms
1 can (4-1/4 ounces) chopped ripe olives, drained
1 cup (4 ounces) shredded part-skim mozzarella cheese

■ Cook the pasta according to package directions. Meanwhile, in a large skillet, cook the beef, sausage, green pepper and onion until meat is no longer pink; drain. Add the pepperoni, tomatoes, spaghetti sauce, mushrooms and olives; cook and stir for 5 minutes.

■ Drain the pasta; stir into meat mixture. Heat through. Sprinkle with cheese. Remove from the heat; cover and let stand until cheese is melted.

Yield: 6 servings.

Sirloin in Wine Sauce

Beefy Tomato Rice Skillet*

Ellyn Graebert
YUMA, ARIZONA

One day I put this recipe together using what I had on hand. It's quick on busy nights or in the summer when we're camping.

PREP/TOTAL TIME: 25 min.

  1 pound ground beef
  1 cup chopped celery
2/3 cup chopped onion
1/2 cup chopped green pepper
  1 can (11 ounces) whole kernel corn, drained
  1 can (10-3/4 ounces) condensed tomato soup, undiluted
  1 cup water
  1 teaspoon Italian seasoning
  1 cup uncooked instant rice

■ In a large skillet over medium heat, cook the beef, celery, onion and pepper until meat is no longer pink and vegetables are tender; drain.

■ Add the corn, soup, water and Italian seasoning; bring to a boil. Stir in the rice; cover and remove from the heat. Let stand for 10 minutes or until rice is tender.

Yield: 6 servings.

∗Nutrition Facts: 1 cup equals 266 calories, 7 g fat (3 g saturated fat), 37 mg cholesterol, 506 mg sodium, 30 g carbohydrate, 2 g fiber, 17 g protein. **Diabetic Exchanges:** 2 lean meat, 2 vegetable, 1 starch, 1 fat.

Barbara Kamm
WILMINGTON, DELAWARE

This recipe is a family favorite as well as an easy dish to fix for company. The tender sirloin steak is coated in a tasty mushroom-wine sauce, and it's fantastic over pasta.

Sirloin in Wine Sauce*

PREP/TOTAL TIME: 30 min.

  2 tablespoons all-purpose flour
1/8 teaspoon ground mustard
  1 pound beef top sirloin steak, thinly sliced
  2 tablespoons butter
  1 can (10-1/2 ounces) condensed beef consomme, undiluted
1/2 cup dry red wine *or* beef broth
  1 jar (4-1/2 ounces) sliced mushrooms, drained
1/4 cup chopped green onions
  1 teaspoon Worcestershire sauce
Hot cooked linguine

■ In a large resealable plastic bag, combine flour and mustard. Add beef, a few pieces at a time, and shake to coat. In a large skillet, brown beef in butter.

■ Add the consomme and wine. Stir in the mushrooms, onions and Worcestershire sauce. Bring to a boil. Reduce heat; simmer, uncovered, for 10-15 minutes or until sauce is thickened. Serve with linguine.

Yield: 4 servings.

∗Nutrition Facts: 3/4 cup equals 258 calories, 10 g fat (5 g saturated fat), 61 mg cholesterol, 748 mg sodium, 7 g carbohydrate, 1 g fiber, 28 g protein. **Diabetic Exchanges:** 4 lean meat, 1 fat, 1/2 starch.

Cajun Pepper Steak

Open-Faced Pizza Burgers

Sharon Schwartz
BURLINGTON, WISCONSIN
I'm not sure where I first saw this burger recipe, but I'm glad I did! My family requests them often.

PREP/TOTAL TIME: 30 min.

1-1/2	pounds ground beef
1/4	cup chopped onion
1	can (15 ounces) pizza sauce
1	can (4 ounces) mushroom stems and pieces, drained
1	tablespoon sugar
1/2	teaspoon dried oregano
6	hamburger buns, split and toasted
1-1/2	cups (6 ounces) shredded part-skim mozzarella cheese

■ In a large skillet, cook beef and onion over medium heat until meat is no longer pink; drain. Stir in pizza sauce, mushrooms, sugar and oregano; mix well. Spoon onto buns; sprinkle with mozzarella cheese.

■ Place on ungreased baking sheets. Broil 4 in. from the heat for 2 minutes or until cheese is melted.

■ To freeze for quick lunches later, place the split and toasted buns on a baking sheet. Spoon the meat mixture onto buns; freeze for 1 hour. Transfer to heavy-duty resealable plastic bags or airtight containers.

■ **TO USE FROZEN BURGERS:** Thaw burgers in refrigerator; sprinkle with cheese. Broil 4-in. from heat for 2 minutes or until cheese is melted.

Yield: 12 servings.

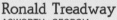

Ronald Treadway
ACWORTH, GEORGIA
The spicy seasonings in this recipe turn strips of beef, onion, and sweet peppers into a zesty dish you'll want to serve again and again.

Cajun Pepper Steak

PREP: 20 min. ■ COOK: 1-1/4 hours

1-1/2	pounds beef top round steak, cubed	4	teaspoons Worcestershire sauce
2	tablespoons butter	1	tablespoon chili powder
2	medium onions, halved and sliced	1	tablespoon soy sauce
2	medium green peppers, julienned	1/2	to 1 teaspoon Cajun seasoning
1	medium sweet red pepper, julienned	1/4	teaspoon hot pepper sauce, optional
1	celery rib, sliced	2	tablespoons cornstarch
1-1/2	cups water	2	tablespoons cold water
			Hot cooked egg noodles *or* rice

■ In a large skillet, brown beef in butter over medium heat; drain. Stir in the onions, peppers and celery; cook and stir for 2 minutes.

■ Add the water, Worcestershire sauce, chili powder, soy sauce, Cajun seasoning and pepper sauce if desired. Bring to a boil. Reduce heat; cover and simmer for 1 to 1-1/2 hours or until meat is tender.

■ Mix cornstarch and cold water; stir into meat. Bring to a boil; cook and stir for 2 minutes or until thickened. Serve with noodles or rice.

Yield: 4 servings.

Paula Pelis
LENHARTSVILLE,
PENNSYLVANIA

Most everyone has a recipe they know by heart. This is mine. It's easy because the ingredients, except the salt, are in measurements of two.

Apple Beef Stew

Apple Beef Stew

PREP: 10 min. ■ COOK: 1 hour 55 min.

2	pounds boneless beef chuck roast, cut into 1-inch cubes
2	tablespoons butter
2	medium onions, cut into wedges
2	tablespoons all-purpose flour
1/8	teaspoon salt

2	cups water
2	tablespoons apple juice
2	bay leaves
2	whole allspice
2	whole cloves
2	medium carrots, sliced
2	medium apples, peeled and cut into wedges

■ In a Dutch oven, over medium heat, brown the cubes of beef in butter. Add the onions; cook until lightly browned. Sprinkle with the flour and salt. Gradually add the water and apple juice. Bring to a boil; cook and stir for 2 minutes.

■ Place the bay leaves, whole allspice and cloves in a double thickness of cheesecloth; bring up the corners of cloth and tie with string to form a bag. Add to pan.

■ Reduce the heat; cover and simmer for 1-1/2 hours or until the meat is almost tender.

■ Add the carrots and apples; cover and simmer 15 minutes longer or until the meat, carrots and apples are tender. Discard the spice bag. Thicken if desired.

Yield: 4 servings.

Chuck Wagon Wraps*

Wendy Conger
WINFIELD, ILLINOIS

If you're a fan of baked beans, you'll love these robust wraps. I mix a can of baked beans with beef, corn and cheese, then roll it all up in tortillas.

PREP/TOTAL TIME: 25 min.

1	pound lean ground beef (90% lean)
1	can (28 ounces) barbecue-flavored baked beans
2	cups frozen corn, thawed
4-1/2	teaspoons Worcestershire sauce
1	cup (4 ounces) shredded reduced-fat cheddar cheese
12	flour tortillas (8 inches), warmed
3	cups shredded lettuce
1-1/2	cups chopped fresh tomatoes
3/4	cup reduced-fat sour cream

■ In a large nonstick skillet, cook beef over medium heat until no longer pink; drain. Stir in the beans, corn and Worcestershire sauce. Bring to a boil. Reduce heat; simmer, uncovered, for 4-5 minutes or until heated through. Sprinkle with cheese; cook 1-2 minutes longer. Spoon 1/2 cup of beef mixture off center onto each tortilla; top with lettuce, tomatoes and sour cream. Roll up.

Yield: 12 servings.

✱Nutrition Facts: 1 wrap equals 373 calories, 11 g fat (4 g saturated fat), 27 mg cholesterol, 605 mg sodium, 50 g carbohydrate, 4 g fiber, 20 g protein. **Diabetic Exchanges:** 3 starch, 2 lean meat, 1/2 fat.

Poultry

134

126

128

There's always time for a home-cooked dinner when you have a great recipe! In this chapter, you'll find delicious dishes that use versatile chicken or turkey. Plus, every one-dish wonder cooks up in a flash on the stovetop.

Sweet and Sour Chicken

Lori Burtenshaw
TERRETON, IDAHO

I first tasted this yummy dish at our friends' home. I asked for the recipe, and we've enjoyed it ever since. We like to call it "favorite chicken" at our house!

Sweet and Sour Chicken

PREP: 20 min. + marinating ■ **COOK:** 15 min.

1 tablespoon plus 2 teaspoons reduced-sodium soy sauce, *divided*	1 can (20 ounces) unsweetened pineapple chunks
1 tablespoon sherry *or* reduced-sodium chicken broth	2 tablespoons plus 1/3 cup cornstarch, *divided*
1/2 teaspoon salt	2 tablespoons sugar
1/2 teaspoon garlic powder	1/4 cup cider vinegar
1/2 teaspoon ground ginger	1/4 cup ketchup
1 pound boneless skinless chicken breasts, cut into 1-inch cubes	1 tablespoon canola oil
	2 cups hot cooked rice
	Sliced green onion, optional

■ In a large resealable plastic bag, combine 1 tablespoon soy sauce, sherry or broth, salt, garlic powder and ginger; add chicken. Seal bag and turn to coat; refrigerate for 30 minutes.

■ Drain the pineapple, reserving juice; set pineapple aside. Add enough water to the juice to measure 1 cup. In a small bowl, combine 2 tablespoons of the cornstarch, sugar and pineapple juice mixture until smooth; stir in the vinegar, ketchup and remaining soy sauce. Set aside.

■ Drain the chicken and discard marinade. Place the remaining cornstarch in a large resealable plastic bag. Add chicken, a few pieces at a time, and shake to coat. In a large nonstick skillet or wok coated with cooking spray, stir-fry chicken in oil until no longer pink. Remove and keep warm.

■ Stir pineapple juice mixture and add to the pan. Bring to a boil; cook and stir for 2 minutes or until thickened. Add chicken and reserved pineapple; heat through. Serve with cooked rice. Garnish with green onion if desired.

Yield: 4 servings.

Brenda Lion
WARREN, PENNSYLVANIA
This out-of-the-ordinary meal is perfect for cool nights with family, friends or company. With cinnamon and brown sugar, it's slightly sweet, and the toasted walnuts add a wonderful toasty-nutty crunch.

Autumn Turkey Tenderloins

Autumn Turkey Tenderloins*

PREP/TOTAL TIME: 30 min.

1-1/4	pounds turkey breast tenderloins
1	tablespoon butter
1	cup unsweetened apple juice
1	medium apple, sliced
1	tablespoon brown sugar
2	teaspoons chicken bouillon granules

1/4	teaspoon ground cinnamon
1/4	teaspoon ground nutmeg
1	tablespoon cornstarch
2	tablespoons cold water
1/2	cup chopped walnuts, toasted

■ In a large skillet, brown turkey in butter. Add the apple juice, apple, brown sugar, bouillon, cinnamon and nutmeg. Bring to a boil. Reduce heat; cover and simmer for 10-12 minutes or until turkey is no longer pink.

■ Using a slotted spoon, remove the turkey and apple slices to a serving platter; keep warm. Combine the cornstarch and water until smooth; stir into the pan juices. Bring to a boil; cook and stir for 2 minutes or until thickened. Spoon over turkey and apple. Sprinkle with walnuts.

Yield: 5 servings.

*Nutrition Facts: 1 serving equals 274 calories, 11 g fat (2 g saturated fat), 62 mg cholesterol, 423 mg sodium, 16 g carbohydrate, 2 g fiber, 30 g protein. **Diabetic Exchanges:** 4 very lean meat, 2 fat, 1 fruit.

Garlic Pineapple Chicken

Jayme Webb
ANDERSON, SOUTH CAROLINA
I found this recipe on the Internet. It makes a wonderfully quick, light meal and tastes great. This is a deliciously different kind of stir-fry without the usual Asian flavors.

PREP/TOTAL TIME: 25 min.

1-1/2	pounds boneless skinless chicken breasts, cut into 1-1/2-inch cubes
2	cups uncooked instant rice
1	can (20 ounces) unsweetened pineapple chunks, undrained
1/2	cup fat-free French salad dressing
1/3	cup chopped green pepper
2	tablespoons salt-free garlic herb seasoning blend

■ In a large skillet coated with cooking spray, cook and stir the chicken over medium heat until it is no longer pink. Meanwhile, cook the rice according to the package directions.

■ Stir pineapple, salad dressing, green pepper and seasoning blend into the chicken. Bring to a boil. Reduce the heat; cook, uncovered, for 3-5 minutes or until heated through. Serve with rice.

Yield: 5 servings.

Editor's Note: This recipe was prepared with McCormick Salt Free Garlic & Herb Seasoning.

Chipotle Chicken and Beans

Jenny Kniesly
DOVER, OHIO

*I was skeptical about this recipe due to its combination
of ingredients, but it immediately became one of our
all-time favorites.*

Chipotle Chicken and Beans

PREP: 15 min. ■ **COOK:** 30 min.

3/4 cup water, *divided*

1/2 cup reduced-sodium chicken broth

1/2 cup uncooked long grain rice

6 boneless skinless chicken breast halves (4 ounces *each*)

1/4 teaspoon salt

3 bacon strips, diced

1 cup chopped onion

3 garlic cloves, minced

1 cup chopped plum tomatoes

1/2 teaspoon ground cumin

1/4 teaspoon ground cinnamon

1/2 cup whole-berry cranberry sauce

4-1/2 teaspoons minced chipotle peppers in adobo sauce

1-1/2 teaspoons lime juice

1 can (15 ounces) black beans, rinsed and drained

1 can (15 ounces) white kidney *or* cannellini beans, rinsed and drained

■ In a small saucepan, bring 1/2 cup water and broth to a boil. Stir in rice. Reduce heat; cover and simmer for 15-18 minutes or until rice is tender.

■ Meanwhile, cut each chicken breast half widthwise into six strips. Sprinkle with salt. In a large nonstick skillet coated with cooking spray, cook the chicken for 5 minutes on each side or until lightly browned. Remove and keep warm.

■ In the same skillet, cook the bacon over medium heat until crisp. Using a slotted spoon, remove bacon to paper towels; drain, reserving 1/2 teaspoon drippings. In drippings, saute onion until tender. Add the garlic; cook 1 minute longer. Add the tomatoes, cumin and cinnamon; cook for 2 minutes. Stir in the cranberry sauce, chipotle peppers, lime juice and the remaining water. Bring to a boil.

■ Return the chicken to the pan. Reduce the heat; cover and simmer for 6-10 minutes or until chicken is no longer pink. Remove and keep warm. Add rice and beans to the skillet; heat through. Serve the chicken over the bean mixture; sprinkle with bacon.

Yield: 6 servings.

Chicken and Barley Boiled Dinner

Susan Greeley
MORRIL, MAINE

I began putting this meal-in-one on my menu because it's nutritious and adequately feeds the big appetites in my family. For a hearty, home-style dinner, it's surprisingly easy to prepare. That's especially nice when I don't have a lot of time to spend in the kitchen.

PREP: 30 min. ■ **COOK:** 1-1/4 hours

- 2 broiler/fryer chickens (about 3 pounds *each*), cut up and skin removed
- 3 tablespoons canola oil
- 2 quarts chicken broth
- 1 cup uncooked brown rice
- 1/2 cup medium pearl barley
- 1 medium onion, chopped
- 2 bay leaves
- 1/2 teaspoon dried basil
- 2 teaspoons salt
- 1/4 teaspoon pepper
- 8 carrots, cut into 1-inch pieces
- 2-1/2 cups frozen cut green beans
- 2 celery ribs, cut into 1-inch pieces

■ In an Dutch oven, brown chicken in oil. Remove chicken and set aside. Drain. In same kettle, combine broth, rice, barley, onion, bay leaves, basil, salt and pepper; bring to a boil. Reduce heat.

■ Return chicken to pan; cover and simmer for 45 minutes or until chicken juices run clear.

■ Stir in carrots, beans and celery. Cook over medium heat for 30 minutes or until grains are tender. Discard bay leaves.

Yield: *6-8 servings.*

To give celery that's gone limp a second chance when seasoning entrees, soups and stews, cut the ends from the stalks. Place in a jar or glass of cold water and refrigerate for several hours or overnight.

Santa Fe Chicken

PREP/TOTAL TIME: 30 min.

- 1 large onion, chopped
- 1 to 2 tablespoons chopped seeded jalapeno pepper
- 1 garlic clove, minced
- 1 tablespoon olive oil
- 1-1/4 cups reduced-sodium chicken broth
- 1 can (10 ounces) diced tomatoes and green chilies, undrained
- 1 cup uncooked long grain rice
- 4 boneless skinless chicken breast halves (4 ounces *each*)
- 1/2 teaspoon salt
- 1/4 teaspoon pepper
- 1/4 teaspoon ground cumin
- 3/4 cup shredded reduced-fat cheddar cheese

Minced fresh cilantro, optional

■ In a large skillet, saute onion, jalapeno and garlic in oil until tender. Add the broth and the tomatoes; bring to a boil. Stir in the rice.

■ Sprinkle the chicken with salt, pepper and cumin; place over rice mixture. Cover and simmer for 10-15 minutes on each side or until chicken juices run clear.

■ Remove from heat. Sprinkle with the cheese; cover and let stand for 5 minutes. Garnish with cilantro if desired.

Yield: **4 servings.**

Editor's Note: When cutting hot peppers, disposable gloves are recommended. Avoid touching your face.

Jon Carole Gilbreath
TYLER, TEXAS

Chicken and rice are dressed up with a zippy sauce for a complete meal that's ready in a dash. Garnished with fresh cilantro, it's a festive weeknight supper or special-occasion menu. You can adjust the seasonings and jalapeno peppers to your family's taste.

Chicken Pasta Dinner

Taste of Home Test Kitchen
Green beans add nice crunch and a bit of color to this tasty pasta-and-chicken dish from our home economists. It appeals to all ages.

Chicken Pasta Dinner*

PREP: 15 min. ■ **COOK:** 20 min.

4	cups uncooked spiral pasta
1/2	pound fresh green beans, trimmed and cut into 1/4-inch pieces
3/4	pound boneless skinless chicken breasts, cut into 1/2-inch pieces
3	teaspoons olive oil, *divided*
1	jar (7 ounces) roasted sweet red peppers, drained
1	garlic clove, minced
3/4	cup reduced-sodium chicken broth
3/4	cup fat-free evaporated milk, *divided*
1/4	cup minced fresh basil *or* 4 teaspoons dried basil
1/2	teaspoon salt
1/4	teaspoon pepper
2	teaspoons cornstarch
5	tablespoons shredded Parmesan cheese

■ Cook the pasta according to the package directions, adding the green beans during the last 2 minutes. Meanwhile, in a large nonstick skillet, saute chicken in 2 teaspoons oil until no longer pink. Remove and keep warm. In the same pan, saute red peppers and garlic in remaining oil for 1 minute.

■ Stir in the broth, 1/2 cup milk, basil, salt and pepper. Bring to a boil. Reduce heat; simmer, uncovered, for 3 minutes or until slightly thickened. Remove from the heat; cool slightly. Transfer to a blender; cover and process until smooth. Return to the pan.

■ Add the chicken to the pepper mixture. Combine cornstarch and the remaining milk until smooth; gradually stir into the chicken mixture. Bring to a boil; cook and stir for 2 minutes or until thickened.

■ Drain pasta mixture; toss with sauce. Sprinkle each serving with 1 tablespoon cheese.

Yield: *5 servings.*

***Nutrition Facts:** 1-1/4 cups equals 345 calories, 6 g fat (2 g saturated fat), 42 mg cholesterol, 625 mg sodium, 44 g carbohydrate, 3 g fiber, 25 g protein. **Diabetic Exchanges:** 2 lean meat, 2-1/2 starch, 1 vegetable, 1/2 fat.

To mince fresh

garlic, crush a garlic clove with the blade of a chef's knife. Peel away the skin and mince as directed.

Barbara Christensen
ARVADA, COLORADO

This is one of my favorite recipes because it's so quick and easy, but it looks and tastes like I spent all day cooking it. And it has all of my favorite ingredients in it!

Chicken Pesto Pasta

Chicken Pesto Pasta

PREP/TOTAL TIME: 25 min.

1 package (16 ounces) bow tie pasta
1 cup cut fresh asparagus (1-inch pieces)
1-1/4 cups sliced fresh mushrooms
1 medium sweet red pepper, sliced
2 tablespoons olive oil
1-1/2 teaspoons minced garlic
2 cups cubed cooked chicken
1 can (14 ounces) water-packed artichoke hearts, rinsed, drained and quartered
2 jars (3-1/2 ounces *each*) prepared pesto
1 jar (7 ounces) oil-packed sun-dried tomatoes, drained and chopped
1 teaspoon salt
1/8 teaspoon crushed red pepper flakes
1 cup (4 ounces) shredded Parmesan cheese
2/3 cup pine nuts, toasted

■ Cook the pasta according to package directions, adding the asparagus during the last 3 minutes of cooking.

■ Meanwhile, in a large skillet, saute the mushrooms and red pepper in oil until tender. Add the garlic; cook 1 minute longer. Reduce heat; stir in the chicken, artichokes, pesto, tomatoes, salt and pepper flakes. Cook 2-3 minutes longer or until heated through.

■ Drain the pasta; toss with the chicken mixture. Sprinkle with cheese and pine nuts.

Yield: 8 servings.

Turkey Fried Rice

Lorna Plett
RIVERTON, MANITOBA

My husband, our two young sons and I enjoy this delicious fried rice dish made with brown rice.

PREP: 50 min. + chilling
COOK: 10 min.

2 cups reduced-sodium chicken broth
1 cup uncooked brown rice
2 cups cubed cooked turkey breast
3 tablespoons reduced-sodium soy sauce
1 egg, lightly beaten
1 small onion, chopped
1/4 cup chopped green pepper
1/4 cup chopped celery
1 tablespoon canola oil
1 cup shredded romaine

■ In a large saucepan, bring broth to a boil. Stir in the rice. Reduce the heat; cover and simmer for 45-50 minutes or until liquid is absorbed and rice is tender. Remove from the heat; cool. Cover and refrigerate overnight.

■ In a small bowl, combine the turkey and soy sauce; cover and refrigerate. In a large nonstick skillet, cook and stir egg over medium heat until completely set. Remove and set aside.

■ In the same skillet, saute the onion, green pepper and celery in oil until tender. Add rice and turkey; cook and stir over medium heat for 6-8 minutes. Add lettuce and reserved egg; cook and stir for 1-2 minutes. Serve immediately.

Yield: 4 servings.

Sandra
Netherton
MARIETTA, GEORGIA

This creamy pasta is a great use for extra turkey and ham. This recipe has undergone a few changes, but it remains one of our favorites.

Turkey Cordon Bleu Pasta

Turkey Cordon Bleu Pasta

PREP/TOTAL TIME: 30 min.

 2 cups sliced fresh mushrooms
1/2 cup sliced green onions
1/4 cup chopped green pepper
 2 tablespoons butter
 2 cups cubed cooked turkey
 1 cup cubed fully cooked ham

 1 can (10-3/4 ounces) condensed cream of mushroom soup, undiluted
1/2 cup water
1/4 cup sherry *or* chicken broth
Hot cooked linguine
1/4 cup shredded Swiss cheese

■ In a large skillet, saute the mushrooms, onions and green pepper in butter for 4-5 minutes or until crisp-tender.

■ In a large bowl, combine the turkey, ham, soup, water and sherry. Stir into the vegetables. Bring to a boil. Reduce the heat to medium; cook, uncovered, for 3-4 minutes or until heated through. Serve with linguine. Sprinkle with cheese.

Yield: 4 servings.

When a recipe calls for green onions, to avoid using a cutting board, cut the onions with a pair of kitchen scissors rather than with a knife. If you need quite a bit, grab a bunch at one time and snip away. You'll be done before you know it.

Chicken Pasta Toss

Margaret Penaflor
THORNTON, COLORADO

Flavored with lots of herbs and seasonings, this dish will satisfy any family member's appetite. The rich and creamy sauce takes minimal effort.

PREP/TOTAL TIME: 25 min.

 10 ounces uncooked spaghetti
 1 teaspoon minced garlic
 2 tablespoons butter
3/4 pound boneless skinless chicken breasts, cubed
1/3 cup chopped green onions
 1 teaspoon salt
1/2 teaspoon dried thyme
1/4 teaspoon *each* onion powder, rubbed sage, white pepper and black pepper
Dash cayenne pepper
 1 cup heavy whipping cream
1/2 cup shredded Parmesan cheese
 2 tablespoons minced fresh parsley

■ Cook spaghetti according to package directions. Meanwhile, in a large skillet, saute the garlic in butter for 1 minute. Add the chicken, onions and seasonings; cook, uncovered, for 3-5 minutes or until juices run clear.

■ Stir in the cream. Bring to a boil. Reduce the heat; simmer, uncovered, for 4-5 minutes or until slightly thickened. Drain spaghetti; toss with chicken mixture. Sprinkle with cheese and parsley.

Yield: 4 servings.

Ragu Bolognese

Mary Bilyeu
ANN ARBOR, MICHIGAN

I cook this hearty sauce slowly, making it absolutely yummy. The veggies add fiber, and skim milk and turkey sausage keep it lighter. The dish is great for family or company.

Ragu Bolognese

PREP: 30 min. ■ **COOK:** 1-1/4 hours

1/2 pound Italian turkey sausage links, casings removed	2 tablespoons balsamic vinegar
1 large carrot, finely chopped	1/4 teaspoon crushed red pepper flakes
1 celery rib, finely chopped	3/4 cup fat-free milk
1 small onion, finely chopped	4 cups uncooked whole wheat spiral pasta
1 can (15 ounces) crushed tomatoes	2 tablespoons prepared pesto
1/2 cup reduced-sodium chicken broth	1 tablespoon chopped ripe olives

■ Crumble sausage into a nonstick Dutch oven. Add carrot, celery and onion. Cook; stir over medium heat until meat is no longer pink. Drain.

■ Stir in the tomatoes, broth, vinegar and pepper flakes. Bring to a boil. Stir in milk. Reduce heat; simmer, uncovered, for 1 to 1-1/4 hours or until thickened, stirring occasionally.

■ Cook pasta according to package directions. Stir pesto and olives into meat sauce. Drain pasta; serve with meat sauce.

Yield: 4 servings.

Chicken Stew*

Taste of Home Test Kitchen

Try this satisfying stew with tender chicken and veggies in a smooth gravy. There are only a handful of ingredients, but it still delivers that old-fashioned flavor. Serve it with the grilled cheese, or with fresh-from-the-oven biscuits.

PREP/TOTAL TIME: 30 min.

   1 pound boneless skinless chicken breasts, cut into 1-inch cubes

   1 tablespoon olive oil

   1 package (16 ounces) frozen vegetables for stew

   1 jar (12 ounces) chicken gravy

1/2 teaspoon dried thyme

1/4 teaspoon rubbed sage

1/4 teaspoon pepper

■ In a large saucepan, brown the chicken in oil over medium heat for 4-6 minutes or until no longer pink. Drain if necessary.

■ Stir in remaining ingredients. Bring to a boil. Reduce the heat; cover and simmer for 15 minutes or until the vegetables are tender.

Yield: 4 servings.

✱Nutrition Facts: 1 cup (prepared with fat-free gravy) equals 240 calories, 6 g fat (1 g saturated fat), 70 mg cholesterol, 574 mg sodium, 19 g carbohydrate, 1 g fiber, 26 g protein. **Diabetic Exchanges:** 3 very lean meat, 1 starch, 1 vegetable.

Betty Kleberger
FLORISSANT, MISSOURI

I like using boxed rice and pasta mixes as the basis for quick meals. This colorful dish is simple to cook on the stovetop using fried rice mix, tender turkey and convenient frozen vegetables.

Tasty Turkey Skillet

Tasty Turkey Skillet*

PREP: 10 min. ■ COOK: 35 min.

1 pound turkey breast tenderloins, cut into 1/4-inch strips

1 package (6.2 ounces) fried rice mix

1 tablespoon butter

2 cups water

1/8 teaspoon cayenne pepper

1-1/2 cups frozen corn, thawed

1 cup frozen broccoli cuts, thawed

2 tablespoons chopped sweet red pepper, optional

■ In a nonstick skillet coated with cooking spray, cook turkey over medium heat until no longer pink; drain. Remove turkey and keep warm.

■ Set aside seasoning packet from rice. In the same skillet, saute the rice in butter until lightly browned. Stir in the water, cayenne and contents of seasoning packet.

■ Bring to a boil. Reduce heat; cover and simmer for 15 minutes. Stir in the corn, broccoli, red pepper if desired and turkey. Return to a boil. reduce heat; cover and simmer for 6-8 minutes or until the rice and vegetables are tender.

Yield: 4-6 servings.

*Nutrition Facts: 1 cup equals 238 calories, 4 g fat (2 g saturated fat), 42 mg cholesterol, 650 mg sodium, 31 g carbohydrate, 3 g fiber, 22 g protein. Diabetic Exchanges: 2 very lean meat, 2 starch.

Chicken and Egg Hash

Joyce Price
WHITEFISH, ONTARIO

This recipe is one of my daughter's favorites. To reduce cooking time and clean out the fridge, dice up leftover potatoes and use cooked chicken or ham instead.

PREP/TOTAL TIME: 30 min.

4 bacon strips, diced

1 medium onion, chopped

2 garlic cloves, minced

1 pound boneless skinless chicken breasts, cubed

2 large potatoes, peeled and diced

1 tablespoon canola oil

1/2 cup frozen peas, thawed

1/2 cup frozen corn, thawed

2 tablespoons minced fresh parsley

3/4 teaspoon salt

1/8 teaspoon pepper

4 eggs

■ In a large skillet, cook bacon until crisp. Remove bacon with a slotted spoon to paper towels to drain. In the drippings, saute onion until tender. Add garlic; cook 1 minute longer. Stir in the chicken, potatoes and oil.

■ Cover and cook for 10 minutes or until the chicken is no longer pink, stirring once. Stir in peas, corn, parsley, salt and pepper.

■ Make four wells in the hash; break an egg into each well. Cover and cook over low heat for 8-10 minutes or until eggs are completely set. Sprinkle with bacon.

Yield: 4 servings.

Chicken & Kielbasa with Curried Rice

Taste of Home Test Kitchen
Chicken and sausage form a hearty foundation for this quick-to-the-table meal that has everything you need for dinner. Curry powder adds loads of flavor, while mild-tasting coconut milk balances the dish out.

Chicken & Kielbasa with Curried Rice

PREP: 25 min. ■ **COOK:** 15 min.

3/4 pound boneless skinless chicken breasts, cut into 1/2-inch cubes

1/4 pound smoked kielbasa *or* Polish sausage, cut into 1/4-inch slices

1/2 cup chopped onion

1 tablespoon olive oil

3 cups frozen chopped broccoli, thawed

1 can (14 ounces) coconut milk

1 can (10-3/4 ounces) condensed cream of celery soup, undiluted

1 cup uncooked instant rice

1/3 cup water

1 tablespoon curry powder

1/4 teaspoon salt

1 medium tomato, chopped

■ In a large skillet, saute the chicken, kielbasa and onion in oil until chicken is no longer pink. Add the broccoli, coconut milk, soup, rice, water, curry and salt.

■ Bring to a boil. Reduce heat; cover and simmer for 10-15 minutes or until rice is tender. Garnish with tomato.

Yield: 4 servings.

Creole Chicken*

Susan Shields
ARCADIA, FLORIDA

Chili powder lends just a hint of heat to this full-flavored and oh-so-easy chicken entree.

PREP: 15 min.
COOK: 25 min.

2 boneless skinless chicken breast halves (4 ounces *each*)

1 teaspoon canola oil

1 can (14-1/2 ounces) stewed tomatoes, cut up

1/3 cup julienned green pepper

1/4 cup chopped celery

1/4 cup sliced onion

1/2 to 1 teaspoon chili powder

1/2 teaspoon dried thyme

1/8 teaspoon pepper

1 cup hot cooked rice

■ In a small nonstick skillet coated with cooking spray, cook chicken in oil over medium heat for 5-6 minutes on each side or a meat thermometer reads 170°. Remove and keep warm.

■ In the same skillet, combine the tomatoes, green pepper, celery, onion, chili powder, thyme and pepper. Bring to a boil. Reduce heat; cover and simmer for 10 minutes or until vegetables are crisp-tender. Return chicken to pan; heat through. Serve with rice.

Yield: 2 servings.

*Nutrition Facts: 1 chicken breast half with 2/3 cup sauce and 1/2 cup rice equals 320 calories, 5 g fat (1 g saturated fat), 63 mg cholesterol, 447 mg sodium, 41 g carbohydrate, 3 g fiber, 27 g protein. **Diabetic Exchanges:** 3 very lean meat, 1-1/2 starch, 3 vegetable, 1/2 fat.

Chicken Paprikash with Spaetzle

John Niklasch
TERRE HAUTE, INDIANA

When my folks came here from Austria in the early 1900s, they brought with them many of the recipes they enjoyed in the old country. This wonderful dish is one of them.

PREP: 15 min. ■ **COOK:** 1 hour

- 1 jar (16 ounces) whole onions, drained
- 4 tablespoons butter, cubed
- 1 large onion, chopped
- 1/2 cup all-purpose flour
- 2 tablespoons paprika, *divided*
- 1 broiler/fryer chicken (2-1/2 to 3 pounds), cut up
- 1/2 teaspoon salt
- 3 tablespoons chopped fresh parsley
- 1-1/4 cups chicken broth
- 1 cup (8 ounces) sour cream
- 3 tablespoons capers with juice

SPAETZLE:
- 1-1/2 cups all-purpose flour
- 2 eggs, lightly beaten
- 1/2 cup milk
- 3/4 teaspoon salt
- 1/4 teaspoon baking powder
- 1 tablespoon butter, melted

■ In a heavy skillet, saute whole onions in butter until lightly browned. Remove and set aside. In the same skillet, saute chopped onions until tender. Set aside.

■ In a large plastic resealable bag, combine flour and 1-1/2 teaspoons paprika; add chicken, a few pieces at a time and shake to coat.

■ Place chicken in skillet; brown on all sides. Add the salt, parsley, broth and remaining paprika. Cover and cook over low heat until juices run clear, about 45 minutes.

■ For spaetzle, in a large bowl, stir the flour, eggs, milk, salt and baking powder until smooth (dough will be sticky). In a large saucepan, bring water to a boil. Pour dough into a colander or spaetzle maker coated with cooking spray; place over boiling water.

■ With a wooden spoon, press dough until small pieces drop into boiling water. Cook for 2 minutes or until the dumplings are tender and float. Remove with a slotted spoon; toss with butter.

■ Remove chicken from skillet; set aside. In the same skillet, stir in the sour cream, capers and juice and onions. Return chicken to the skillet and gently heat through. Place spaetzle on a platter and top with chicken. Serve with sauce.

Yield: 6-8 servings.

Chicken Alfredo

PREP/TOTAL TIME: 15 min.

- 1 package (8 ounces) cream cheese, cubed
- 6 tablespoons butter, cubed
- 1/2 cup milk
- 1/2 teaspoon garlic powder
- Salt and pepper to taste
- 2 boneless skinless chicken breast halves, cooked and cubed (about 1-1/2 cups)
- 2 cups frozen chopped broccoli, thawed
- 2 small zucchini, julienned
- 1/2 cup julienned sweet red pepper
- 6 ounces cooked fettuccine

■ In a large skillet over low heat, melt cream cheese and butter; stir until smooth. Add the milk, garlic powder, salt and pepper. Cook and stir for 3 minutes or until thickened.

■ Add chicken, broccoli, zucchini and red pepper. Cook over medium heat for 3 minutes. Reduce heat; cover and cook 5 minutes longer or until the vegetables are tender. Serve with fettuccine.

Yield: 4-6 servings.

To "julienne"

means to cut foods into matchstick shapes about 2 inches long and 1/8 inch thick. For zucchini, cut lengthwise into 1/8-inch-thick slices, then cut into 2-inch-long pieces. Finally, cut, or julienne, into matchsticks.

Jody Stewart
GOLDSBORO, NORTH CAROLINA

Bright green broccoli, fresh zucchini and sweet red pepper lend a fresh taste to this classically rich and creamy chicken and pasta entree. Cream cheese makes the smooth sauce extra delicious and a snap to stir up. The dish is a real people-pleaser!

Becky Taaffe
SAN JOSE, CALIFORNIA

A tasty blend of peppers makes this skillet meal popular. I've prepared it for everyday meals, but also for church dinners, potluck suppers and family get-togethers.

Mexican Stir-Fry

Mexican Stir-Fry

PREP/TOTAL TIME: 20 min.

1/2 cup chopped onion	1/2 teaspoon chili powder
2 teaspoons canola oil	1/2 teaspoon chicken bouillon granules
2 garlic cloves, minced	
1/2 cup finely chopped green pepper	1/4 teaspoon salt
	Pinch cayenne pepper
1/2 cup finely chopped sweet red pepper	1-1/3 cups diced cooked chicken
2 tablespoons minced jalapeno pepper	2/3 cup canned kidney beans, rinsed and drained
3/4 cup water	1 cup cooked rice
1/2 cup tomato puree	1/2 cup shredded cheddar cheese

■ In a large skillet, saute onion in oil for 3 minutes or until crisp-tender. Add garlic; cook 1 minute longer. Add peppers; saute until crisp-tender, about 2 minutes.

■ Stir in the water, tomato puree, chili powder, bouillon, salt and cayenne; bring to a boil. Reduce heat; simmer, uncovered, for 5 minutes. Add the chicken, beans and rice; heat through. Sprinkle with cheese.

Yield: 2-4 servings.

Editor's Note: When cutting hot peppers, disposable gloves are recommended. Avoid touching your face.

Balsamic Chicken and Peppers*

Valerie Moore
STILWELL, KANSAS

I like using a colorful blend of peppers to brighten this skillet specialty—and a little balsamic vinegar to flavor the tender chicken. If you prefer a stronger flavor, add a little more!

PREP/TOTAL TIME: 25 min.

4 boneless skinless chicken breast halves (4 ounces *each*)

1/4 teaspoon pepper

1/8 teaspoon salt

2 tablespoons olive oil, *divided*

1 *each* medium sweet yellow, red and orange peppers, julienned

1 small onion, sliced

2 tablespoons balsamic vinegar

■ Sprinkle chicken with pepper and salt. In a large skillet, cook the chicken in 1 tablespoon oil for 4-6 minutes on each side or until a meat thermometer reads 170°; drain. Remove the chicken and keep warm.

■ In the same skillet, saute the peppers and onion in remaining oil for 3-4 minutes or until tender. Return the chicken to the pan. Add vinegar; heat through.

Yield: 4 servings.

*Nutrition Facts: 1 chicken breast half with 1 cup peppers equals 220 calories, 10 g fat (2 g saturated fat), 63 mg cholesterol, 133 mg sodium, 9 g carbohydrate, 2 g fiber, 24 g protein. **Diabetic Exchanges:** 3 very lean meat, 2 vegetable, 1-1/2 fat.

Cashew Chicken

Linda Avila
TOONE, TENNESSEE

Whenever my friends and I get together for a potluck, they always ask me to bring this dish. The recipe has a distinct Chinese flavor from all the spices.

Cashew Chicken

PREP: 20 min. + marinating ■ COOK: 15 min.

3 tablespoons reduced-sodium soy sauce, *divided*

1 tablespoon sherry *or* reduced-sodium chicken broth

3/4 teaspoon sesame oil, *divided*

1 pound boneless skinless chicken breasts, cut into 1-inch pieces

1 tablespoon cornstarch

1/3 cup reduced-sodium chicken broth

1 tablespoon sugar

1 tablespoon rice vinegar

1 tablespoon hoisin sauce

1/2 teaspoon minced fresh gingerroot

1/4 teaspoon salt

2 teaspoons canola oil, *divided*

1-1/2 cups fresh snow peas

2 medium carrots, julienned

1 can (8 ounces) sliced water chestnuts, drained

1/4 cup unsalted cashews, toasted

Hot cooked rice, optional

■ In a large resealable plastic bag, combine 2 tablespoons soy sauce, sherry or broth and 1/2 teaspoon sesame oil; add the chicken. Seal the bag and turn to coat. Refrigerate for 30 minutes.

■ In a small bowl, combine the cornstarch and broth until smooth. Stir in sugar, vinegar, hoisin sauce, ginger, salt, and the remaining soy sauce and sesame oil; set aside.

■ Drain the chicken and discard marinade. In a large nonstick wok or skillet, stir-fry chicken in 1 teaspoon oil until no longer pink. Remove and keep warm.

■ In the same pan, stir-fry the peas and carrots in remaining oil until crisp-tender. Add the water chestnuts.

■ Return the chicken to the pan. Stir the sauce mixture and stir into chicken mixture. Bring to a boil; cook and stir for 1 minute or until thickened. Sprinkle with the cashews. Serve with the rice if desired.

Yield: 4 servings.

Hoisin sauce is a sweet, salty and spicy soy-based ingredient used in Chinese cuisine. It's used to flavor sauces for stir-fry dishes or as a condiment for Moo Shoo Pork or Peking Duck. You can find hoisin in Asian markets or in the ethnic section of grocery stores.

Pork

149

147

144

The savory taste of pork is irresistible, whether it's the smoky flavor of bacon or kielbasa, sizzling pork chops, juicy tenderloin or robust roasts. From home-style pasta tosses to spicy stews, there's a delicious dish for every occasion in this chapter.

Prosciutto Pasta Toss

Pork Tenderloin With Raspberry Sauce

Norma Pimental
ACUSHNET, MASSACHUSETTS

Here's an easy, elegant dinner that's perfect for any special occasion. The colorful raspberry sauce adds just the right amount of sweetness to the moist and tender pork.

PREP/TOTAL TIME 20 min.

  1 pork tenderloin (1 pound)
1/8 teaspoon cayenne pepper, optional
  2 teaspoons butter
1/4 cup seedless raspberry preserves
  2 teaspoons red wine vinegar
  1 tablespoon ketchup
1/2 teaspoon soy sauce
1/8 to 1/4 teaspoon prepared horseradish
  1 garlic clove, minced
Fresh raspberries, optional

- Cut the tenderloin into eight pieces; flatten each piece to 1-in. thickness. Sprinkle cayenne on both sides if desired. In a large skillet, cook the pork over medium heat for 3-4 minutes on each side or until pork is no longer pink.

- Meanwhile, in a small saucepan, combine the preserves, vinegar, ketchup, soy sauce and the horseradish. Add the garlic; cook 1 minute longer. Simmer, uncovered, for 3 minutes, stirring occasionally. Serve with the tenderloin; garnish with the raspberries if desired.

Yield: 4 servings.

Laura Murphy-Ogden
CHARLOTTE, NORTH CAROLINA

I love quick, simple pasta dishes, and this is one of my favorites. I prepare a tossed green salad while the pasta cooks and serve up a lovely light supper in minutes!

Prosciutto Pasta Toss

PREP/TOTAL TIME: 20 min.

  1 package (16 ounces) linguine
1/2 cup frozen peas
  2 tablespoons minced garlic
  1 tablespoon Italian seasoning
  1 teaspoon pepper
1/4 cup olive oil
1/2 pound thinly sliced prosciutto *or* deli ham, chopped
1/4 cup shredded Parmesan cheese

- Cook linguine according to package directions, adding the peas during the last 3 minutes. Meanwhile, in a large skillet, saute the garlic, Italian seasoning and pepper in oil for 1 minute or until the garlic is tender. Stir in prosciutto.

- Drain linguine; add to skillet and toss to coat. Sprinkle with cheese.

Yield: 6 servings.

Teriyaki Pork

Molly Gee
PLAINWELL, MICHIGAN

I season pork loin and an assortment of fresh vegetables with soy sauce and an easy-to-make garlic marinade for this scrumptious stir-fry.

Teriyaki Pork*

PREP: 10 min. + marinating ■ COOK: 20 min.

3/4 cup reduced-sodium chicken broth, *divided*

1/3 cup reduced-sodium soy sauce

2 tablespoons red wine vinegar

2 teaspoons honey

2 teaspoons garlic powder

1 pound boneless pork loin chops, cut into thin strips

1 tablespoon canola oil

2 cups fresh broccoli florets

3 medium carrots, sliced

3 celery ribs, sliced

4 cups shredded cabbage

6 green onions, sliced

1 tablespoon cornstarch

Hot cooked rice, optional

■ In a small bowl, combine 1/4 cup broth, soy sauce, vinegar, honey and garlic powder. Pour 1/3 cup marinade into a large resealable plastic bag; add the pork. Seal bag and turn to coat; refrigerate for 1 hour. Cover and refrigerate remaining marinade.

■ Drain and discard the marinade from pork. In large nonstick skillet or wok, stir-fry pork in oil for 2-3 minutes or until no longer pink. Remove and keep warm. In the same pan, stir-fry broccoli and carrots in reserved marinade for 2 minutes. Add celery; stir-fry for 2 minutes. Add the cabbage and green onions; stir-fry 2-3 minutes longer or until vegetables are crisp-tender.

■ Combine the cornstarch and remaining broth until smooth; stir into the vegetable mixture. Bring to a boil; cook and stir until thickened. Return pork to the pan; heat through. Serve with rice if desired.

Yield: 4 servings.

✱Nutrition Facts: 1-1/2 cups stir-fry mixture (calculated without rice) equals 302 calories, 11 g fat (3 g saturated fat), 63 mg cholesterol, 802 mg sodium, 20 g carbohydrate, 5 g fiber, 30 g protein. **Diabetic Exchanges:** 3 lean meat, 1 starch, 1/2 fat.

This delicious and easy pork entree would be extra tasty topped with toasted sesame seeds, slivered almonds, pecans or even crunchy chow mein noodles.

Italian Sausage Stew

Ann Erney
MIDDLEBURY CENTER, PENNSYLVANIA

One day I was experimenting with using Italian sausage in a recipe, and ended up with this stew. My husband and I like it very much.

Italian Sausage Stew

PREP: 10 min. ■ **COOK:** 1-1/2 hours

1-1/2 pounds Italian sausage links, cut into 1-inch pieces
3 cups water
4 medium potatoes, peeled and cut into chunks
2 medium carrots, cut into chunks
2 celery ribs, cut into chunks
2 small onions, cut into wedges
1/4 cup Worcestershire sauce
1 teaspoon dried oregano
1/2 teaspoon *each* dried basil, thyme and rosemary, crushed
1 bay leaf
Salt and pepper to taste
3/4 cup ketchup
1/2 large green *or* sweet red pepper, cut into chunks
1 tablespoon minced fresh parsley
1 tablespoon cornstarch
1 tablespoon cold water

■ In a Dutch oven, over medium heat, brown sausage; drain. Add the water, potatoes, carrots, celery, onions, Worcestershire sauce and seasonings. Bring to a boil. Reduce heat; cover and cook over low heat for 1 hour or until sausage is no longer pink and vegetables are tender.

■ Add the ketchup, green pepper and parsley; cook 12-15 minutes longer or until pepper is tender. Discard bay leaf.

■ Combine cornstarch and cold water until smooth; gradually stir into stew. Bring to a boil; cook and stir for 2 minutes or until thickened.

Yield: 6 servings.

Tex-Mex Ham & Eggs

Page Alexander
BALDWIN CITY, KANSAS

For a satisfying combo, you can't beat ham, eggs, potatoes and cheese, plus salsa for zip.

PREP/TOTAL TIME: 20 min.

1 cup cubed fully cooked ham
1/2 cup chopped onion
2 tablespoons olive oil, *divided*
2 cups frozen shredded hash brown potatoes
2 eggs
2 tablespoons milk
Salt and pepper to taste
1/2 cup shredded cheddar cheese
2 to 3 tablespoons salsa *or* picante sauce

■ In a large skillet, saute ham and onion in 1 tablespoon of oil until ham is lightly browned and onion is tender; remove and keep warm. Add remaining oil to skillet; cook the potatoes over medium heat until tender, turning to brown.

■ In a small bowl, whisk the eggs, milk, salt and pepper; add to skillet. As eggs set, lift edges, letting uncooked portion flow underneath. When the eggs are set, spoon ham mixture over top; heat through. Sprinkle with the cheese; top with salsa. Cut into wedges.

Yield: 2 servings.

Bacon and Macaroni

Stephanie Savage
RUSHVILLE, MISSOURI

I've prepared this dish on the stovetop and in the microwave...either way, it's a down-home dinner that my husband can't resist. The blend of bacon and cheese is unbeatable.

PREP/TOTAL TIME: 25 min.

14 bacon strips, diced
1 can (15 ounces) tomato sauce
1 can (6 ounces) tomato paste
3 tablespoons minced fresh parsley, *divided*
1/2 teaspoon sugar
1/4 teaspoon garlic powder
1/8 teaspoon pepper
2 cups elbow macaroni, cooked and drained
1/4 cup grated Parmesan cheese

- In a large skillet, cook bacon; drain. Reserve 1 tablespoon drippings in skillet. Add the tomato sauce, tomato paste, 2 tablespoons parsley, sugar, garlic powder and pepper to drippings; cover and simmer for 8-10 minutes. Stir in the macaroni; heat through, stirring occasionally. Combine cheese and remaining parsley; sprinkle over casserole.

- **MICROWAVE DIRECTIONS:** In a 2-qt. microwave-safe baking dish, heat the bacon on high for 2-1/2 minutes; discard fat. Microwave on high 2-3 minutes more or until bacon is crisp. Reserve 1 tablespoon drippings; stir in the tomato sauce, tomato paste, 2 tablespoons parsley, sugar, garlic powder and pepper. Cover and cook on high for 2-3 minutes, stirring occasionally. Stir in the macaroni; cover and cook on high for 1-2 minutes or until heated through. Combine the cheese and remaining parsley; sprinkle over the casserole.

Yield: 8 servings.

Always check the date stamp on packages of vacuum-sealed bacon to make sure it's fresh. The date indicates the last date of sale. Once the package is opened, bacon should be used within a week. For long-term storage, freeze bacon for up to 1 month.

Asian Pork Patties

Shirley Nordblum
YOUNGSVILLE, PENNSYLVANIA

While on the road, my husband can't find many good Chinese restaurants. When he's home, I cook Asian dishes like this one.

PREP/TOTAL TIME: 30 min.

1/2 cup bread crumbs
1 egg, lightly beaten
2 tablespoons soy sauce
3/4 teaspoon ground ginger
3/4 teaspoon ground mustard
1 pound ground pork
1 can (20 ounces) unsweetened pineapple chunks, undrained
1 medium green pepper, cut into chunks
3 green onions, sliced
3 tablespoons white vinegar
3 tablespoons water
3 tablespoons brown sugar
2 tablespoons cornstarch
Hot cooked rice

- In a large bowl, combine the first five ingredients. Crumble pork over mixture and mix well. Shape into four patties.

- In a large skillet, over medium heat, brown patties on both sides until a meat thermometer reads 160° and juices run clear; drain. Add the pineapple, juice, green pepper and onions; bring to a boil. Reduce heat; cover and simmer for 10 minutes.

- Combine vinegar, water, brown sugar and cornstarch; add to pineapple mixture. Bring to a boil; cook and stir for 2 minutes. Serve with rice.

Yield: 4 servings.

Orange-Topped Chops

Sausage Potato Wraps

Julia Rathburn
BEGGS, OKLAHOMA

With our busy schedules, we are always on the lookout for quick recipes. My husband came up with these mouthwatering wraps. We frequently rely on them during the morning rush.

PREP/TOTAL TIME: 30 min.

- 1 pound bulk hot pork sausage
- 1 package (28 ounces) frozen O'Brien potatoes
- 4 eggs
- 1/2 cup milk

Salt and pepper to taste

- 12 flour tortillas (8 inches)

Sour cream and salsa, optional

- ◼ In a large skillet, cook sausage over medium heat until no longer pink; drain. Add the potatoes and cook until lightly browned, about 15 minutes.

- ◼ In a large bowl, whisk the eggs, milk, salt and pepper; add to sausage mixture. Cook and stir over medium heat until eggs are completely set. Divide the mixture between tortillas; roll up tightly.

- ◼ Place in a greased 13-in. x 9-in. baking dish. Microwave, uncovered, on high for 2-4 minutes or until heated through, or microwave individually for 30 seconds. Serve wraps with sour cream and salsa if desired.

Yield: 6-8 servings.

Cindy Milleson
BOZEMAN, MONTANA

This recipe has just two main ingredients, plus a few simple seasonings. As the chops simmer, they'll pick up the fruity flavor. You can substitute any canned fruit for the oranges.

Orange-Topped Chops

PREP/TOTAL TIME: 30 min.

- 6 bone-in pork loin chops (8 ounces *each*)
- 1 tablespoon canola oil
- 1 can (11 ounces) mandarin oranges, drained
- 1/2 teaspoon ground cloves

Pepper to taste

- ◼ In a large skillet, brown pork chops in oil on both sides. Top with the oranges; sprinkle with cloves and pepper.

- ◼ Cover; simmer over medium-high heat for 20-25 minutes or until a meat thermometer reads 160°.

Yield: 6 servings.

Chops with Mixed Fruit

Phyllis Leslie
TOLEDO, OHIO
Prunes, apricots and pineapple lend winter fruit flavor to this meal that preps in 10 minutes.

PREP: 10 min.
COOK: 30 min.

- 4 boneless pork loin chops (4 ounces *each*)
- 3/4 cup chopped onion
- 3/4 cup thinly sliced celery
- 8 pitted prunes
- 3/4 cup pineapple tidbits
- 1/3 cup dried apricots
- 1/3 cup plus 2 tablespoons water, *divided*
- 4 teaspoons reduced-sodium soy sauce

Dash dried marjoram

- In a large nonstick skillet coated with cooking spray, cook pork chops over medium heat for 4-5 minutes on each side or until a meat thermometer reads 160°. Remove and keep warm.

- In the same skillet, saute the onion and celery for 3 minutes. Stir in the prunes, pineapple, apricots, 1/3 cup water, soy sauce and marjoram. Bring to a boil. Reduce heat; cover and simmer for 15 minutes.

- Return pork to the pan. Stir in remaining water; return to a boil. Reduce heat; cover and simmer for 7-11 minutes or until meat is tender.

Yield: 4 servings.

Sausage 'n' Sauerkraut

Mary Lyon
SPOTSYLVANIA, VIRGINIA
Three young children involved in different activities keep me running year-round. I created this quick-and-easy dish so I can throw it together in no time on those extra-busy nights.

Sausage 'n' Sauerkraut

PREP/TOTAL TIME: 30 min.

- 4 medium potatoes, peeled and cubed
- 2 tablespoons canola oil
- 1 small onion, halved and sliced
- 1 pound smoked sausage, cut into 1/4-inch pieces
- 1 package (16 ounces) sauerkraut, rinsed and well drained
- 1/4 teaspoon pepper
- 1/8 teaspoon salt

- In a large skillet, saute potatoes in oil for 5-6 minutes or until lightly browned. Stir in onion; saute for 3-4 minutes or until the potatoes are tender. Add the sausage, sauerkraut, pepper and salt. Cook, uncovered, over medium heat for 4-5 minutes or until heated through, stirring mixture occasionally.

Yield: 4 servings.

Terri Glauser
APPLETON, WISCONSIN
Sliced peaches and red pepper strips add pretty color to these fast-to-fix pork slices. A hint of Dijon mustard and fresh gingerroot perks up the slightly sweet sauce.

Peachy Ginger Pork

Peachy Ginger Pork*

PREP/TOTAL TIME: 25 min.

1 pork tenderloin (1 pound), cut into 1/2-inch slices	1 cup canned sliced peaches in extra-light syrup
1/2 teaspoon salt	1/2 cup reduced-sodium chicken broth
1/8 teaspoon pepper	1/3 cup peach spreadable fruit
1 teaspoon olive oil	1 tablespoon Dijon mustard
1 medium sweet red pepper, julienned	2 teaspoons minced fresh gingerroot

■ Flatten pork to 1/4-in. thickness; sprinkle with salt and pepper. In a large nonstick skillet coated with cooking spray, saute pork in oil in batches until meat is no longer pink. Remove and keep warm.

■ In the same skillet, saute red pepper and peaches until red pepper is tender. Add the broth, spreadable fruit, mustard and ginger. Cook and stir over medium heat for 4 minutes. Return pork to the pan. Reduce heat; cover and simmer until heated through.

Yield: 4 servings.

*Nutrition Facts: 1 serving equals 236 calories, 5 g fat (2 g saturated fat), 63 mg cholesterol, 517 mg sodium, 23 g carbohydrate, 1 g fiber, 23 g protein. **Diabetic Exchanges:** 3 lean meat, 1 fruit.

Fresh gingerroot is available in your grocer's produce section and should have a smooth skin. If it's wrinkled and cracked, the root is dry and past its prime. When stored in a heavy-duty resealable plastic bag, unpeeled gingerroot can be frozen for up to 1 year. When needed, simply peel and grate.

One-Pan Pork A la Orange

Shirley Smith
ORANGE, CALIFORNIA
When I want to serve family and friends something special without a lot of fuss, this is the recipe I reach for.

PREP/TOTAL TIME: 30 min.

       2 cups dry instant chicken stuffing mix
   1-1/2 cups orange juice, *divided*
       4 pork cutlets (4 ounces each)
     1/4 cup all-purpose flour
       2 tablespoons canola oil
       2 cups frozen tiny whole carrots
       2 cups frozen broccoli cuts
     1/8 teaspoon salt
     1/8 teaspoon pepper

■ Combine the stuffing mix and 3/4 cup orange juice; let stand for 3-4 minutes or until liquid is absorbed, stirring occasionally. Flatten the cutlets to 1/4-in. thickness; top each with about 1/3 cup of the stuffing. Roll up jelly-roll style and secure with toothpicks; coat with flour.

■ In a large skillet, brown roll-ups in oil; drain. Add the remaining orange juice; bring to a boil. Reduce heat; cover and simmer for 7 minutes. Add the remaining ingredients; cover and simmer 7-10 minutes longer or until meat is no longer pink. Remove the toothpicks.

Yield: 4 servings.

Stick-to-Your-Ribs Supper

Cynthia Chapman
ALLENDALE, SOUTH CAROLINA

This sausage and bean skillet dish appears on my Sunday dinner menu at least once a month. For a little extra zest, add more chili powder and cayenne pepper.

PREP: 10 min. ■ **BAKE:** 30 min.

- 2 medium green peppers, chopped
- 1 large onion, chopped
- 1 can (4 ounces) mushroom stems and pieces, drained
- 1 tablespoon canola oil
- 2 garlic cloves, minced
- 1 pound smoked kielbasa *or* smoked Polish sausage, thinly sliced
- 1-1/2 cups water
- 1 can (16 ounces) kidney beans, rinsed and drained
- 1 can (15 ounces) pinto beans, rinsed and drained
- 1 can (14-1/2 ounces) diced tomatoes, undrained
- 2 teaspoons chili powder
- 1 teaspoon ground cumin
- 1/2 teaspoon salt
- 1/8 teaspoon cayenne pepper
- 3/4 cup uncooked long grain rice
- 1 cup (4 ounces) shredded part-skim mozzarella cheese

■ In a large skillet, saute the green peppers, onion and mushrooms in oil until tender. Add garlic; cook 1 minute longer. Add the sausage, water, beans, tomatoes, chili powder, cumin, salt and cayenne. Bring to a boil Stir in the rice.

■ Reduce heat; cover and simmer for 20-25 minutes or until rice is tender. Sprinkle with the cheese; cover and cook for 5 minutes longer or until cheese is melted.

Yield: 10 servings.

When it comes to rice, long, medium and short grain refers to the length of the grain. Long grain has a long, slender kernel and it is separate, light and fluffy when cooked. Medium grain is shorter and wider, and when cooked, it is moist, tender, and the grains cling together. Short grain has short, plump, almost round kernels. When cooked it has a soft texture, and the individual grains cling together.

Cinnamon-Apple Pork Chops*

Christina Price
WHEELING, WEST VIRGINIA

I found this recipe years ago, and it quickly became a favorite. The ingredients are convenient and the dish goes together quickly, One-pan cleanup is a bonus.

PREP/TOTAL TIME: 25 min.

- 4 boneless pork loin chops (4 ounces *each*)
- 2 tablespoons reduced-fat butter, *divided*
- 3 tablespoons brown sugar
- 1 teaspoon ground cinnamon
- 1/2 teaspoon ground nutmeg
- 1/4 teaspoon salt
- 4 medium tart apples, thinly sliced
- 2 tablespoons chopped pecans

■ In a large skillet over medium heat, cook the pork chops in 1 tablespoon butter for 4-5 minutes on each side or until a meat thermometer reads 160°. Meanwhile, in a small bowl, combine the brown sugar, cinnamon, nutmeg and salt.

■ Remove chops and keep warm. Add apples, pecans, brown sugar mixture and remaining butter to pan; cook and stir until apples are tender. Serve with chops.

Yield: 4 servings.

✱Nutrition Facts: 1 pork chop with 2/3 cup apples equals 316 calories, 12 g fat (4 g saturated fat), 62 mg cholesterol, 232 mg sodium, 31 g carbohydrate, 4 g fiber, 22 g protein. **Diabetic Exchanges:** 3 lean meat, 1 starch, 1 fruit, 1 fat.

Editor's Note: This recipe was tested with Land O'Lakes light stick butter.

Jennifer Enzer
MANCHESTER, MICHIGAN

I based the recipe for these noodles on a similar dish I found in a magazine. I changed a few things around, and my husband and I loved it. It's just as good when the pork is replaced with seafood.

Chinese Pork 'n' Noodles

Chinese Pork 'n' Noodles*

PREP: 20 min. ■ COOK: 15 min.

6 ounces uncooked angel hair pasta

3 tablespoons hoisin sauce

2 tablespoons reduced-sodium soy sauce

2 teaspoons sesame oil

1 pork tenderloin (1 pound), thinly sliced and halved

3 teaspoons canola oil, *divided*

3/4 cup julienned sweet red pepper

3/4 cup halved fresh snow peas

1/2 cup sliced onion

1 cup sliced cabbage

1/4 cup minced fresh cilantro

■ Cook pasta according to package directions. Meanwhile, in a small bowl, combine the hoisin sauce, soy sauce and sesame oil; set aside.

■ In a large nonstick skillet or wok, stir-fry pork in 2 teaspoons canola oil for 3 minutes or until no longer pink. Remove and keep warm. In the same skillet, stir-fry the red pepper, peas and onion in remaining oil for 3 minutes. Add cabbage; stir-fry 2 minutes longer or until vegetables are crisp-tender.

■ Stir reserved hoisin sauce mixture and stir into skillet. Return pork to the pan; heat through. Drain pasta and add to skillet; toss to coat. Sprinkle each serving with 1 tablespoon cilantro.

Yield: 4 servings.

*Nutrition Facts: 1-1/2 cups equals 398 calories, 11 g fat (2 g saturated fat), 64 mg cholesterol, 550 mg sodium, 43 g carbohydrate, 3 g fiber, 30 g protein. **Diabetic Exchanges:** 3 lean meat, 2-1/2 starch, 1 vegetable, 1 fat.

Flavorful Frittata

Annette Self
JUNCTION CITY, OHIO

Basil adds Italian flair to this cheesy egg dish that cooks on the stovetop. Canned mushrooms and store-bought spaghetti sauce cut minutes off the prep time. Spicy pork sausage adds to the appeal, but it's tasty when made with ham, too.

PREP/TOTAL TIME: 30 min.

1 cup cooked bulk pork sausage

1 small onion, chopped

1 jar (4-1/2 ounces) sliced mushrooms, drained

1 to 2 tablespoons canola oil

12 eggs

1/4 cup half-and-half cream

1 teaspoon dried basil

1/2 teaspoon salt

1 cup (4 ounces) shredded part-skim mozzarella cheese

2 cups meatless spaghetti sauce, warmed

■ In a large nonstick skillet, saute sausage, onion and mushrooms in oil until the onion is tender. Meanwhile, in a large bowl, whisk eggs, cream, basil and salt; pour over sausage mixture.

■ As the eggs set, lift the edges, allowing uncooked portion to flow underneath. When eggs are nearly set, sprinkle with cheese. Cook until the cheese is melted. Cut into wedges; serve with spaghetti sauce.

Yield: 8 servings.

Angie Smith
CLARKSVILLE, TENNESSEE

This is my most requested dish. I like the thicker texture of the sauce, which is great with any hearty pasta, such as whole wheat tortellini or penne.

Creamy Ham Fettuccine

Creamy Ham Fettuccine

PREP/TOTAL TIME: 25 min.

- 1 package (12 ounces) fettuccine
- 3 tablespoons finely chopped onion
- 3 tablespoons butter
- 2 tablespoons plus 1 teaspoon all-purpose flour
- 3 cups heavy whipping cream
- 2 cups fresh broccoli florets
- 2 cups cubed fully cooked ham
- 1 cup shredded Parmesan cheese, *divided*
- 1/2 to 3/4 teaspoon garlic salt
- 1/4 teaspoon pepper
- 1/4 teaspoon dried oregano
- 1/4 teaspoon ground nutmeg

■ Cook the fettuccine according to package directions. Meanwhile, in a large saucepan, saute the onion in butter until tender. Stir in flour until blended. Gradually stir in the cream. Bring to a boil over medium heat, stirring constantly.

■ Add broccoli. Reduce heat; simmer, uncovered, for 7-10 minutes or until broccoli is crisp-tender, stirring occasionally. Stir in the ham, 1/2 cup cheese, garlic salt, pepper, oregano and nutmeg. Drain fettuccine; serve with sauce. Sprinkle with remaining cheese.

Yield: 6 servings.

Whipping cream is a rich cream that ranges from 36-40% butterfat and doubles in volume when whipped. The carton is often labeled as either heavy cream or whipping cream.

Creole Pork Chops

Ann Rogers
OCALA, FLORIDA

I've had this recipe for over 20 years and love it. Since the children are grown, I now cook just half the recipe for my husband and I. And it's so easy! You'll be in and out of the kitchen in no time.

PREP/TOTAL TIME: 30 min.

- 1/2 teaspoon salt
- 1/2 teaspoon dried basil
- 1/2 teaspoon paprika
- 1/2 teaspoon pepper
- 1/4 teaspoon ground cumin
- 1/8 to 1/4 teaspoon cayenne pepper
- 4 boneless pork loin chops (4 ounces *each*)
- 2 tablespoons canola oil
- 1 can (8 ounces) tomato sauce
- 1/2 cup chopped onion
- 1/2 cup chopped green pepper
- 1/4 cup chopped celery
- 1 tablespoon Worcestershire sauce
- 1/2 teaspoon minced garlic

■ In a small bowl, combine the first six ingredients; rub over both sides of pork.

■ In a large skillet, brown pork chops in oil over medium heat. Add the remaining ingredients. Cover and cook 15-20 minutes longer or until a meat thermometer reads 160°.

Yield: 4 servings.

Sweet Potato Pork Stew

Susan Schlenvogt
WAUKESHA, WISCONSIN
I'm an avid recipe collector and have fun trying new dishes. Fortunately, my family doesn't mind experimenting with new tastes. Everyone loves the blend of flavors in this stew.

Sweet Potato Pork Stew

PREP: 10 min. ■ COOK: 1 hour 5 min.

3 tablespoons Dijon mustard
2 pounds boneless pork, trimmed and cut into 1-inch cubes
1/2 cup all-purpose flour
3 tablespoons brown sugar
3 tablespoons canola oil
2 garlic cloves, minced

2-1/3 cups chicken broth
4 to 5 small onions, quartered
2 medium sweet potatoes, peeled and cubed
1/2 teaspoon salt
1/4 teaspoon pepper
1/4 cup minced fresh parsley

■ Rub mustard over pork. In a large resealable plastic bag, combine the flour and brown sugar; add the pork and shake to coat.

■ In a large skillet, over medium-high heat, brown pork in oil. Add the garlic; cook 1 minute longer. Add the broth; bring to a boil. Scrape the bottom of skillet to loosen any browned bits. Reduce heat; cover and simmer for 30 minutes or until pork is no longer pink.

■ Add onions, sweet potatoes, salt and pepper; cover and simmer for 30 minutes more or until the pork and potatoes are tender. Stir in parsley.

Yield: 6-8 servings (2 quarts).

To keep fresh
parsley in the refrigerator for several weeks, wash the bunch in warm water, shake off excess moisture, wrap in paper towels and seal in a plastic bag. If you need a longer storage time, remove the paper towels and place the sealed bag in the freezer. Then simply break off and crumble the amount of parsley you need for soups, stews and other cooked dishes.

- In a large bowl, combine 1 tablespoon of the cornstarch and the sherry until smooth; add pork and toss to coat. In a second bowl, combine sugar and remaining cornstarch. Stir in the water, cider vinegar, soy sauce and ketchup until the mixture is smooth; set aside.

- In a large nonstick skillet or wok, stir-fry the pork in hot oil until no longer pink. Add the cashews, onions, ginger and garlic; stir-fry for 1 minute. Add peas and pineapple; stir-fry 3 minutes longer or until peas are crisp-tender.

- Stir cornstarch mixture and add to the pan. Bring to a boil; cook and stir for 1-2 minutes or until sauce is thickened. Serve over rice if desired.

Yield: 4 servings.

Sweet 'n' Sour Cashew Pork

Janet Rodakowski
WENTZVILLE, MISSOURI

A simple homemade sauce blends the tangy flavors in this stir-fry. Ginger, garlic and pineapple give it a traditional taste, and snow peas, green onions and cashews add a little crunch.

Sweet 'n' Sour Cashew Pork

PREP/TOTAL TIME: 30 min.

2 tablespoons cornstarch, *divided*

1 tablespoon sherry *or* chicken broth

1 pork tenderloin (1 pound), cut into 1-inch pieces

1/4 cup sugar

1/3 cup water

1/4 cup cider vinegar

3 tablespoons reduced-sodium soy sauce

3 tablespoons ketchup

1 tablespoon canola oil

1/3 cup unsalted cashews

1/4 cup chopped green onions

2 teaspoons minced fresh gingerroot

2 garlic cloves, minced

1/2 pound fresh snow peas (3 cups)

1 can (8 ounces) unsweetened pineapple chunks, drained

Hot cooked rice, optional

To store fresh

snow peas, refrigerate them, unwashed, in an aerated plastic bag for up to 3 days. To prepare, wash, cut off the stems and pull off any attached strings. To brighten the color of snow peas, submerge in boiling water for about 30 seconds, then plunge in ice water.

Vicki Blaine
PLYMOUTH, MICHIGAN

This recipe came out of necessity! I love to cook but hate to grocery shop. One day I found myself with nothing but pork chops, canned black beans and canned tomatoes. This is the dish I came up with, and my husband loved it.

Southwestern Pork Chops

Southwestern Pork Chops

PREP/TOTAL TIME: 30 min.

1	medium onion, chopped
2	tablespoons olive oil, *divided*
1-1/2	teaspoons minced garlic
2	cans (14-1/2 ounces *each*) diced tomatoes, drained
1	can (15 ounces) black beans, rinsed and drained
3/4	cup chicken broth
1-1/2	teaspoons chili powder
1/2	teaspoon dried oregano

1/2	teaspoon ground cumin
1/8	teaspoon crushed red pepper flakes
4	bone-in pork loin chops (1/2 inch thick and 6 ounces *each*)
1/4	teaspoon salt
1/4	teaspoon pepper

Hot cooked rice

2	tablespoons minced fresh cilantro, optional

■ In a large skillet, saute the onion in 1 tablespoon oil for 3-4 minutes or until tender. Add the garlic; cook 1 minute longer. Stir in the tomatoes, beans, broth, chili powder, oregano, cumin and pepper flakes. Bring to a boil. Reduce the heat; simmer, uncovered, for 4-5 minutes or until heated through.

■ Meanwhile, in another skillet, brown the pork chops on both sides in remaining oil over medium-high heat. Sprinkle with salt and pepper. Pour tomato mixture over chops. Cover and simmer for 10-15 minutes or until a meat thermometer reads 160°. Serve with a slotted spoon over rice. Sprinkle with cilantro if desired.

Yield: 4 servings.

Pork 'n' Potato Skillet*

Mary Tallman
ARBOR VITAE, WISCONSIN

This scrumptious dinner makes an ideal fuss-free entree. Round out the meal with steamed vegetables or a salad.

PREP/TOTAL TIME: 30 min.

4	boneless pork loin chops (1 inch thick and 4 ounces *each*)
1/4	teaspoon pepper
1	tablespoon olive oil
4	medium red potatoes, thinly sliced
1	medium onion, sliced
1	teaspoon dried oregano
1	cup chicken broth
1/2	cup diced roasted sweet red peppers

■ Sprinkle the pork chops with pepper. In a large skillet, brown the chops in oil on both sides; drain. Remove and keep warm.

■ In the same skillet, saute the potatoes, onion and oregano for 6-8 minutes or until the potatoes are almost tender. Stir in broth and red peppers; bring to a boil.

■ Top with the pork chops. Reduce the heat; cover and simmer for 10-15 minutes or until the potatoes are tender and a meat thermometer reads 160°, stirring occasionally.

Yield: 4 servings.

*Nutrition Facts: 1 serving (prepared with reduced-sodium broth) equals 292 calories, 10 g fat (3 g saturated fat), 55 mg cholesterol, 297 mg sodium, 24 g carbohydrate, 3 g fiber, 26 g protein. **Diabetic Exchanges:** 3 lean meat, 1 starch, 1 vegetable.

Fish & Seafood

155

161

156

For a refreshing change from traditional meat and potatoes fare, try creating a meal with fish or seafood. The recipes in this chapter can be prepared quickly, which is a boon for busy cooks. Plus, they add a healthier option to your weekly menu.

Orange Roughy Italiano

Sherry Fletcher
HIGHLAND, ILLINOIS

I'm not a big fan of fish unless it's fried. But this recipe is so simple and good that it's become a favorite! It's also low in fat and packed with vitamin-rich veggies and Italian flavor.

Orange Roughy Italiano*

PREP/TOTAL TIME: 30 min.

2 cups sliced zucchini	1/4 teaspoon salt
1/2 cup thinly sliced onion	1/8 teaspoon pepper
1 teaspoon dried oregano	1 medium tomato, chopped
1 tablespoon olive oil	1/2 cup shredded part-skim mozzarella cheese
4 orange roughy fillets (4 ounces *each*)	

■ In a large nonstick skillet coated with cooking spray, saute the zucchini, onion and oregano in oil for 5 minutes or until onion is tender.

■ Sprinkle the fillets with salt and pepper; place over zucchini mixture. Sprinkle with tomato. Reduce heat; cover and simmer for 10 minutes or until fish flakes easily with a fork. Sprinkle with cheese; cover and let stand for 2 minutes or until cheese is melted.

Yield: 4 servings.

✳Nutrition Facts: 1 serving equals 167 calories, 7 g fat (2 g saturated fat), 31 mg cholesterol, 290 mg sodium, 5 g carbohydrate, 2 g fiber, 21 g protein. **Diabetic Exchanges:** 3 very lean meat, 1 vegetable, 1 fat.

Salsa Fish Skillet*

Taste of Home Test Kitchen

Zucchini and yellow summer squash add seasonal flair to this colorful fish dish from our home economists.

PREP/TOTAL TIME: 20 min.

   1 pound halibut steaks *or* other firm whitefish, cut into 1-inch pieces

   3 teaspoons canola oil, *divided*

   1 medium yellow summer squash, julienned

   1 medium zucchini, julienned

   1 cup sliced fresh mushrooms

1/4 to 1/2 teaspoon ground cumin

   2 garlic cloves, minced

1-1/2 cups chunky salsa

   4 teaspoons minced fresh cilantro

■ In a large nonstick skillet or wok, stir-fry halibut in 2 teaspoons hot oil for 3-4 minutes or until the fish flakes easily with a fork; remove and keep warm.

■ Add yellow squash, zucchini, mushrooms, cumin and the remaining oil to pan. Stir-fry for 2-3 minutes or until vegetables are crisp-tender. Add garlic; cook 1 minute longer. Return fish to the pan. Add salsa; heat through. Sprinkle with cilantro.

Yield: 4 servings.

✳Nutrition Facts: 1 cup equals 210 calories, 6 g fat (1 g saturated fat), 36 mg cholesterol, 485 mg sodium, 8 g carbohydrate, 5 g fiber, 25 g protein. **Diabetic Exchanges:** 3 lean meat, 2 vegetable.

Couscous Paella

- In a large nonstick skillet coated with cooking spray, saute the red pepper in oil for 2 minutes. Add the onions and garlic; cook 1 minute longer.

- Stir in broth and seasonings; bring to a boil. Add shrimp; cook for 2-3 minutes or just until shrimp turn pink. Return to a boil. Stir in the couscous, peas and butter.

- Remove from the heat; cover and let stand for 5 minutes. Fluff with a fork. Sprinkle with almonds and parsley. Serve with lemon.

Yield: 8 servings.

Marcella Stevenson
WESTMINSTER, CALIFORNIA

Featuring aromatic seasonings—including coriander, turmeric and garlic—this shrimp paella makes eating well enjoyable.

Couscous Paella

PREP: 25 min. **COOK:** 20 min.

1 medium sweet red pepper, chopped	1/8 teaspoon cayenne pepper
1 tablespoon canola oil	2 pounds uncooked medium shrimp, peeled and deveined
6 green onions, thinly sliced	2 cups uncooked couscous
4 garlic cloves, minced	2 cups frozen peas, thawed
2 cans (14-1/2 ounces *each*) vegetable broth	1 tablespoon butter
2 teaspoons ground coriander	2 tablespoons chopped almonds, toasted
1 teaspoon ground turmeric	2 tablespoons minced fresh parsley
1/2 teaspoon salt	Lemon wedges
1/4 teaspoon pepper	

To easily peel

and devein shrimp, start on the underside by the head area to remove the shell. Pull the legs and the first section of the shell to one side. Continue pulling the shell up, around the top and to the other side. Pull off the shell by the tail if desired. Make a shallow slit with a paring knife along the back from head area to tail. Rinse under cold water to remove the vein.

Mildred Sherrer
FORT WORTH, TEXAS

I give fish a healthy flavor lift with a homemade relish. Tangy vinegar and tarragon lend zest to the tasty condiment, and chopped cucumber and radishes add garden-fresh color.

Perch with Cucumber Relish

Salmon Fettuccine

Lisa Royston
WASILLA, ALASKA

We like to make this dish when we have leftover cooked salmon. It's also great with canned salmon.

PREP/TOTAL TIME: 20 min.

- 8 ounces uncooked fettuccine
- 1-1/2 cups sliced fresh mushrooms
- 1 small zucchini, sliced
- 2 tablespoons chopped onion
- 2 tablespoons butter
- 1 tablespoon all-purpose flour
- 3/4 cup milk
- 3/4 cup canned *or* fully cooked salmon chunks
- 1/2 cup frozen peas, thawed
- 1/2 cup diced fresh tomato
- 1 tablespoon minced parsley
- 1/4 teaspoon salt
- 1/8 to 1/4 teaspoon pepper
- 1/8 teaspoon dried basil
- 1/8 teaspoon dried oregano

- ■ Cook fettuccine according to package directions. Meanwhile in a large skillet, saute the mushrooms, zucchini and onion in butter until crisp-tender.

- ■ Stir in the flour until blended. Gradually add milk. Bring to a boil; cook and stir for 1 minute or until thickened. Add the salmon, peas, tomato, parsley and seasonings; heat through. Drain fettuccine; serve with salmon mixture.

Yield: 4 servings.

Perch with Cucumber Relish

PREP/TOTAL TIME: 25 min.

- 2/3 cup chopped seeded cucumber
- 1/2 cup chopped radishes
- 2 tablespoons white vinegar
- 1 teaspoon canola oil
- 1/4 teaspoon sugar
- 1/4 teaspoon dried tarragon
- 1/8 teaspoon salt
- 2 tablespoons butter
- 4 perch *or* tilapia fillets (6 ounces *each*)

- ■ For relish, in a small bowl, combine the cucumber, radishes, vinegar, oil, sugar, tarragon and salt; set aside.

- ■ In a large skillet, melt the butter over medium-high heat. Cook fillets for 3-4 minutes on each side or until fish flakes easily with a fork. Serve with relish.

Yield: 4 servings.

For fish fillets, check for doneness by inserting a fork at an angle into the thickest part of the fish and gently parting the meat. When it is opaque and flakes into sections, it is cooked.

Seafood Stir-Fry*

Robin Chamberlin
LA COSTA, CALIFORNIA

This delightfully different stir-fry features tuna steaks, broccoli and pasta. The sauce offers a delicate balance of flavors, ranging from zesty red pepper flakes to Parmesan cheese.

PREP/TOTAL TIME: 25 min.

- 6 ounces uncooked linguine, broken in half
- 1 tablespoon cornstarch
- 3/4 cup dry white wine *or* reduced-sodium chicken broth
- 1/2 cup additional reduced-sodium chicken broth
- 1 teaspoon dried thyme
- 1/2 teaspoon salt
- 1/8 to 1/4 teaspoon crushed red pepper flakes
- 2 cups broccoli florets
- 4 teaspoons canola oil
- 1 large sweet yellow, red *or* green pepper, julienned
- 2 garlic cloves, minced
- 2 tuna *or* swordfish steaks (8 ounces *each*), cut into 1-inch cubes
- 1/4 cup shredded Parmesan cheese

- Cook pasta according to package directions. In a small bowl, combine the cornstarch, wine, additional chicken broth, thyme, salt and pepper flakes until smooth; set aside.

- Meanwhile, in a large nonstick skillet, stir-fry the broccoli in hot oil for 4 minutes. Add the sweet pepper; stir-fry for 4 minutes. Add garlic; cook 1 minute longer.

- Stir cornstarch mixture and gradually add to the pan along with tuna; stir-fry 3-4 minutes for medium-rare or until slightly pink in the center. Drain pasta; add to stir-fry and toss to coat. Sprinkle with cheese.

Yield: 4 servings.

*Nutrition Facts: 1-1/2 cups equals 399 calories, 9 g fat (2 g saturated fat), 57 mg cholesterol, 521 mg sodium, 39 g carbohydrate, 3 g fiber, 35 g protein. **Diabetic Exchanges:** 4 lean meat, 2 starch, 1 vegetable.

Tuscan Salmon Pasta

PREP/TOTAL TIME: 20 min.

- 4 ounces uncooked linguine
- 1 salmon fillet (10 ounces), cut into 1-inch cubes
- 1 teaspoon minced fresh rosemary
- 5 tablespoons olive oil, *divided*
- 3/4 cup white kidney *or* cannellini beans, rinsed and drained
- 2 small plum tomatoes, chopped
- 6 garlic cloves, minced

Salt and pepper to taste

- Cook the linguine according to package directions. Meanwhile, in a small skillet, saute salmon and rosemary in 2 tablespoons oil for 5 minutes or until the salmon flakes easily with a fork. Add beans, tomatoes, garlic, salt and pepper; heat through.

- Drain the linguine; and transfer to a large bowl. Add salmon mixture; toss gently. Drizzle with remaining oil.

Yield: 2 servings.

When cooking with white wine, the general rule is to use wine that you would enjoy drinking with the meal. For Seafood Stir-Fry, consider using dry whites such as Chardonnay, Chablis, Chenin Blanc, Sauvignon Blanc or Pinot Grigio.

Dianne Alvine
TOMS RIVER, NEW JERSEY

White kidney beans and plum tomatoes are tossed with salmon and linguine in this fast-to-fix entree that works for special dinners or every day. If you like, you can double or triple the recipe to serve more people. To balance the meal, serve the pasta with crusty bread and a crisp side salad.

- In a small saucepan, saute the onion in butter until tender. Remove from the heat. Add the tuna, zucchini, eggs, parsley, lemon juice, seasonings and 1/2 cup bread crumbs. Stir until well combined. Shape into six 1/2-in.-thick patties; coat with remaining bread crumbs.

- In a large skillet, heat oil. Cook patties for 3 minutes on each side or until golden brown.

Yield: 3 servings.

You can freeze
zucchini with a bit of preparation. Shred the zucchini, steam it for 1-2 minutes or until translucent, then drain. Pack in measured and labeled amounts into freezer containers, leaving 1/2 inch of space at the top, or in heavy-duty resealable bags. Cool, seal and freeze.

Tuna Zucchini Cakes

Billie Blanton
KINGSPORT, TENNESSEE

Here's a great combination of seafood and a bountiful garden vegetable! People seem to like its nice color and texture...not to mention the wonderful flavor!

Tuna Zucchini Cakes

PREP/TOTAL TIME: 25 min.

1/2 cup finely chopped onion	1/3 cup minced fresh parsley
1 tablespoon butter	1 teaspoon lemon juice
1 can (6-1/2 ounces) light water-packed tuna, drained and flaked	1/2 teaspoon salt
	1/8 teaspoon pepper
1 cup shredded zucchini	1 cup seasoned bread crumbs, *divided*
2 eggs, lightly beaten	2 tablespoons canola oil

Scallop Stir-Fry*

Taste of Home Test Kitchen

This saucy seafood stir-fry from our home economists features scallops, curry, ginger and a colorful medley of vegetables.

PREP/TOTAL TIME: 15 min.

- 12 ounces fresh *or* frozen sea scallops, thawed
- 1 tablespoon cornstarch
- 1 teaspoon sugar
- 1/4 teaspoon salt
- 1 cup water
- 2 teaspoons reduced-sodium soy sauce
- 2 medium carrots, thinly sliced
- 3 celery ribs, thinly sliced
- 3 teaspoons canola oil, *divided*
- 4 ounces fresh mushrooms, quartered
- 4 green onions, cut into 1-inch pieces
- 4 garlic cloves, minced
- 1 teaspoon curry powder
- 2 teaspoons minced fresh gingerroot

Hot cooked rice, optional

- If scallops are large, cut in half and set aside. In a small bowl, combine the cornstarch, sugar and salt. Stir in water and soy sauce until smooth; set aside.

- In a nonstick skillet, saute the carrots and celery in 1-1/2 teaspoons hot oil for 4 minutes. Add the mushrooms and green onions; stir-fry for 2-3 minutes or until crisp-tender. Add garlic, curry powder and ginger; stir-fry for 1 minute longer. Remove vegetable mixture and set aside.

- In the same skillet, stir-fry scallops in remaining oil for 2-3 minutes or until scallops turn opaque. Stir sauce and add to the pan. Bring to a boil; cook and stir for 1-2 minutes or until thickened. Return vegetables to the pan; heat through. Serve over hot cooked rice if desired.

Yield: 3 servings.

***Nutrition Facts:** 1 cup stir-fry mixture, calculated without rice, equals 213 calories, 6 g fat (trace saturated fat), 37 mg cholesterol, 581 mg sodium, 18 g carbohydrate, 3 g fiber, 22 g protein. **Diabetic Exchanges:** 3 lean meat, 2 vegetable, 1/2 starch.

To prepare mushrooms for cooking,
gently remove any dirt by rubbing with a mushroom brush or by wiping with a damp paper towel. Or quickly rinse under cold water, drain and pat dry with paper towels. Do not peel mushrooms, but trim stems.

Lobster & Artichoke Quesadillas

Allene Bary-Cooper
WICHITA FALLS, TEXAS

Lobster, artichokes, cheese and spices are some of my favorite foods. Put them together in a quesadilla and it is fantastic fare. I like to serve these quesadillas with fresh avocados seasoned with lemon juice and pepper.

PREP/TOTAL TIME: 30 min.

- 1/2 cup grated Parmesan cheese
- 1/2 cup fat-free mayonnaise
- 1 can (14 ounces) water-packed artichoke hearts, rinsed, drained and chopped
- 4-1/2 teaspoons chopped roasted sweet red pepper
- 1 garlic clove, minced
- 6 flour tortillas (10 inches)
- 1 cup cooked lobster meat *or* canned flaked lobster meat
- 1/2 cup shredded part-skim mozzarella cheese

- In a small bowl, combine the Parmesan cheese, mayonnaise, artichokes, red pepper and garlic. Spread over the three tortillas. Top with the lobster, mozzarella cheese and the remaining tortillas; press down lightly.

- On a griddle coated with cooking spray, cook the quesadillas over medium heat for 2 minutes on each side or until the cheese is melted. Cut each quesadilla into six wedges.

Yield: 6 servings.

Cod with Sweet Peppers*

Judy Grebetz
RACINE, WISCONSIN

This quick and delicious dish is a family favorite. I like to use three or four different colors of peppers.

PREP/TOTAL TIME: 25 min.

- 1 medium onion, halved and sliced
- 1 cup reduced-sodium chicken broth
- 1 tablespoon lemon juice
- 3 garlic cloves, minced
- 1-1/2 teaspoons dried oregano
- 1/2 teaspoon grated lemon peel
- 1/4 teaspoon salt
- 4 cod fillets (6 ounces *each*)
- 3/4 cup julienned green pepper
- 3/4 cup julienned sweet red pepper
- 2-1/2 teaspoons cornstarch
- 1 tablespoon cold water
- 1 medium lemon, halved and sliced

■ In a large nonstick skillet, combine the first seven ingredients. Bring to a boil. Reduce the heat; cover and simmer for 6-8 minutes or until onion is tender.

■ Arrange the fish and peppers over onion mixture. Cover and simmer for 6-9 minutes or until the fish flakes easily with a fork and peppers are tender. Remove fish and vegetables and keep warm.

■ Combine cornstarch and water until smooth; gradually stir into pan juices. Bring to a boil; cook and stir for 2 minutes or until thickened. Spoon over fish and vegetables. Serve with lemon.

Yield: 4 servings.

❋Nutrition Facts: 1 fish fillet with 1/3 cup vegetable mixture and 1/4 cup sauce equals 168 calories, 1 g fat (trace saturated fat), 65 mg cholesterol, 398 mg sodium, 10 g carbohydrate, 2 g fiber, 29 g protein. **Diabetic Exchanges:** 4 very lean meat, 1 vegetable.

Other types of fish you can use instead of cod for the Cod with Sweet Peppers recipe include any white and flaky fish, such as haddock, tilapia or halibut.

Shrimp And Grits

Judith King
MADISONVILLE, TENNESSEE

I serve a mixture of shrimp and vegetables alongside dressed-up grits for a lip-smacking sweet and spicy meal.

PREP/TOTAL TIME: 30 min.

- 2 cups water
- 1 cup fat-free half-and-half
- 4 teaspoons butter, *divided*
- 1/4 teaspoon salt
- 1/4 teaspoon pepper
- 3/4 cup quick-cooking grits
- 1 medium onion, chopped
- 3 celery ribs, chopped
- 1 pound uncooked medium shrimp, peeled and deveined
- 1/4 cup ketchup
- 1 tablespoon honey
- 2 teaspoons lemon juice
- 1/2 to 1 teaspoon hot pepper sauce
- 1 cup (4 ounces) shredded reduced-fat cheddar cheese

■ In a small saucepan, combine water, half-and-half, 2 teaspoons butter, salt and pepper. Bring to a boil. Stir in grits. Reduce heat; simmer, uncovered, for 5-7 minutes or until the grits are thickened.

■ Meanwhile, in a large skillet, saute the onion and celery in remaining butter until tender. Add shrimp; cook and stir until shrimp turn pink. Combine the ketchup, honey, lemon juice and hot pepper sauce; stir into skillet. Stir cheese into grits. Serve with shrimp mixture.

Yield: 4 servings.

- Cook the pasta according to package directions. Meanwhile, in a large nonstick skillet, saute the asparagus in butter for 4 minutes. Add shrimp; cook and stir for 3-4 minutes or until shrimp turn pink. Remove and keep warm.

- In a small bowl, combine flour, salt and cream until smooth; gradually add to the skillet. Bring to a boil; cook and stir for 1-2 minutes or until thickened. Stir in 1/4 cup cheese.

- Remove from the heat. Drain pasta; toss with shrimp mixture and sauce. Sprinkle with the remaining cheese.

Yield: 4 servings.

Shrimp and Asparagus Penne

Diane Shipley
MENTOR, OHIO

This pretty pasta has only a few ingredients, so it's a breeze to whip up. We prepare it with half-and-half to cut down on the fat content, and it tastes just as good.

Shrimp and Asparagus Penne

PREP/TOTAL TIME: 30 min.

3 cups uncooked penne pasta
1 pound fresh asparagus, trimmed and cut into 1-inch pieces
1 tablespoon butter
1 pound uncooked medium shrimp, peeled and deveined

2 teaspoons all-purpose flour
1/4 teaspoon salt
1/2 cup half-and-half cream
1/2 cup grated Parmesan cheese, *divided*

Peak months for buying asparagus are April and May. When buying, look for uniform-size spears that are firm and straight. The tips should be closed with crisp stalks. It's best to use asparagus within a few days of purchase. For a longer storage, place bundled stalks upright in a bowl filled with 1 inch of water and refrigerate.

Joe Hable
MADISON, WISCONSIN

No need to order takeout with this approachable recipe. Tender scallops and crunchy cashews star at dinnertime tonight! This recipe calls for sea scallops, but you could also use their sweeter, smaller relative, the bay scallop.

Scallops with Thai Sauce

PREP/TOTAL TIME: 30 min.

1 tablespoon cornstarch
1 can (14-1/2 ounces) vegetable broth
2 tablespoons creamy peanut butter
1 to 2 tablespoons Thai chili sauce
1 pound sea scallops
2 tablespoons canola oil, *divided*
1 small onion, sliced
1 large sweet red pepper, julienned
1/2 cup salted cashews
2 garlic cloves, minced
1 can (8-3/4 ounces) whole baby corn, drained
Hot cooked angel hair pasta, optional

- In a small bowl, combine the cornstarch, broth, peanut butter and chili sauce until smooth; set aside.

- In a large skillet, saute scallops in 1 tablespoon oil for 2-3 minutes on each side or until opaque. Remove with a slotted spoon and keep warm.

- In the same pan, saute the onion, red pepper and cashews in remaining oil for 3-5 minutes or until vegetables are crisp-tender. Add garlic; cook 1 minute longer.

- Stir cornstarch mixture and add to pan. Bring to a boil; cook and stir for 1-2 minutes or until thickened. Add scallops and corn; heat through. Serve over pasta if desired.

Yield: *5 servings.*

Sea scallops are about 1-1/2 inches in diameter, whereas bay scallops are about 1/2 inch in diameter. Sea scallops are more available and affordable than bays, and come to about 30 per pound. Look for ones that are pale beige to creamy pink in color.

Linguine in Clam Sauce

Louis Fabin Vouk
KIRKLAND, OHIO

I make this for my daughter's birthday celebration each year at her request. The zucchini adds a nice touch to this traditional dish.

PREP: 20 min.
COOK: 15 min.

1 package (1 pound) linguine
1 large onion, finely chopped
2 tablespoons olive oil
1 medium zucchini, diced
1 garlic clove, minced
3 cans (6-1/2 ounces *each*) chopped clams
1/2 pound sliced fresh mushrooms
2 teaspoons chicken bouillon granules
1 teaspoon minced fresh basil
1/8 teaspoon pepper
Shredded Parmesan cheese

- Cook linguine according to package directions. Meanwhile, in a large skillet, saute onion in oil until tender. Add zucchini; cook for 2 minutes or until crisp-tender. Stir in garlic; cook 1 minute longer or until the garlic is tender.

- Drain clams, reserving 1/2 cup juice. Add clams, mushrooms, bouillon, basil, pepper and reserved juice to skillet. Bring to a boil. Reduce heat; simmer, uncovered, for 5 minutes or until vegetables are tender. Drain linguine; top with clam mixture. Sprinkle with cheese.

Yield: *4-6 servings.*

Tropical Mahi Mahi

Fish Primavera

Charolette Westfall
HOUSTON, TEXAS

This colorful blend of vegetables, fish and pasta is so satisfying.

PREP/TOTAL TIME: 30 min.

- 4 green onions, chopped
- 2 tablespoons olive oil
- 5 garlic cloves, minced
- 1 can (14-1/2 ounces) chicken broth
- 2 tablespoons dried parsley flakes
- 1/2 teaspoon salt
- 1/4 teaspoon pepper
- 1/4 teaspoon ground cumin
- 2 tablespoons cornstarch
- 1/2 cup apple juice
- 1/2 pound orange roughy, haddock *or* red snapper fillets, cut into 1-inch pieces
- 1 medium tomato, seeded and chopped
- 1 cup chopped fresh broccoli florets
- 8 ounces uncooked thin spaghetti
- 1/4 cup sliced ripe olives

■ In a large skillet, saute onions in oil until tender. Add garlic; cook 1 minute. Stir in broth, parsley and seasonings. Cover and simmer for 2 minutes. Mix cornstarch and apple juice until smooth; slowly pour into the skillet. Cook and stir for 1-2 minutes or until thickened.

■ Stir in fish, tomato and broccoli. Cover; cook for 2 minutes or until fish easily flakes with a fork. Meanwhile, cook spaghetti according to package directions; drain. Toss with olives. Serve with fish and vegetables.

Yield: 2 servings.

Bob Gebhardt
WAUSAU, WISCONSIN

My favorite foods to prepare are fish and seafood. This easy creation of mine is the result of combining two Hawaiian recipes. The tropical fruit and cilantro make it a wonderful, aromatic dish.

Tropical Mahi Mahi

PREP: 15 min. ■ COOK: 30 min.

- 2 cups all-purpose flour
- 1 teaspoon seasoned salt, *divided*
- 1/2 teaspoon pepper, *divided*
- 6 mahi mahi fillets (4 ounces each)
- 2 tablespoons butter
- 2 tablespoons olive oil
- 1 cup fresh cilantro leaves, chopped
- 1 cup white grape juice
- 1-1/2 cups heavy whipping cream
- 1 can (15-1/4 ounces) mixed tropical fruit, drained
- 1/2 cup chopped macadamia nuts

■ In a large resealable plastic bag, combine flour, 1/2 teaspoon seasoned salt and 1/4 teaspoon pepper; add fillets. Seal bag and turn to coat.

■ In a large skillet, heat butter and oil. Cook the mahi mahi over medium-high heat for 2-3 minutes on each side. Remove and keep warm.

■ Saute cilantro in pan drippings for 1 minute. Add grape juice; cook until reduced by half. Add cream; cook until reduced by half. Stir in the fruit and remaining seasoned salt and pepper; heat through. Serve with mahi mahi; sprinkle with macadamia nuts.

Yield: 6 servings.

Crab and Shrimp Gumbo

- In a large skillet, cook the bacon over medium heat until crisp. Using a slotted spoon, remove to paper towels to drain, reserving 1 tablespoon drippings. In same skillet, saute onions and garlic in drippings until tender.

- Pour into a Dutch oven or soup kettle. Add the tomatoes, consomme and water. Cover and bring to a boil; add the leeks, carrot and okra. Reduce the heat; simmer, uncovered, for 25 minutes, stirring occasionally. Add the shrimp, crab, salt and cayenne; simmer, uncovered, for 5 minutes.

- In a small bowl, combine flour and cold water until smooth. Stir into the gumbo mixture. Bring to a boil; cook and stir for 2 minutes or until slightly thickened. Stir in the parsley and reserved bacon. Serve immediately with rice.

Yield: 16-20 servings (about 5 quarts).

La Vonne Vrooman
DOTHAN, ALABAMA
I found this recipe in a magazine over 30 years ago. It's a dish that is versatile, so I change it from time to time to suit my family's tastes.

Crab and Shrimp Gumbo

PREP: 10 min. ■ COOK: 1 hour 25 min.

- 6 bacon strips, diced
- 2 large onions, chopped
- 2 garlic cloves, minced
- 2 cans (one 29 ounces, one 14-1/2 ounces) diced tomatoes
- 3 cans (10-1/2 ounces *each*) condensed beef consomme, undiluted
- 2 cups water
- 4 medium leeks, cut into 1/4-inch slices
- 1 medium carrot, diced
- 2 pounds fresh *or* frozen sliced okra

- 1-1/2 pounds uncooked medium shrimp, peeled and deveined
- 1 pound fresh *or* frozen crabmeat, flaked and cartilage removed
- 1/2 teaspoon salt
- 1/2 teaspoon cayenne pepper
- 1/3 cup all-purpose flour
- 1/3 cup cold water
- 3 tablespoons minced fresh parsley

Hot cooked rice

When okra is

sliced, it releases a substance that naturally thickens the liquid it is cooked in. Its mild flavor is similar to that of green beans or eggplant, which can be substituted for okra in soups and stews. However, without okra's natural thickener, flour or cornstarch may have to be added.

OVEN
ENTREES

Beef & Ground Beef

180

177

170

Delicious, hearty and reliable beef main dishes, fresh from the oven, are must-have recipes for any busy cook. You'll find tasty new twists on classics such as pot roast, pizza, beefy baked pasta casseroles and meat loaf. You can't go wrong with these robust one-dish dinners.

Stuffed Steak Spirals

Margaret Pache
MESA, ARIZONA

When looking for a special entree to serve guests, I rely on this impressive and appealing recipe. Swirled with tomato stuffing, it's a sensational way to showcase flank steak.

Stuffed Steak Spirals*

PREP: 35 min. ■ BAKE: 30 min. + standing

1/4 cup chopped sun-dried tomatoes (not packed in oil)

1/2 cup boiling water

1/2 cup grated Parmesan cheese

1/4 cup minced fresh parsley

1 tablespoon prepared horseradish, drained

1 to 1-1/2 teaspoons coarsely ground pepper

1 beef flank steak (1-1/2 pounds)

2 teaspoons canola oil

■ Place the tomatoes in a small bowl; add water. Cover and let stand for 5 minutes; drain. Stir in cheese, parsley, horseradish and pepper; set aside.

■ Cut steak horizontally from a long side to within 1/2 in. of opposite side. Open the meat so it lies flat; cover with the plastic wrap. Flatten to 1/4-in. thickness. Remove plastic; spoon tomato mixture over meat to within 1/2 in. of edges. Roll up tightly jelly-roll style, starting with a long side. Tie with kitchen string.

■ Line a shallow roasting pan with heavy-duty foil; coat foil with cooking spray. In a large nonstick skillet coated with cooking spray, brown meat in oil on all sides. Place in the prepared pan.

■ Bake, uncovered, at 400° for 30-40 minutes or until the meat reaches desired doneness (for medium-rare, thermometer should read 145°; medium, 160°; and well-done, 170°). Let meat stand for 10-15 minutes. Remove string and cut into slices.

Yield: 6 servings.

*Nutrition Facts: 3 ounces cooked beef equals 214 calories, 12 g fat (5 g saturated fat), 53 mg cholesterol, 229 mg sodium, 2 g carbohydrate, 1 g fiber, 22 g protein. **Diabetic Exchanges:** 3 lean meat, 1 fat.

Spinach-Stuffed Beef Tenderloin*

Taste of Home Test Kitchen

Make this elegant but easy entree the centerpiece of Christmas dinner...and you're sure to be serving up seconds.

PREP: 30 min. ■ **BAKE:** 40 min. + standing

1/2 pound fresh mushrooms, chopped	1 teaspoon salt, *divided*
4 green onions, sliced	1/8 to 1/4 teaspoon cayenne pepper
2 tablespoons olive oil, *divided*	1 beef tenderloin roast (3-1/2 pounds)
2 garlic cloves, minced, *divided*	1/4 teaspoon onion powder
2 packages (10 ounces *each*) fresh spinach leaves	1/4 teaspoon coarsely ground pepper

■ In a large nonstick skillet, saute mushrooms and onions in 1 tablespoon oil until mushrooms are tender. Add half the garlic; cook 1 minute longer. Add the spinach, 1/2 teaspoon salt and cayenne. Cook until spinach is wilted. Remove from the heat; set aside.

■ Cut a lengthwise slit down the center of the tenderloin to within 3/4 in. of the bottom. Open so meat lies flat. Spread with spinach stuffing. Fold one side of the meat over stuffing; tie several times with kitchen string. Rub the remaining oil over beef. Combine the onion powder, pepper and remaining garlic and salt; rub over beef. Place on a rack in a shallow roasting pan.

■ Bake, uncovered, at 425° for 40-55 minutes or until a meat thermometer reaches desired doneness (for medium-rare, meat thermometer should read 145°; medium, 160°; well-done, 170°). Let stand for about 10 minutes. Remove string before slicing.

Yield: 12 servings.

*Nutrition Facts: 4 ounces stuffed beef equals 242 calories, 12 g fat (4 g saturated fat), 82 mg cholesterol, 293 mg sodium, 3 g carbohydrate, 1 g fiber, 29 g protein. **Diabetic Exchanges:** 3 lean meat, 1 vegetable, 1 fat.

Sloppy Joe Pizza

PREP/TOTAL TIME: 25 min.

- 2 tubes (13.8 ounces *each*) refrigerated pizza crust
- 1 pound ground beef
- 1 can (15-1/2 ounces) sloppy joe sauce
- 2 cups (8 ounces) shredded part-skim mozzarella cheese
- 1 cup (4 ounces) shredded cheddar cheese
- 1/2 cup grated Parmesan cheese

■ Unroll pizza dough; place on two greased 12-in. pizza pans. Bake at 425° for 6-7 minutes or until golden brown.

■ In a large skillet, cook beef over medium heat until no longer pink; drain. Add sloppy joe sauce. Spread over crusts. Sprinkle with cheeses. Bake at 425° for 6-8 minutes or until cheese is melted.

Yield: 2 pizzas (8 slices each).

For a crispy pizza crust and better browning, use a pizza stone. Before preheating the oven, place the stone on an oven rack in the lower third of the oven. If you don't have a pizza stone, a preheated baking sheet will work. Sprinkle the sheet with a little cornmeal to help slide the dough on and off.

Brenda Rohlman
KINGMAN, KANSAS

If your children like sloppy joes, they'll love this change-of-pace pizza. It has all the same flavors as the popular sandwich. The six-ingredient recipe has kid-pleasing taste and goes together so quickly, it will grace your table time and again.

Tortilla Lasagna

Lynn Smith
WARRENSBURG, MISSOURI

After adjusting a recipe I found online, this was the result. It was an instant hit with my family! They love spicy food, and this simple lasagna has become a new favorite.

Tortilla Lasagna

PREP: 25 min. ■ **BAKE:** 50 min. + standing

1   pound ground beef
1   cup water
1   envelope taco seasoning
1/2   teaspoon garlic powder
1/4   teaspoon cayenne pepper
1-1/2   cups (12 ounces) sour cream
1-1/2   teaspoons chili powder

2   cups (8 ounces) shredded Monterey Jack cheese
2   cups (8 ounces) shredded cheddar cheese
1   tablespoon cornmeal
10   flour tortillas (6 inches)
1   cup salsa
1   small onion, sliced

■ In a large skillet, cook beef over medium heat until no longer pink; drain. Stir in the water, taco seasoning, garlic powder and cayenne. Bring to a boil. Reduce the heat and simmer, uncovered, for 10 minutes.

■ Meanwhile, combine sour cream and chili powder. In a large bowl, combine cheeses; set aside. Sprinkle the cornmeal into a greased 13-in. x 9-in. baking dish.

■ Arrange five of the tortillas, overlapping, in the bottom of prepared dish; spread with 1/2 cup salsa. Layer with half of the meat mixture, onion and sour cream mixture. Sprinkle with 1-1/2 cups cheese mixture. Repeat layers.

■ Bake, uncovered, at 375° for 40 minutes. Sprinkle with the remaining cheese mixture. Bake 10 minutes longer or until the cheese is melted. Let stand for 10 minutes before cutting.

Yield: 8 servings.

When browning

ground beef or other ground meat, consider using a pastry blender to break up large pieces shortly before the meat is completely cooked.

Seasoned Swiss Steak

Edna Hoffman
HEBRON, INDIANA

This main dish combines moist beef and vegetables with a gravy that blends tomato, brown sugar and mustard.

PREP: 35 min. ■ **COOK:** 1-1/2 hours

1/4 cup all-purpose flour	1/2 cup chopped onion
1 tablespoon ground mustard	1/2 cup chopped green pepper
1 teaspoon salt, *divided*	1 tablespoon brown sugar
1/4 teaspoon pepper, *divided*	1 tablespoon Worcestershire sauce
1-1/2 pounds beef top round steak (about 1 inch thick), cut into serving-size pieces	1 can (14-1/2 ounces) diced tomatoes, undrained
2 tablespoons canola oil	1/4 cup cold water
1 cup diced carrots	

■ Combine the flour, mustard, 1/2 teaspoon salt and 1/8 teaspoon pepper; set aside 2 tablespoons for gravy. Rub remaining flour mixture over steak. Pound meat with a mallet to tenderize.

■ In a large skillet, brown the steak in oil over medium-high heat. Transfer to a greased 2-1/2-qt. baking dish. Top with the carrots, onion, green pepper, brown sugar and Worcestershire sauce. Pour tomatoes over all.

■ Cover and bake at 350° for 1-1/2 to 2 hours or until the meat and vegetables are tender.

■ Transfer meat and vegetables to a serving dish; keep warm. Strain pan juices into a measuring cup; add water to measure 1 cup.

■ In a small saucepan, combine the reserved flour mixture with cold water until smooth. Whisk in pan juices. Bring to a boil; cook and stir for 2 minutes or until thickened. Add the remaining salt and pepper. Serve with steak.

Yield: 6 servings.

A crisp green salad partners well with Seasoned Swiss Steak. For an easy yet delicious dressing, try Maple Balsamic Dressing. For 1 cup of dressing, in a blender, combine 1/3 cup each of balsamic vinegar and maple syrup. Slowly drizzle 1/3 cup olive oil into the vinegar mixture as it blends.

Swiss Pot Roast

Darlene Brenden
SALEM, OREGON

My gang loves the taste of this tender roast. It's easy to prepare and even makes its own gravy. The house smells wonderful when it cooks.

PREP: 20 min.
BAKE: 2-1/2 hours

1 boneless beef chuck roast (3 pounds)
1 tablespoon canola oil
8 medium potatoes, peeled and quartered
8 medium carrots, cut into chunks
1 medium onion, sliced
3 tablespoons all-purpose flour
1 cup water
1 can (8 ounces) tomato sauce
1 teaspoon beef bouillon granules
1/2 teaspoon salt
1/2 teaspoon pepper

■ In a Dutch oven, brown roast on all sides in oil; drain. Add the potatoes, carrots and onion. In a large bowl, combine the flour, water, tomato sauce, bouillon, salt and pepper until smooth. Pour over roast and vegetables.

■ Cover; bake at 325° for 2-1/2 to 3 hours or until meat is tender.

Yield: 8 servings.

Patricia Teller
LEWISTON, IDAHO

This is an old family favorite I made when my boys were growing up. It was such a tasty dish, there were never any leftovers.

Hamburger Noodle Bake

Hamburger Noodle Bake

PREP: 20 min. ■ **BAKE:** 35 min.

5 cups uncooked egg noodles

2 pounds ground beef

1 cup chopped onion

1/2 cup chopped green pepper

2 cans (10-3/4 ounces *each*) condensed tomato soup, undiluted

2 cups (8 ounces) shredded cheddar cheese

1-1/2 cups water

1/2 cup chili sauce

1-1/2 cups soft bread crumbs

3 tablespoons butter, melted

■ Cook noodles according to package directions until almost tender; drain. In a large skillet, cook the beef, onion and green pepper over medium-high heat for 10-12 minutes or until meat is no longer pink; drain. Stir in the noodles, soup, cheese, water and chili sauce. Transfer to two greased 8-in. square baking dishes.

■ Toss the bread crumbs and butter; sprinkle over casseroles. Bake one casserole, uncovered, at 350° for 35-40 minutes or until bubbly and golden brown. Cover; freeze the remaining casserole for up to 3 months.

■ **TO USE FROZEN CASSEROLE:** Remove from the freezer 30 minutes before baking (do not thaw). Cover and bake at 350° for 60 minutes. Uncover; bake 10-15 minutes longer or until heated through.

Yield: 2 casseroles (4 servings each).

Oven Beef Stew

Bettina Turner
KERNERSVILLE, NORTH CAROLINA

This is a great cold-weather dish. I love it because it's a one-pot meal.

PREP: 20 min.
BAKE: 2-1/4 hours

6 tablespoons all-purpose flour, *divided*

1/4 teaspoon salt, optional

1/2 teaspoon pepper, *divided*

1-1/2 pounds boneless beef chuck roast, cut into 1-inch cubes

1 medium onion, chopped

1 tablespoon canola oil

3 garlic cloves, minced

3 cups beef broth

1 can (14-1/2 ounces) stewed tomatoes, cut up

3/4 teaspoon dried thyme

3 large potatoes, peeled and cut into 1-inch cubes

3 medium carrots, cut into 1/4-inch slices

1/2 cup frozen peas, thawed

■ In a large resealable plastic bag, combine 4 tablespoons flour, salt if desired and 1/4 teaspoon pepper. Add beef, a few pieces at a time, and shake to coat.

■ In a Dutch oven, cook beef and onion in oil over medium-high heat until meat is browned. Add garlic; cook 1 minute. Stir in remaining flour and pepper until blended. Slowly stir in broth, tomatoes and thyme. Cover; bake at 350° for 1-1/4 hours.

■ Add the potatoes and carrots. Cover; bake 1 hour or until meat and veggies are tender. Stir in peas; cover. Let stand for 5 minutes before serving.

Yield: 6 servings.

Wagon Wheel Casserole

- In a large nonstick skillet, cook the beef, mushrooms and onion over medium heat until meat is no longer pink; drain. In a shallow 3-qt. baking dish coated with cooking spray, layer the pasta, Parmesan cheese, green pepper, beef mixture and spaghetti sauce.

- Cover and bake at 350° for 30 minutes. Uncover; sprinkle with mozzarella cheese. Bake 10 minutes longer or until the cheese is melted. Let stand for 10 minutes before serving.

Yield: 8 servings.

✱Nutrition Facts: 1 serving equals 257 calories, 9 g fat (5 g saturated fat), 32 mg cholesterol, 576 mg sodium, 23 g carbohydrate, 3 g fiber, 22 g protein. **Diabetic Exchanges:** 2 lean meat, 1 starch, 1 vegetable, 1 fat.

Barbara Hopkins
LUSBY, MARYLAND

My ground beef hot dish is a crowd-pleaser. We love the delicious combination of flavors, it isn't difficult to prepare, and by the end of dinner, the plates are always clean.

Wagon Wheel Casserole*

PREP: 20 min. ■ BAKE: 40 min. + standing

- 1 pound lean ground beef (90% lean)
- 1 pound sliced fresh mushrooms
- 1 large onion, chopped
- 8 ounces wagon wheel pasta, cooked and drained
- 1/3 cup grated Parmesan cheese
- 1 large green pepper, thinly sliced
- 1 jar (26 ounces) meatless spaghetti sauce
- 1 cup (4 ounces) shredded part-skim mozzarella cheese

To transport a
casserole dish to a potluck dinner, put the dish inside a clear plastic oven bag. Just slide the dish in and seal with a twist tie. The bag won't melt, it catches spills and organizers can see what's inside.

Taste of Home Test Kitchen

Our home economists put a zesty twist on a dinnertime staple with this colorful main course. Garlic, chili powder, cumin and more season the ground beef so well, you won't even miss the salt. You can vary the toppings to your liking.

South-of-the-Border Stuffed Peppers*

PREP: 25 min. ■ BAKE: 25 min.

- 1 pound lean ground beef (90% lean)
- 2/3 cup chopped sweet red pepper
- 1/2 cup chopped onion
- 2 garlic cloves, minced
- 1-3/4 cups chopped seeded tomatoes, *divided*
- 4 teaspoons chili powder
- 1 teaspoon cornstarch
- 1 teaspoon ground cumin
- 1/2 teaspoon dried oregano
- 1/4 teaspoon cayenne pepper
- 1/2 cup water
- 4 medium green peppers
- 2 tablespoons reduced-fat sour cream
- 2 tablespoons shredded cheddar cheese
- 2 green onions, chopped
- 4 grape tomatoes, halved, optional

■ In a large nonstick skillet, cook the beef, red pepper and onion over medium heat until meat is no longer pink. Add garlic; cook 1 minute longer. Drain. Stir in 1/2 cup tomatoes, chili powder, cornstarch, cumin, oregano and cayenne. Gradually stir in water. Bring to a boil. Reduce the heat; simmer, uncovered, for 5 minutes.

■ Cut the green peppers in half lengthwise and remove seeds. In a large kettle, cook peppers in boiling water for 3-5 minutes. Drain and rinse in cold water. Spoon about 1/3 cup of beef mixture into each pepper half.

■ Place in a 13-in. x 9-in. baking dish coated with cooking spray. Cover and bake at 350° for 25-30 minutes or until peppers are crisp-tender and filling is heated through.

■ Top with remaining tomatoes. Garnish with the sour cream, cheese, green onions and grape tomatoes if desired.

Yield: 4 servings.

*Nutrition Facts: 2 stuffed pepper halves equals 268 calories, 11 g fat (5 g saturated fat), 62 mg cholesterol, 137 mg sodium, 18 g carbohydrate, 5 g fiber, 26 g protein. **Diabetic Exchanges:** 3 lean meat, 2 vegetable, 1 fat.

To remove the seeds from a tomato, cut it in half horizontally and remove the stem. Holding a tomato half over a bowl or sink, scrape out seeds with a small spoon or squeeze the tomato to force out the seeds. Then slice or dice as directed in the recipe.

Zippy Beef Bake

Gay Kelley
TUCSON, ARIZONA

With its Tex-Mex flavor, this filling meal-in-one is a much-requested recipe in our home. We like it so much, we have it about once a week!

PREP: 15 min.
BAKE: 20 min.

- 3/4 pound ground beef
- 1 tablespoon butter
- 2 medium zucchini, thinly sliced
- 1/4 pound sliced fresh mushrooms, sliced
- 2 tablespoons sliced green onions
- 1-1/2 teaspoons chili powder
- 1 teaspoon salt
- 1/8 teaspoon garlic powder
- 1-1/2 cups cooked rice
- 1 can (4 ounces) chopped green chilies
- 1/2 cup sour cream
- 1 cup (4 ounces) shredded Monterey Jack cheese, *divided*

■ In a large skillet, cook beef over medium heat until no longer pink; drain. Add butter, zucchini, mushrooms and onions; cook and stir until vegetables are tender. Drain. Stir in the chili powder, salt and garlic powder. Add the rice, chilies, sour cream and half of the cheese.

■ Transfer to a greased 2-qt. baking dish and sprinkle with the remaining cheese. Bake, uncovered, at 350° for 20-22 minutes or until the cheese is melted.

Yield: 4 servings.

Beef 'n' Bean Braid

Val O'Connell
HOTCHKISS, COLORADO

This robust recipe makes a big impression when I bring it to a potluck. Each slice of the beautiful loaf contains some of the hearty filling for a truly satisfying meal.

PREP: 30 min. + rising ■ **BAKE:** 20 min.

1 package (1/4 ounce) active dry yeast	1 medium onion, chopped
3/4 cup warm water (110° to 115°)	1 teaspoon garlic salt
2 tablespoons butter, melted	1 can (16 ounces) kidney beans, rinsed and drained
1 tablespoon sugar	2/3 cup water
1/2 teaspoon salt	2 tablespoons chili powder
1 egg	1/4 teaspoon ground cumin
2 cups all-purpose flour	1/4 teaspoon cayenne pepper
FILLING:	1-1/2 cups (6 ounces) shredded cheddar cheese
1 pound ground beef	1 egg, lightly beaten

■ In a large bowl, dissolve yeast in warm water. Add the butter, sugar, salt, egg and 1-1/2 cups flour; beat until smooth. Stir in enough remaining flour to form a soft dough.

■ Turn onto a floured surface; knead until smooth and elastic, about 6-8 minutes. Place in a greased bowl, turning once to grease top. Cover and let rise in a warm place until doubled, about 1 hour.

■ Meanwhile, in a large skillet, cook the beef, onion and garlic salt over medium heat until the meat is no longer pink; drain. Stir in the beans, water and seasonings; bring to a boil. Reduce the heat and simmer, uncovered, for 5-10 minutes or until thickened.

■ Punch dough down. Turn onto a lightly floured surface; roll into a 16-in. x 11-in. rectangle. Transfer to a greased 15-in. x 10-in. baking sheet. Spread the beef mixture down center of dough; sprinkle with the cheese. On each long side, cut 1-in.-wide strips about 1/2 in. from filling. Starting at one end, fold alternating strips at an angle across filling; seal the ends. Cover and let rise until doubled, 30 minutes.

■ Brush the egg over the dough. Bake at 350° for 20-25 minutes or until golden brown. Remove to a wire rack. Let stand for 5 minutes before slicing.

Yield: 6-8 servings.

Ground Beef Biscuit Stew

Darlene Brenden
SALEM, OREGON

Preparation time for this hearty meal is only 10 minutes!

PREP: 10 min.
BAKE: 30 min.

- 1 pound ground beef
- 1 medium onion, chopped
- 1 can (14-1/2 ounces) stewed tomatoes, cut up
- 1 package (10 ounces) frozen mixed vegetables
- 1 can (8 ounces) tomato sauce
- 1 cup all-purpose flour
- 1-1/2 teaspoons baking powder
- 2 tablespoons shortening
- 2/3 cup milk
- 1 teaspoon prepared mustard
- 1/2 cup shredded cheddar cheese, *divided*

■ In a large skillet, cook beef and onion over medium heat until meat is no longer pink; drain. Stir in the tomatoes, vegetables and tomato sauce.

■ Transfer to a greased 11-in. x 7-in. baking dish. Cover and bake at 400° for 15 minutes.

■ Meanwhile, for biscuits, combine flour and baking powder. Cut in shortening until the mixture resembles coarse crumbs. Stir in the milk and mustard until the mixture forms a soft dough. Add 6 tablespoons cheese.

■ Drop by tablespoonfuls onto stew. Bake for 15-20 minutes or until golden brown; sprinkle with remaining cheese.

Yield: 6 servings.

- In a large skillet, cook beef over medium heat until no longer pink; drain and set aside. In the same skillet, cook the bacon, onion and oregano until bacon is crisp. Add the garlic; cook 1 minute longer. Stir in the tomato sauce, corn and the reserved beef. Bring to a boil. Reduce the heat and simmer, uncovered, for 10 minutes.

- Meanwhile, in a large bowl, combine the mashed potatoes, eggs, butter, parsley and salt. Spread half of potato mixture onto the bottom and up the sides of a greased 9-in. pie plate. Top with beef mixture and remaining potato mixture.

- Bake at 375° for 20 minutes. Brush with the melted butter. Bake 10 minutes longer or until top is golden brown.

Yield: 6-8 servings.

Shepherd's Pie

Chris Eschweiler
DALLAS, TEXAS

This recipe creates a savory crust using mashed potatoes. The bacon flavor in the filling is fabulous! With a tossed salad or vegetable and dessert, you'll have a complete meal!

Shepherd's Pie

PREP: 30 min. ■ BAKE: 30 min.

- 1 pound ground beef
- 3 bacon strips, diced
- 1 small onion, chopped
- 1/4 teaspoon dried oregano
- 2 garlic cloves, minced
- 1/2 cup tomato sauce
- 1 can (11 ounces) Mexicorn, drained
- 5-1/2 cups hot mashed potatoes (prepared without milk and butter)

- 2 eggs, lightly beaten
- 2 tablespoons butter, softened
- 1 to 2 tablespoons minced fresh parsley
- 1/4 teaspoon salt

Additional butter, melted

If you don't want to make mashed potatoes for the Shepherd's Pie, combine a can of cream of celery soup with milk and frozen hash browns, then layer that mixture on top of the meat and vegetables. It's easy and oh-so delicious.

In a large skillet, cook the beef, green pepper and onion over medium heat until the meat is no longer pink; drain. Add the potatoes, beans, tomatoes, corn, salsa, rice, chili powder and salt. Sprinkle 1/4 cup cheese off-center on each tortilla; top with about 1 cup beef mixture. Fold sides and ends over filling.

Wrap burritos individually in foil and freeze for up to 3 months. Or place burritos seam side down on a baking sheet.

Bake at 350° for 25 minutes or until heated through. Serve with the sour cream, tomatoes, guacamole, additional cheese and salsa if desired.

TO USE FROZEN BURRITOS: Thaw burritos in refrigerator overnight. Bake and serve as directed.

Yield: 8 burritos.

A tasty way to use leftover tortillas is to brush them with butter and sprinkle with herbs or cinnamon-sugar, then bake on a cookie sheet until crisp.

Hearty Burritos

Janelle McEachern
RIVERSIDE, CALIFORNIA

These beyond-compare burritos are chock-full of delicious ingredients and frozen individually, so on busy mornings you can bake only as many as are needed.

Hearty Burritos

PREP: 20 min. ■ **BAKE:** 25 min.

1/2 pound ground beef	1/2 cup salsa
1 large green pepper, chopped	1/2 cup cooked rice
1 medium onion, chopped	2 teaspoons chili powder
1 package (16 ounces) frozen cubed hash brown potatoes, thawed	1/2 teaspoon salt
	2 cups (8 ounces) shredded cheddar cheese
1 can (15 ounces) black beans, rinsed and drained	8 flour tortillas (10 inches), warmed
1 can (14-1/2 ounces) Mexican diced tomatoes, undrained	Sour cream, chopped tomatoes, guacamole, additional shredded cheddar cheese and salsa, optional
1 cup frozen corn, thawed	

Old-Fashioned Cabbage Rolls

Florence Krantz

It was an abundance of dill in my garden that led me to try this. My family liked the flavor so much that, from then on, I always made my cabbage rolls with dill.

PREP: 25 min. ■ BAKE: 1-1/2 hours

1	medium head cabbage (3 pounds)	1	tablespoon dried parsley flakes
1/2	pound uncooked ground beef	1/2	teaspoon salt
1/2	pound uncooked ground pork	1/2	teaspoon dill weed
1	can (15 ounces) tomato sauce, *divided*	1/8	teaspoon cayenne pepper
1	small onion, chopped	1	can (14-1/2 ounces) diced tomatoes, undrained
1/2	cup uncooked long grain rice	1/2	teaspoon sugar

■ In a Dutch oven, cook cabbage in boiling water just until leaves fall off head. Remove 12 large leaves for the rolls; set aside remaining cabbage. Cut out the thick vein from the bottom of each reserved leaf, making a V-shaped cut to enclose filling.

■ In a small bowl, combine the beef, pork, 1/2 cup tomato sauce, onion, rice, parsley, salt, dill and cayenne. Place about 1/4 cup of the meat mixture on each cabbage leaf; overlap the cut ends of the leaf. Fold in sides, beginning from cut end. Roll up completely to enclose filling.

■ Slice the remaining cabbage; place in Dutch oven. Arrange the cabbage rolls seam side down over sliced cabbage. Combine the tomatoes, sugar and remaining tomato sauce; pour over the rolls.

■ Cover and bake at 350° for 1-1/2 hours or until tender and a meat thermometer reads 160°.

Yield: 6 servings.

When buying cabbage, look for heads with crisp-looking leaves that are firmly packed. The head should feel heavy for its size. Store the cabbage tightly wrapped in a plastic bag in the refrigerator for up to 2 weeks.

Beefy Bake

Monika Rahn

This dish is easy to make, tastes just great and freezes well.

PREP: 40 min.
BAKE: 25 min.

1	package (16 ounces) spiral pasta
2	pounds ground beef
2/3	cup chopped onion
1	teaspoon minced garlic
2	jars (28 ounces *each*) spaghetti sauce
2	tablespoons tomato paste
1	teaspoon dried basil
1	teaspoon dried oregano
4	cups (16 ounces) shredded part-skim mozzarella cheese

■ Cook the pasta according to directions; drain. Meanwhile, in a Dutch oven, cook beef and onion over medium heat until meat is no longer pink. Add garlic; cook 1 minute. Drain. Stir in spaghetti sauce, tomato paste, basil and oregano. Bring to a boil. Reduce heat; simmer, uncovered, for 5-10 minutes.

■ Stir pasta into meat. Transfer to two greased 13-in. x 9-in. baking dishes. Sprinkle each with 2 cups cheese. Cover; freeze 1 casserole for up to 3 months.

■ Bake the second casserole, uncovered, at 350° for 25-30 minutes or until heated through.

■ **TO USE FROZEN CASSEROLE:** Thaw in refrigerator overnight. Bake, uncovered, at 350° for 35-40 minutes or until heated.

Yield: 2 casseroles (8-10 servings each).

OVEN ENTREES Beef & Ground Beef   181

Enchiladas El Paso*

Loraine Meyer
BEND, OREGON

These enchiladas have more of a spaghetti sauce-tomato taste than most typical Southwestern dishes. I found this recipe many years ago, and it quickly became a family favorite. It is even better when it is prepared one day and served the next, because the flavors are more pronounced.

PREP: 20 min. ■ **BAKE:** 30 min.

1 pound lean ground beef (90% lean)	3 teaspoons chili powder
1/2 cup chopped onion	1-1/4 teaspoons salt
1 can (14-1/2 ounces) diced tomatoes, drained	1/4 teaspoon pepper
1 can (6 ounces) tomato paste	10 flour tortillas (8 inches), warmed
1/2 cup water	2 cups (8 ounces) shredded cheddar cheese

■ In a large skillet, cook the ground beef and onion over medium heat until the meat is no longer pink; drain. Stir in the diced tomatoes, tomato paste, water, chili powder, salt and pepper.

■ Spoon about 1/3 cup meat sauce down the center of each tortilla. Top each with about 2 tablespoons shredded cheese. Roll up and place the filled tortillas seam side down in an ungreased 13-in. x 9-in. baking dish. Top with the remaining meat sauce and cheese.

■ Cover and refrigerate overnight. Or cover and bake at 375° for 25 minutes. Uncover; bake 3-5 minutes longer or until heated through.

■ **TO USE FROZEN ENCHILADAS:** Remove from refrigerator 30 minutes before baking. Bake as directed.

Yield: 10 servings.

✱ Nutrition Facts: 1 enchilada (prepared with lean ground beef, no-salt added tomato paste, fat-free tortillas and reduced-fat cheese) equals 283 calories, 8 g fat (5 g saturated fat), 38 mg cholesterol, 799 mg sodium, 34 g carbohydrate, 3 g fiber, 19 g protein. **Diabetic Exchanges:** 2 lean meat, 2 vegetable, 1-1/2 starch.

Beef 'n' Turkey Meat Loaf

PREP: 15 min.
BAKE: 50 min. + standing

- 2 egg whites
- 2/3 cup ketchup, *divided*
- 1 medium potato, peeled and finely shredded
- 1 medium green pepper, finely chopped
- 1 small onion, grated
- 3 garlic cloves, minced
- 1 teaspoon salt
- 1 teaspoon dried thyme
- 1/2 teaspoon pepper
- 3/4 pound lean ground beef
- 3/4 pound lean ground turkey

■ In a large bowl, combine the egg whites and 1/3 cup ketchup. Stir in the shredded potato, green pepper, onion, garlic, salt, thyme and pepper. Crumble the beef and turkey over the mixture and mix well. Shape into a 10-in. x 4-in. loaf.

■ Line a 15-in. x 10-in. x 1-in. baking pan with heavy-duty foil and coat the foil with cooking spray. Place the loaf in the pan. Bake, uncovered, at 375° for 45 minutes and drain. Brush the loaf with the remaining ketchup. Bake 5-10 minutes longer or until a meat thermometer inserted into the center of the meat loaf reads 165°. Let stand for 10 minutes before slicing.

Yield: 6 servings.

Fern Nead
FLORENCE, KENTUCKY

Lean ground beef, ground turkey and shredded potatoes bulk up this hefty meat loaf but keep it light. Seasonings, such as onion, garlic and dried thyme, make it flavorful. With a side of vegetables, this entree makes a lovely meal.

Kathleen Hendrick
ALEXANDRIA, KENTUCKY

Who can resist a juicy ribeye steak topped with mushrooms and onions in a rich gravy? Simply add a green salad and an impressive dinner is served.

Mushroom Ribeyes

Mushroom Ribeyes

PREP/TOTAL TIME: 30 min.

> 2 beef ribeye steaks (8 ounces *each*)
> 1/4 teaspoon seasoned salt
> 1/8 teaspoon pepper
> 2 teaspoons canola oil
> 1 small onion, thinly sliced
> 1 cup sliced fresh mushrooms
> 1 envelope brown gravy mix
> 1/3 cup sour cream

■ Sprinkle the steaks with seasoned salt and pepper. In a large skillet, brown the steaks on both sides in the canola oil. Transfer to an 11-in. x 7-in. baking dish.

■ In the same skillet, saute onion and mushrooms until tender. Spoon over steaks. Prepare gravy mix according to package directions; stir in sour cream. Pour over steaks.

■ Cover and bake at 350° for 10-15 minutes or until meat reaches desired doneness (for medium-rare, a meat thermometer should read 145°; medium, 160°; well-done, 170°).

Yield: 2 servings.

To test a steak for doneness, insert an instant-read thermometer horizontally from the side, making sure to get the reading in the center of the steak.

Baked Spaghetti

Betty Rabe
MAHTOMEDI, MINNESOTA

This pasta bake pleases young and old, family and friends... everyone! To round out a memorable menu, add breadsticks and hot fudge sundaes.

PREP: 20 min.
BAKE: 30 min. + standing

> 8 ounces uncooked spaghetti, broken into thirds
> 1 egg
> 1/2 cup milk
> 1/2 teaspoon salt
> 1/2 pound ground beef
> 1/2 pound bulk Italian sausage
> 1 small onion, chopped
> 1/4 cup chopped green pepper
> 1 jar (14 ounces) meatless spaghetti sauce
> 1 can (8 ounces) tomato sauce
> 1 to 2 cups (4 to 8 ounces) shredded part-skim mozzarella cheese

■ Cook spaghetti according to package directions; drain. In a large bowl, beat the egg, milk and salt. Add spaghetti; toss to coat. Transfer to a greased 13-in. x 9-in. baking dish.

■ In a large skillet, cook the beef, sausage, onion and green pepper over medium heat until meat is no longer pink; drain. Stir in spaghetti sauce and tomato sauce. Spoon over the spaghetti mixture.

■ Bake, uncovered, at 350° for 20 minutes. Sprinkle with cheese. Bake 10 minutes longer or until cheese is melted. Let stand for 10 minutes before cutting.

Yield: 6-8 servings.

Spiced Beef Roast

Barb Bredthauer
OMAHA, NEBRASKA

In the South, this tangy roast is traditionally served cold or at room temperature, but we like it piping hot. It's excellent for special occasions, and the leftovers are fantastic.

Spiced Beef Roast*

PREP: 25 min. + marinating ■ BAKE: 2-1/4 hours + standing

1 medium onion, thinly sliced	1/2 teaspoon pepper
1 cup white vinegar	1/8 teaspoon cayenne pepper
1/2 cup beef broth	1 beef sirloin tip roast *or* 1 beef bottom round roast (2 pounds)
1/2 cup packed brown sugar	
1 bay leaf	3/4 cup *each* chopped dried plums and apricots
1 teaspoon ground ginger	
3/4 teaspoon salt	1/4 cup golden raisins
1/2 teaspoon *each* ground allspice, cinnamon and nutmeg	1 teaspoon cornstarch
	2 tablespoons cold water

- For marinade, combine the onion, vinegar, broth, brown sugar, bay leaf and seasonings in a small saucepan. Cook and stir over medium heat until sugar is dissolved. Cool to room temperature.

- Pierce the roast several times with a meat fork; place in a large resealable plastic bag. Add cooled marinade. Seal bag and turn to coat; refrigerate for 8 hours or overnight.

- Place meat and marinade in an ungreased 11-in. x 7-in. baking dish. Bake, uncovered, at 325° for 1-1/2 hours. Stir in dried fruit and raisins. Bake 45-55 minutes longer or until meat and fruit are tender. Discard bay leaf. Remove roast to a platter; let stand for 10 minutes before slicing.

- For gravy, combine cornstarch and water until smooth. Pour pan juices into a saucepan; gradually stir in cornstarch mixture. Bring to a boil; cook and stir for 2 minutes or until thickened. Serve with beef.

Yield: 8 servings.

*Nutrition Facts: 3 ounces cooked beef with 2 tablespoons gravy equals 317 calories, 6 g fat (2 g saturated fat), 71 mg cholesterol, 285 mg sodium, 38 g carbohydrate, 4 g fiber, 26 g protein. **Diabetic Exchanges:** 3 lean meat, 1-1/2 fruit, 1 starch.

Poultry

189

202

196

From comforting casseroles to golden roasts, this chapter is chock-full of oven-baked dinners that use chicken or turkey plus other wholesome ingredients. These recipes are perfect for potlucks, weeknight dinners and gatherings with friends.

Romano Chicken Supreme

- In a large skillet coated with cooking spray, brown chicken on both sides over medium heat. Transfer to a 13-in. x 9-in. baking dish coated with cooking spray; sprinkle with salt.

- In the same skillet, saute the mushrooms, lemon juice and basil in butter. Add garlic and cook for 1 minute or until tender. Stir in the broth and orange juice; bring to a boil. Reduce the heat; simmer, uncovered, for 2-3 minutes or until heated through. Spoon over chicken; sprinkle with bread crumbs and cheese.

- Bake, uncovered, at 400° for 20-25 minutes or until a meat thermometer reads 170°.

Yield: 6 servings.

*Nutrition Facts: 1 chicken breast half with about 1/4 cup mushroom mixture equals 274 calories, 11 g fat (6 g saturated fat), 100 mg cholesterol, 413 mg sodium, 8 g carbohydrate, 1 g fiber, 34 g protein. **Diabetic Exchanges:** 4-1/2 very lean meat, 1/2 starch, 2 fat.

Anna Minegar
ZOLFO SPRINGS, FLORIDA
Plenty of Romano cheese and golden-brown bread crumbs add flavor and crunch to this tender and delicious chicken and mushroom recipe.

Romano Chicken Supreme*

PREP: 20 min. ■ BAKE: 20 min.

  6 boneless skinless chicken breast halves (5 ounces *each*)
1/4 teaspoon salt
  1 pound fresh mushrooms, chopped
  1 tablespoon lemon juice
  1 teaspoon dried basil

  3 tablespoons butter
  2 garlic cloves, minced
1/2 cup reduced-sodium chicken broth
  2 tablespoons orange juice
  1 cup soft bread crumbs
1/3 cup grated Romano cheese

To make soft

bread crumbs, tear a few slices of bread into 1-1/2-in. pieces and place in a food processor or blender container. Cover and pulse until the bread turns to crumbs. You can process a sprig of fresh parsley or another herb along with the bread for added flavor.

Virginia Shaw
MODESTO, CALIFORNIA
Whether for an everyday meal or a special occasion, this is a fun and creative way to serve lasagna. Chicken and almonds add a tasty new twist.

Chicken Lasagna Rolls

Chicken Lasagna Rolls

PREP: 45 min. ■ **BAKE:** 25 min.

1 medium onion, chopped
1/2 cup chopped sweet red pepper
1/2 cup chopped almonds
1/3 cup butter
1/2 cup cornstarch
1-1/2 teaspoons salt
2 cans (10-1/2 ounces *each*) condensed chicken broth, undiluted
2 cups chopped cooked chicken
1 package (10 ounces) frozen chopped spinach, thawed and well drained
1/4 teaspoon pepper
1/4 teaspoon ground nutmeg
10 lasagna noodles, cooked and drained
2 cups milk
1 cup (4 ounces) shredded Swiss cheese, *divided*
1/4 cup dry white wine *or* water

■ In a large saucepan, saute the onion, red pepper and almonds in butter until onion is tender and almonds are toasted. Stir in the cornstarch and salt until blended. Stir in the broth. Bring to a boil; cook and stir for 2 minutes or until thickened.

■ Transfer half of the sauce to a large bowl; stir in the chicken, spinach, pepper and nutmeg. Spread about 3 tablespoons over each lasagna noodle. Roll up and place seam side down in a greased 11-in. x 7-in. baking dish.

■ Add milk, 1/2 cup Swiss cheese and wine to remaining sauce. Cook and stir over medium heat until thickened and bubbly. Pour over roll-ups.

■ Bake, uncovered, at 350° for 20-25 minutes. Sprinkle with remaining cheese; bake 5 minutes longer or until cheese is melted.

Yield: 5 servings.

Turkey and Swiss Calzones

Suzie Salle
RENTON, WASHINGTON
These stuffed sandwiches are a fun change of pace.

PREP: 25 min. + rising
BAKE: 25 min.

4 cups all-purpose flour
4-1/2 teaspoons quick-rise yeast
2 teaspoons brown sugar
1/4 teaspoon salt
1-1/2 cups water
3 tablespoons olive oil
3-1/2 cups cubed cooked turkey
1-1/2 cups (6 ounces) shredded Swiss cheese
3 tablespoons Dijon mustard
1 egg, beaten

■ In a large bowl, combine 3 cups flour, yeast, brown sugar and salt. In a small saucepan, heat water and oil to 120°-130°. Add to dry ingredients; beat until smooth. Stir in enough remaining flour to form a soft dough.

■ Turn onto a floured surface; knead until smooth and elastic (4 minutes). Cover and let rest in a warm place for 15 minutes.

■ In a large bowl, combine turkey, cheese and mustard. Divide dough into eight pieces.

■ On a floured surface, roll each piece into a 7-in. circle. Place filling on half of each circle. Fold dough over filling; pinch seams to seal.

■ Place on greased baking sheets. Brush with egg. Bake at 375° for 25-30 minutes or until golden brown.

Yield: 8 servings.

Chicken Burritos

Sonya Nightingale
BURLEY, IDAHO
This mouthwatering Southwestern recipe makes enough for two casseroles, so you can enjoy one today and freeze the other for a busy weeknight.

Chicken Burritos

PREP: 20 min. + freezing ■ **BAKE:** 55 min.

1 large onion, chopped	1/2 teaspoon salt
1/4 cup chopped green pepper	1 can (15 ounces) chili with beans
6 tablespoons butter	1 package (8 ounces) cream cheese, cubed
1/2 cup all-purpose flour	8 cups cubed cooked chicken
3 cups chicken broth	24 flour tortillas (6 inches), warmed
1 can (10 ounces) diced tomatoes and green chilies	6 cups (24 ounces) shredded Colby-Monterey Jack cheese
2 tablespoons chopped jalapeno pepper, optional	Salsa, optional
1 teaspoon ground cumin	
1 teaspoon chili powder	
1/2 teaspoon garlic powder	

- ■ In a large skillet, saute the chopped onion and green pepper in butter until tender. Stir in the flour until blended. Gradually stir in the broth.

- ■ Bring to a boil; cook and stir for 2 minutes. Reduce heat; add the tomatoes, jalapeno pepper if desired and seasonings. Cook for 5 minutes or until heated through. Stir in the chili and cream cheese until cheese is melted. Stir in the chicken.

- ■ Spoon about 1/2 cupful down the center of each tortilla; sprinkle each with 1/4 cup Colby-Monterey Jack cheese. Fold ends and sides over filling. Place in two greased 13-in. x 9-in. baking dishes.

- ■ Cover and freeze one casserole for up to 3 months. Cover and bake the remaining casserole at 350° for 35-40 minutes or until heated through. Serve with salsa if desired.

- ■ **TO USE FROZEN BURRITOS:** Thaw burritos in refrigerator overnight. Bake at 350° for 50-55 minutes or until burritos are heated through.

Yield: 2 casseroles
(1 dozen burritos each).

Editor's Note: When cutting hot peppers, disposable gloves are recommended. Avoid touching your face.

Bernice Morris
MARSHFIELD, MISSOURI

I combine chicken and pasta with a variety of vegetables to make this all-in-one entree. It's a nice change of pace from the usual creamy casseroles. I make one for dinner and keep the other in the freezer for unexpected company.

Colorful Chicken Casserole*

PREP: 25 min. ■ BAKE: 30 min.

- 1 cup chopped celery
- 1 cup chopped green pepper
- 3/4 cup chopped onion
- 2 tablespoons butter
- 1 cup chicken broth
- 1 cup frozen corn
- 1 cup frozen peas
- 1 teaspoon salt, optional
- 1/4 teaspoon pepper

- 3 cups cubed cooked chicken
- 1 package (7 ounces) ready-cut spaghetti *or* elbow macaroni, cooked and drained
- 1 jar (4-1/2 ounces) sliced mushrooms, drained
- 1 cup (4 ounces) shredded cheddar cheese

■ In a large skillet, saute celery, green pepper and onion in butter until tender. Add the broth, corn, peas and salt if desired and pepper; heat through. Stir in chicken and spaghetti.

■ Divide between two 11-in. x 7-in. baking dishes coated with cooking spray. Top with the mushrooms and cheese.

■ Cover and freeze one casserole for up to 3 months. Cover and bake the second casserole at 350° for 20 minutes. Uncover and bake 10 minutes longer or until heated through.

■ TO USE FROZEN CASSOROLE: Remove from freezer 30 minutes before baking. Bake at 350° for 35 minutes. Uncover; bake 15 minutes longer or until heated through.

Yield: 2 casseroles (4 servings each).

*Nutrition Facts: 1 cup (prepared with reduced-fat butter, reduced-sodium broth and reduced-fat cheese; calculated without salt) equals 295 calories, 9 g fat (4 g saturated fat), 62 mg cholesterol, 334 mg sodium, 30 g carbohydrate, 3 g fiber, 25 g protein. **Diabetic Exchanges:** 3 lean meat, 1-1/2 starch, 1 vegetable.

Whole wheat pasta is fast becoming a popular choice for today's family cooks. Featuring more fiber and a slightly stronger flavor than other pasta, the healthy alternative makes a nice switch from traditional pasta dishes.

Chicken Asparagus Bake

Margaret Carlson
AMERY, WISCONSIN

Layers of crunchy Triscuits sandwich a chicken and vegetable filling in this down-home casserole. A friend served this deliciously different dish for an evening meal, and I couldn't resist asking for the recipe.

PREP: 20 min.
BAKE: 30 min.

- 1 package (9-1/2 ounces) Triscuits
- 2 cups cubed cooked chicken
- 2 cans (10-3/4 ounces *each*) condensed cream of chicken soup, undiluted
- 1 package (10 ounces) frozen chopped asparagus, thawed and drained
- 1 can (8 ounces) sliced water chestnuts, drained
- 1 can (4 ounces) mushroom stems and pieces, drained
- 1/2 cup mayonnaise

■ Break two-thirds of crackers into bite-size pieces; place in a greased 2-1/2-qt. baking dish. Top with chicken; spread soup over chicken. In a large bowl, combine the asparagus, water chestnuts, mushrooms and mayonnaise; spoon over soup. Crush the remaining crackers; sprinkle over the top.

■ Bake, uncovered, at 350° for 30-40 minutes or until heated through.

Yield: 4 servings.

Doris Cohn
DENVILLE, NEW JERSEY
I try to keep the ingredients for this creamy casserole on hand for last-minute meals. Whenever I serve this at family dinners and potlucks, it is always well-received.

Swiss Chicken Bake

Swiss Chicken Bake

PREP: 10 min. ■ BAKE: 30 min.

1 package (7 ounces) thin spaghetti, cooked and drained

1 package (10 ounces) frozen chopped spinach, thawed and squeezed dry

1/2 cup half-and-half cream

1/3 cup shredded Parmesan cheese, *divided*

1/2 teaspoon salt

1/4 teaspoon pepper

1/8 to 1/4 teaspoon ground nutmeg

2 cups diced cooked chicken

1 cup (4 ounces) shredded Swiss cheese

1/2 cup sliced fresh mushrooms

2 bacon strips, cooked and crumbled

4 eggs, lightly beaten

1 cup ricotta cheese

1/4 cup chopped onion

1 garlic clove, minced

■ In a large bowl, combine the spaghetti, spinach, cream, 4 tablespoons Parmesan cheese, salt, pepper and nutmeg. Place in a greased 8-in. square baking dish. Top with the chicken, Swiss cheese, mushrooms and bacon.

■ In a small bowl, combine the eggs, ricotta, onion and garlic; spread over chicken. Sprinkle with remaining Parmesan cheese.

■ Bake, uncovered, at 350° for 30-35 minutes or until bubbly.

Yield: 4-6 servings.

Harvest Vegetable Bake

Janet Weisser
SEATTLE, WASHINGTON
This delicious dish is packed with a large assortment of vegetables. Served with a green salad, it makes an excellent entree.

PREP: 10 min.
BAKE: 1-1/2 hours

2-1/2 to 3 pounds boneless skinless chicken thighs

2 bay leaves

4 small red potatoes, cut into 1-inch pieces

4 small onions, quartered

4 small carrots, cut into 2-inch pieces

2 celery ribs, cut into 2-inch pieces

2 small turnips, peeled and cut into 1-inch pieces

1 medium green pepper, cut into 1-inch pieces

12 small fresh mushrooms

2 teaspoons salt

1 teaspoon dried rosemary, crushed

1/2 teaspoon pepper

1 can (14-1/2 ounces) diced tomatoes, undrained

■ Place chicken in a greased 13-in. x 9-in. baking dish; add bay leaves. Top with the potatoes, onions, carrots, celery, turnips, green pepper and mushrooms. Sprinkle with salt, rosemary and pepper. Pour the tomatoes over all.

■ Cover; bake at 375° for 1-1/2 hours or until chicken juices run clear and vegetables are tender. Discard the bay leaves before serving.

Yield: 6-8 servings.

- In a large bowl, combine the vegetables, chicken, soup, milk, cheese, onions and seasoned salt. Transfer to a greased shallow 2-qt. baking dish.

- Unroll crescent roll dough and separate into two rectangles. Seal the perforations; cut each rectangle lengthwise into 1/2-in. strips. Form a lattice crust over the chicken mixture. Bake, uncovered, at 375° for 35-40 minutes or until golden brown.

Yield: 4-6 servings.

Lattice Chicken Potpie

Angie Cottrell
SUN PRAIRIE, WISCONSIN

My sister shared this great recipe with me. The main reason I like to make it for my family is because it features all four food groups, so it's the only dish I have to prepare for dinner.

Lattice Chicken Potpie

PREP: 10 min. ■ BAKE: 35 min.

1 package (16 ounces) frozen California-blend vegetables

2 cups cubed cooked chicken

1 can (10-3/4 ounces) condensed cream of potato soup, undiluted

1 cup milk

1 cup (4 ounces) shredded cheddar cheese

1 can (2.8 ounces) french-fried onions

1/2 teaspoon seasoned salt

1 tube (8 ounces) refrigerated crescent rolls

When taking food to a potluck, welcoming a new family to the neighborhood or bringing meals to someone, use dishes you've purchased at yard sales. That way, you'll never feel bad if the dishes are lost, broken or not returned.

Dawn Owens
PALATKA, FLORIDA

As a working mother with four children, I often prepare casseroles. This lasagna recipe is a little different than the traditional kind, since it doesn't have tomato sauce—just lots of chicken, ham and cheese. I like to fix it with a salad tossed with light dressing for a complete meal.

Broccoli Chicken Lasagna

PREP: 20 min. ■ BAKE: 50 min. + standing

1/2 pound sliced fresh mushrooms	2/3 cup grated Parmesan cheese
1 large onion, chopped	1 package (16 ounces) frozen broccoli cuts, thawed
1/4 cup butter, cubed	9 lasagna noodles, cooked and drained
1/2 cup all-purpose flour	
1/2 teaspoon salt	1-1/3 cups julienned fully cooked ham, *divided*
1/4 teaspoon pepper	
1/8 teaspoon ground nutmeg	2 cups (8 ounces) shredded Monterey Jack cheese, *divided*
1 can (14-1/2 ounces) chicken broth	
1-3/4 cups milk	2 cups cubed cooked chicken

■ In a large skillet, saute mushrooms and onion in the butter until tender. Stir in the flour, salt, pepper and nutmeg until blended. Gradually stir in the broth and milk. Bring to a boil; cook and stir for 2 minutes or until thickened. Stir in the Parmesan cheese and broccoli; heat through.

■ Spread 1/2 cup of the broccoli mixture in a greased 13-in. x 9-in. baking dish. Layer with three noodles, a third of the remaining broccoli mixture, 1 cup ham and 1 cup Monterey Jack cheese. Top with three noodles, half of the remaining broccoli mixture, all of the chicken and 1/2 cup Monterey Jack cheese. Top with the remaining noodles, broccoli mixture and ham.

■ Cover and bake at 350° for 45-50 minutes or until bubbly. Sprinkle with the remaining Monterey Jack cheese. Bake 5 minutes longer or until cheese is melted. Let stand for 15 minutes before cutting.

Yield: 12 servings.

To keep lasagna from becoming watery when baking, it's important to drain the noodles well. Here's a good way to do that: Drain and rinse the cooked noodles in a colander. Take each noodle, shake off excess water and lay flat on pieces of waxed paper until most of the water has evaporated.

Crunchy Turkey Casserole

Lois Koogler
SIDNEY, OHIO

This comforting second-time-around casserole is perfect for a family supper or potluck. With an appealing crunch from water chestnuts, almonds and chow mein noodles, this economical main dish is enjoyed by all.

PREP: 15 min.
BAKE: 30 min.

2 cans (10-3/4 ounces each) condensed cream of mushroom soup, undiluted	
1/2 cup milk *or* chicken broth	
4 cups cubed cooked turkey	
2 celery ribs, thinly sliced	
1 small onion, chopped	
1 can (8 ounces) sliced water chestnuts, drained and halved	
1 tablespoon soy sauce	
1 can (3 ounces) chow mein noodles	
1/2 cup slivered almonds	

■ In a large bowl, combine the soup and milk. Stir in turkey, celery, onion, water chestnuts and soy sauce.

■ Transfer to a greased shallow 2-qt. baking dish. Sprinkle with noodles and almonds. Bake, uncovered, at 350° for 30 minutes or until heated through.

Yield: 6-8 servings.

Georgia Hennings
SCOTTSBLUFF, NEBRASKA

Celery and water chestnuts add crunch to this hearty casserole. I like to fix two so I can serve one and freeze the second.

Turkey Noodle Casserole

Turkey Noodle Casserole

PREP: 30 min. ■ **BAKE:** 30 min.

- 2 pounds ground turkey
- 2 cups chopped celery
- 1/4 cup chopped green pepper
- 1/4 cup chopped onion
- 1 can (10-3/4 ounces) condensed cream of mushroom soup, undiluted
- 1 can (8 ounces) sliced water chestnuts, drained
- 1 jar (4-1/2 ounces) sliced mushrooms, drained
- 1 jar (4 ounces) diced pimientos, drained
- 1/4 cup soy sauce
- 1/2 teaspoon salt
- 1/2 teaspoon lemon-pepper seasoning
- 1 cup (8 ounces) sour cream
- 8 ounces cooked wide egg noodles

■ In a large skillet, cook turkey over medium heat until no longer pink. Add the celery, green pepper and onion; cook until tender. Stir in the soup, water chestnuts, mushrooms, pimientos, soy sauce, salt and lemon-pepper. Reduce heat; simmer for 20 minutes.

■ Remove from the heat; add sour cream and noodles. Spoon half into a freezer container; cover and freeze for up to 3 months. Place remaining mixture in a greased 2-qt. baking dish. Cover and bake at 350° for 30-35 minutes or until heated through.

■ **TO USE FROZEN CASSEROLE:** Thaw in the refrigerator. Transfer to a greased 2-qt. baking dish and bake as directed.

Yield: 2 casseroles (6 servings each).

Baked Chicken with Pasta Sauce

Gert Kaiser
KENOSHA, WISCONSIN

This easy Italian specialty make a satisfying main course becaus it features delicious seasoned chicken breast halves in a tasty pasta sauce. The meal is also ready for the oven in minutes.

PREP: 10 min.
BAKE: 35 min.

- 1 egg
- 1 cup seasoned bread crumbs
- 4 boneless skinless chicke breast halves (6 ounces each)
- 1 jar (26 ounces) garden-style pasta sauc
- 1 cup (4 ounces) shredde part-skim mozzarella cheese

Hot cooked pasta, optional

■ In a shallow bowl, beat the e Place bread crumbs in anoth shallow bowl. Dip the chick in egg, then coat with crum Place in a 13-in. x 9-in. baki dish coated with cooking spr

■ Bake, uncovered, at 400° 20-22 minutes or until a me thermometer reads 170°. Pc pasta sauce over chicke Sprinkle with cheese.

■ Bake 12-14 minutes longer until sauce is bubbly a cheese is melted. Serve w pasta if desired.

Yield: 4 servings.

Chicken Taco Quiche

- Line unpricked pastry shells with a double thickness of heavy-duty foil. Bake at 400° for 4 minutes. Remove foil; bake 4 minutes longer.

- In a small bowl, combine the chicken and one envelope of the taco seasoning; spoon into the pastry shells. Top with salsa and cheese. In a large bowl, whisk the eggs, cream, butter and remaining taco seasoning. Stir in the chilies and olives. Pour over cheese.

- Cover and freeze one quiche for up to 3 months. Cover edges of remaining quiche loosely with foil; place on a baking sheet. Bake at 400° for 33-35 minutes or until a knife inserted near center comes out clean. Let stand for 10 minutes before cutting.

- **TO USE FROZEN QUICHE:** Remove from the freezer 30 minutes before baking (do not thaw). Cover the edges of crust loosely with foil; place on a baking sheet. Bake at 400° for 70-75 minutes or until a knife inserted near the center comes out clean. Let stand for about 10 minutes before cutting.

Yield: 2 quiches
(6 servings each).

Tamie Bradford
GRAND FORKS AFB, NORTH DAKOTA

I wanted to make a quiche but didn't want the usual flavors, so I used ingredients I had on hand to come up with this recipe. It tastes great, and the flavors go well together.

Chicken Taco Quiche

PREP: 20 min. ■ **BAKE:** 35 min. + standing

- 2 unbaked pastry shells (9 inches)
- 2 cups cubed cooked chicken
- 2 envelopes taco seasoning, *divided*
- 2/3 cup salsa
- 2 cups (8 ounces) shredded cheddar cheese
- 8 eggs
- 2 cups half-and-half cream
- 2 tablespoons butter, melted
- 1 can (4 ounces) chopped green chilies
- 1/2 cup sliced ripe olives

Mary Beth Hansen
COLUMBIA, TENNESSEE

Thyme flavors moist, golden-brown chicken surrounded by bright, tender vegetables to make this appealing meal-in-one.

Roasted Chicken with Veggies

Roasted Chicken with Veggies*

PREP: 20 min. ■ BAKE: 1-1/2 hours

1 broiler/fryer chicken (3 to 3-1/2 pounds)	3 medium baking potatoes, cut into 1-1/2-inch pieces
1 tablespoon canola oil	2 medium onions, cut into wedges
1/8 teaspoon salt	
1/8 teaspoon pepper	2 tablespoons butter, melted
6 medium carrots, cut into 1-inch pieces	4 teaspoons minced fresh thyme *or* 1 teaspoon dried thyme
4 celery ribs, cut into 1-inch pieces	

■ Place chicken, breast side up, in a shallow roasting pan. Rub with oil; sprinkle with salt and pepper. Bake, uncovered, at 375° for 45 minutes.

■ Arrange carrots, celery, potatoes and onions around chicken. Combine butter and thyme; drizzle over the chicken and vegetables.

■ Cover and bake 45-60 minutes longer or until a meat thermometer reads 180° and vegetables are tender.

Yield: 6 servings.

＊Nutrition Facts: 4 ounces cooked chicken (skin removed) with 1/2 cup vegetables (prepared with reduced-fat butter) equals 329 calories, 10 g fat (3 g saturated fat), 80 mg cholesterol, 187 mg sodium, 31 g carbohydrate, 5 g fiber, 28 g protein. **Diabetic Exchanges:** 3 lean meat, 1-1/2 starch, 2 vegetable.

Alfredo Chicken 'n' Biscuits

PREP: 20 min.
BAKE: 20 min.

- 2 cups chopped fresh broccoli
- 1-1/2 cups sliced fresh carrots
- 1 cup chopped onion
- 2 tablespoons olive oil
- 2 cups cubed cooked chicken
- 1 carton (10 ounces) refrigerated Alfredo sauce
- 1 cup biscuit/baking mix
- 1/3 cup milk
- 1/4 teaspoon dill weed

■ In a large skillet, saute broccoli, carrots and onion in oil until crisp-tender. Stir in chicken and Alfredo sauce; heat through. Transfer to a lightly greased 8-in. square baking dish.

■ In a small bowl, combine baking mix, milk and dill just until moistened. Drop by rounded tablespoonfuls onto the chicken mixture.

■ Bake, uncovered, at 400° for 18-22 minutes or until bubbly and biscuits are golden brown.

Yield: 4 servings.

Cheryl Miller
FORT COLLINS, COLORADO

Chock-full of veggies and topped off with golden-brown biscuits and Alfredo sauce, this casserole will warm you through. It's fun to prepare and has excellent flavor. It's an easy dish to fix because store-bought sauce and a boxed mix make it very convenient.

Spinach-Stuffed Chicken Breasts

Sandy Friede
NEWBURYPORT, MASSACHUSETTS

Here's a savory entree that's easy to make but elegant enough for company. I double the recipe and freeze individual size portions for those busy days when I don't have time to cook.

Spinach-Stuffed Chicken Breasts

PREP: 30 min. ■ **BAKE:** 40 min.

1/4 cup chopped onion

4-1/2 teaspoons plus 1/4 cup butter, *divided*

1 garlic clove, minced

1 package (10 ounces) frozen chopped spinach, thawed and squeezed dry

6 ounces cream cheese, cubed

1/4 cup seasoned bread crumbs

6 boneless skinless chicken breast halves (6 ounces *each*)

1/2 teaspoon salt

1/2 teaspoon pepper

1/4 cup honey

2 tablespoons stone-ground mustard

1 tablespoon lemon juice

- In a large skillet, saute the onion in 4-1/2 teaspoons butter until tender. Add the garlic; saute 1 minute longer. Add spinach and cream cheese; cook and stir over low heat until blended. Remove from the heat; stir in bread crumbs.

- Flatten the chicken to 1/4-in. thickness; sprinkle both sides with salt and pepper. Place about 1/4 cup spinach mixture down the center of each chicken breast half. Fold the chicken over filling and secure with toothpicks.

- Place chicken bundles seam side down in a greased 11-in. x 7-in. baking dish. Melt the remaining butter; stir in the honey, mustard and lemon juice. Pour over the chicken.

- Bake, uncovered, at 350° for 40-50 minutes or until the meat is no longer pink, basting every 15 minutes with pan juices. Discard toothpicks.

Yield: 6 servings.

Draining and

squeezing the water from cooked spinach is very important when using in a recipe. Without this step, the dish could become too watery. After draining the spinach in a colander, if cooked, allow to cool. Then, with clean hands, squeeze the water out of the spinach.

Doris Russell
FALLSTON, MARYLAND
This recipe is nice if you only want to bake a turkey breast. Prepared with herbs and crisp-tender veggies, no one will miss the rest of the bird.

Turkey Breast with Vegetables

Turkey Breast with Vegetables

PREP: 20 min. ■ BAKE: 2-1/4 hours + standing

1/4 cup plus 1 tablespoon olive oil, *divided*

1 tablespoon minced fresh rosemary

2 teaspoons fennel seed, crushed

3 garlic cloves, minced

1 pound fresh baby carrots

3 large onions, cut into eighths

8 small red potatoes, cut in half

1 bone-in turkey breast (6 pounds)

1/2 teaspoon salt

1/4 teaspoon pepper

1/8 teaspoon garlic powder

1/2 cup chicken broth

■ In a large resealable plastic bag, combine 1/4 cup oil, rosemary, fennel seed and garlic. Add the carrots, onions and potatoes; shake to coat.

■ Place turkey breast in a shallow roasting pan. Rub turkey skin with remaining oil; sprinkle with the salt, pepper and garlic powder. Arrange vegetables around turkey.

■ Bake, uncovered, at 325° for 2-1/4 to 2-3/4 hours or until a meat thermometer reads 170°, basting occasionally with broth. Cover and let stand for 10 minutes before carving.

Yield: 6 servings.

Chicken Rice Casserole

Linda Durnil
DECATUR, ILLINOIS
Mushrooms, celery and water chestnuts add texture and crunch to this comforting casserole. Chicken and rice are perfect partners that always satisfy.

PREP: 10 min.
BAKE: 30 min.

2 cups cubed cooked chicken

2 cups cooked rice

1 can (10-3/4 ounces) condensed cream of chicken soup, undiluted

1 can (8 ounces) sliced water chestnuts, drained

1 jar (4-1/2 ounces) sliced mushrooms, drained

2 celery ribs, thinly sliced

3/4 cup mayonnaise

1 tablespoon chopped onion

1 tablespoon lemon juice

1/2 teaspoon salt

1/3 cup crushed saltines (about 10 crackers)

1 tablespoon butter, melted

■ In a large bowl, combine the first 10 ingredients. Transfer to a greased 2-1/2-qt. baking dish. Combine the cracker crumbs and butter; sprinkle over top.

■ Bake, uncovered, at 350° for 30-35 minutes or until bubbly.

Yield: 4-6 servings.

Lissa Hutson
PHELAN, CALIFORNIA

With turkey and broccoli, this special scalloped potato dish is a meal in itself. A handy jar of Alfredo sauce speeds along the preparation time.

Hearty Alfredo Potatoes

Hearty Alfredo Potatoes

PREP: 20 min. ■ BAKE: 1-1/4 hours + standing

1 jar (16 ounces) Alfredo sauce

1 cup milk

1 teaspoon garlic powder

3 pounds potatoes, peeled and thinly sliced

5 tablespoons grated Parmesan cheese, *divided*

Salt and pepper to taste

2 to 3 cups cubed cooked turkey

3 cups frozen chopped broccoli, thawed

2 cups (8 ounces) shredded Swiss cheese, *divided*

■ In a large bowl, combine the Alfredo sauce, milk and garlic powder. Pour a fourth of the mixture into a greased 13-in. x 9-in. baking dish. Layer with a fourth of the potatoes; sprinkle with 1 tablespoon Parmesan cheese, salt and pepper.

■ In a large bowl, combine the turkey, broccoli and 1-1/2 cups Swiss cheese; spoon a third over potatoes. Repeat layers twice. Top with the remaining potatoes. Sprinkle with remaining Swiss and Parmesan cheeses. Spread with remaining Alfredo sauce mixture.

■ Cover and bake at 400° for 45 minutes. Reduce heat to 350°. Bake, uncovered, 30 minutes longer or until the potatoes are tender. Let stand for 15 minutes before serving.

Yield: 6-8 servings.

Chicken Stuffing Bake

PREP: 5 min.
BAKE: 45 min.

6 boneless skinless chicken breast halves (6 ounces *each*)

6 slices Swiss cheese

1 can (10-3/4 ounces) condensed cream of chicken soup, undiluted

1/3 cup white wine *or* chicken broth

3 cups seasoned stuffing cubes

1/2 cup butter, melted

■ Place the chicken in a greased 13-in. x 9-in. baking dish; top with cheese. In a small bowl, combine soup and wine; spoon over cheese.

■ Combine croutons and butter; sprinkle over the soup. Bake, uncovered, at 350° for 45-55 minutes or until a meat thermometer reads 170°.

Yield: 6 servings.

When melted

butter is called for in a recipe, butter is measured first, then melted. The convenient markings on the wrappers make it easy to slice off the amount you need and melt it.

Nicole Vogl Harding
SPOKANE, WASHINGTON

At my bridal shower a few years ago, each guest brought a recipe card of her best dish. It has been a great way to experiment with new and different dinner menus. My husband and I have tried everyone's recipe, but this is our favorite.

Pork

209

218

222

These meal-in-one delights are made with the savory flavor of pork, whether you're biting into Italian sausage, the smoky flavor of ham and bacon, or juicy tenderloin, roasts and chops. From hearty casseroles to elegant stuffed pork chops, there's a meal for every purpose.

Peachy Pork Chops

- In a large skillet, saute the onion and celery in butter until tender; transfer to a large bowl. Add bread, poultry seasoning, sage and pepper. Fold in the peaches. Combine the eggs, water and parsley; add to the bread mixture. Toss to coat.

- Cut a large pocket in the side of each pork chop; spoon stuffing loosely into pockets. Tie with string to secure the stuffing if necessary. Brush the chops with oil. Sprinkle with garlic salt and pepper.

- In a large skillet, brown the chops on both sides. Place the remaining stuffing in a greased 13-in. x 9-in. baking dish. Top with the pork chops. Spoon preserves over the chops. Cover and bake at 350° for 45 minutes. Uncover and bake 15 minutes longer or until meat juices run clear. If string was used, remove before serving.

Yield: 6 servings.

Brenda DuFresne
MIDLAND, MICHIGAN

Pork and peaches team for a palate-pleasing combination in this hearty main dish. Even the pickiest eaters will love these tempting stuffed chops.

Peachy Pork Chops

PREP: 30 min. ■ BAKE: 1 hour

1-1/2	cups finely chopped onion	2	eggs
1-1/2	cups finely chopped celery	1	cup water
1/3	cup butter, cubed	2	tablespoons minced fresh parsley
6	cups day-old cubed bread	6	boneless pork chops (1-1/4 inches thick and 4 ounces *each*)
1/2	teaspoon poultry seasoning		
1/2	teaspoon rubbed sage		
1/8	teaspoon pepper	3	tablespoons olive oil
1	can (8-1/2 ounces) sliced peaches, drained and diced		Garlic salt and pepper to taste
		1/4	cup peach preserves

When a dish calls for poultry seasoning, you can make your own at home with this mix that yields 1 teaspoon of poultry seasoning. Just combine 3/4 teaspoon rubbed sage and 1/4 teaspoon dried thyme or marjoram.

Hearty Pork Pie

Sue Bacon
GLENCOE, MINNESOTA

My family adores this pie, especially at holiday time. The dough is easy to work with, and the wonderful aroma calls everyone to the table, so I don't have to!

PREP: 45 min. + chilling ■ **BAKE:** 25 min. + standing

- 2 cups all-purpose flour
- 1 teaspoon salt
- 1/2 cup shortening
- 1/2 cup sour cream
- 1 egg, lightly beaten

FILLING:

- 4 bacon strips, diced
- 1-1/2 pounds boneless pork, cut into 1/2-inch cubes
- 3 small onions, chopped
- 1 garlic clove, minced
- 2 tablespoons all-purpose flour
- 1 teaspoon salt
- 1/4 to 1/2 teaspoon pepper
- 1/8 to 1/4 teaspoon ground allspice
- 3/4 cup water
- 1 teaspoon beef bouillon granules
- 3 tablespoons minced fresh parsley
- 1 tablespoon heavy whipping cream

■ In a small bowl, combine the flour and salt. Cut in shortening until the mixture resembles coarse crumbs. Combine sour cream and egg; add to crumb mixture, tossing with a fork until dough forms a ball. Cover and refrigerate for 2 hours.

■ Meanwhile, for filling, in a large skillet, cook bacon over medium heat until crisp. Remove to paper towels; drain, reserving 2 tablespoons drippings. Brown pork in drippings. Add the onions; cook and stir until tender. Add garlic; cook 1 minute longer.

■ Sprinkle with flour, salt, pepper and allspice; stir until blended. Add the water, bouillon, parsley and bacon. Cover and cook over medium-low heat for 30 minutes or until meat is tender.

■ Divide dough in half; roll out one portion to fit a 9-in. pie plate. Transfer to pie plate; trim pastry even with edge. Spoon filling into crust. Roll out remaining pastry to fit top of plate; place over filling. Trim, seal and flute edges. Cut slits in pastry; brush with cream.

■ Bake at 400° for 25-30 minutes or until golden brown. Let stand for 15 minutes before cutting.

Yield: 6-8 servings.

Roast Pork With Cherry-Almond Glaze

PREP: 10 min.
BAKE: 65 min. + standing

- 1 boneless whole pork loin roast (3-1/2 pounds)
- 1 teaspoon salt
- 1 jar (12 ounces) cherry preserves
- 1/4 cup cider vinegar
- 2 tablespoons light corn syrup
- 1/4 teaspoon *each* ground cinnamon, nutmeg and cloves
- 1/4 cup slivered almonds

■ Sprinkle roast with salt; place on a rack in a shallow roasting pan. Bake, uncovered, at 350° for 30 minutes.

■ In a small saucepan, bring the preserves, vinegar, corn syrup and spices to a boil. Reduce heat; simmer, uncovered, for 2 minutes. Set aside 3/4 cup for serving. Stir almonds into remaining mixture.

■ Brush roast with some of glaze. Bake 35-50 minutes longer or until a meat thermometer reads 160°, brushing frequently with remaining glaze. Let stand for 10 minutes before slicing. Serve with the reserved cherry mixture.

Yield: 10 servings.

Joan Laurenzo
JOHNSTOWN, OHIO

Your pork roast will never dry out during cooking with this sweet cherry glaze. You can also spoon the sauce over slices of baked ham. The final dish has such an elegant and special-occasion appearance, but it's so easy to prepare.

Mary Merrill
BLOOMINGDALE, OHIO

As Sunday school teachers, my husband and I often host youth groups, so I dreamed up this "handy" recipe to feed some hungry teenagers. They loved this pizza-like sandwich so much that they still request it when they visit.

Sausage Sandwich Squares

PREP: 35 min. + rising ■ BAKE: 20 min.

1	package (1/4 ounce) active dry yeast
1-1/3	cups warm water (110° to 115°), *divided*
1/2	teaspoon salt
3	to 3-1/2 cups all-purpose flour
1	pound bulk Italian sausage
1	medium sweet red pepper, diced
1	medium green pepper, diced
1	large onion, diced
4	cups (16 ounces) shredded part-skim mozzarella cheese
1	egg
1	tablespoon water
2	tablespoons grated Parmesan cheese
2	tablespoons minced fresh parsley
1/2	teaspoon dried oregano
1/8	teaspoon garlic powder

■ In a large bowl, dissolve the yeast in 1/2 cup warm water. Add the salt, remaining water and 2 cups flour. Beat until smooth. Add enough of the remaining flour to form a firm dough.

■ Turn onto a floured surface; knead until smooth and elastic, about 6 minutes. Place in a greased bowl, turning once to grease top. Cover and let rise in a warm place until doubled, about 50 minutes.

■ In a large skillet, cook sausage over medium heat until no longer pink; remove with a slotted spoon and set aside. In the drippings, saute the peppers and onion until tender; drain.

■ Press half of the dough onto bottom and 1/2 in. up the sides of a greased 15-in. x 10-in. x 1-in. baking pan. Spread the sausage evenly over the crust. Top with peppers and onion. Sprinkle with mozzarella cheese. Roll out remaining dough to fit pan; place over cheese and seal the edges.

■ In a small bowl, beat the egg and water. Add the remaining ingredients; mix well. Brush over the dough. Cut slits in top. Bake at 400° for 20-25 minutes or until golden brown. Cut into squares.

Yield: 12-15 servings.

Apricot Baked Ham

Marge Clark
WEST LEBANON, INDIANA

Ham is a super choice for a holiday meal because once you put it in the oven, it practically takes care of itself until dinnertime. I serve it because everyone in my family loves it! The sugary crust makes the ham beautiful.

PREP: 20 min.
BAKE: 1 hour 40 min.

1/2	fully cooked bone-in ham (5 to 7 pounds)
20	whole cloves
1/2	cup apricot preserves
3	tablespoons ground mustard
1/2	cup packed light brown sugar

■ Place the ham on a rack in a shallow roasting pan. Score the surface of the ham, making diamond shapes 1/2 in. deep; insert a clove in each diamond. Combine the preserves and mustard; spread over the ham. Pat the brown sugar into the apricot mixture.

■ Bake at 325° for 20 minutes per pound or until a meat thermometer reads 140°.

Yield: 10-14 servings.

Leftover ham is great for creating future meals. Just cube the leftovers and store them in the freezer. They are a convenient addition to macaroni and cheese, scrambled eggs and potato or bean soup.

Bernice Morris
MARSHFIELD, MISSOURI

This is a noodle casserole just like Mom used to make! Its down-home taste has great appeal at a family gathering or as a dish to pass. It's quick to prepare and can be assembled ahead of time. No leftovers!

Reunion Casserole

Reunion Casserole

PREP: 15 min. ■ **BAKE:** 45 min.

1 pound ground beef	1 can (10-3/4 ounces) condensed tomato soup, undiluted
1/2 pound bulk hot sausage	
1 cup large onion, chopped	1 can (8 ounces) tomato sauce
2 cups (8 ounces) shredded cheddar cheese, *divided*	1/3 cup sliced pimiento-stuffed olives
1 medium green pepper, chopped	1 garlic clove, minced
1 can (11 ounces) whole kernel corn, drained	1/2 teaspoon salt
	8 ounces wide noodles, cooked and drained

■ In a large Dutch oven, cook the beef, sausage and onion over medium heat until meat is no longer pink; drain. Stir in 1 cup cheese, green pepper, corn, soup, tomato sauce, olives, garlic, salt and noodles.

■ Transfer to a 13-in. x 9-in. baking dish. Sprinkle with remaining cheese. Cover and bake at 350° for 35 minutes. Uncover; bake 10 minutes longer.

Yield: 8-10 servings.

Scalloped Pork Chop Combo

Sherry Schoneman
CEDAR FALLS, IOWA

This meal is made easy by adding vegetables and pork chops to boxed scalloped potatoes.

PREP: 15 min.
BAKE: 30 min. + standing

6 bone-in pork loin chops (1/2 inch thick and 7 ounces *each*)
2 tablespoons canola oil
1 teaspoon salt
2 cups water
1 package (10 ounces) frozen French-style green beans
1 cup thinly sliced carrots
1 package (5 ounces) scalloped potatoes
1 can (10-3/4 ounces) condensed cream of celery soup, undiluted
2/3 cup milk
2 tablespoons butter
1/2 teaspoon Worcestershire sauce

■ In a large skillet, brown pork chops in oil; sprinkle with salt. In a large saucepan, bring the water to a boil; add the beans, carrots, potatoes with contents of sauce packet, soup, milk, butter and Worcestershire sauce. Bring to a boil.

■ Transfer to a greased 13-in. x 9-in. baking dish; top with the pork chops.

■ Cover and bake at 350° for 25 minutes. Uncover; bake 5 minutes longer or until a meat thermometer reads 160°. Let stand for 10 minutes before serving.

Yield: 6 servings.

Hearty Barley Bake

- In a large skillet, saute the mushrooms, carrots and onion in oil until tender. Add garlic; cook 1 minute longer. Transfer to a large bowl.

- In the same skillet, cook the sausage over medium heat until no longer pink; drain. Add to the mushroom mixture. Stir in the barley, corn, spinach, onions, savory, thyme, marjoram and pepper.

- Transfer to a greased shallow 2-qt. baking dish. Cover and bake at 350° for 40 minutes. Sprinkle with the cheese. Bake, uncovered, 5 minutes longer or until the cheese is melted.

Yield: 6 servings.

Savory is an herb used to season soups, vegetables, fish, eggs, lentils and German dishes. The mild summer variety and a stronger winter variety are the most popular. The flavor is similar to a mixture of thyme and mint. You can grow the plants in your garden, or you can buy savory in a dried and crushed leaf or ground form in the spice section of your grocery store.

Jenny Browning
CYPRESS, TEXAS

Barley is a nice change of pace from the usual pasta or rice in this colorful casserole. It's chock-full of spicy sausage and a variety of vegetables including spinach, carrots and corn.

Hearty Barley Bake

PREP: 15 min. ■ **BAKE:** 20 min.

- 2 cups sliced fresh mushrooms
- 1 cup thinly sliced carrots
- 1/2 cup chopped onion
- 2 teaspoons vegetable oil
- 1 garlic clove, minced
- 12 ounces bulk pork sausage
- 1-1/2 cups cooked barley
- 1 can (14-3/4 ounces) cream-style corn

- 1 package (10 ounces) frozen chopped spinach, thawed and squeezed dry
- 3 green onions, sliced
- 1 teaspoon dried savory
- 1 teaspoon dried thyme
- 1/2 teaspoon dried marjoram
- 1/8 teaspoon pepper
- 1/2 cup shredded Parmesan cheese

Rose Enns
ABBOTSFORD, BRITISH COLUMBIA

I've been making this recipe since I discovered it and tweaked it to our family's liking for more than 15 years. You can substitute chopped salami, pepperoni or cooked ground beef for the ham. Any ingredient that you would like on a pizza, such as olives or red peppers, can be added to this dish.

Hawaiian Pizza Pasta

PREP: 30 min. ■ BAKE: 30 min.

- 1/2 pound sliced fresh mushrooms
- 1 medium onion, chopped
- 1 medium green pepper, chopped
- 3 tablespoons canola oil
- 2 garlic cloves, minced
- 1 can (15 ounces) tomato sauce
- 2 bay leaves
- 1 teaspoon dried oregano
- 1 teaspoon dried basil
- 1/2 teaspoon sugar
- 3-1/2 cups uncooked spiral pasta
- 6 cups (24 ounces) shredded part-skim mozzarella cheese, *divided*
- 1 can (20 ounces) pineapple chunks, drained
- 1 cup cubed fully cooked ham

■ In a large saucepan, saute the mushrooms, onion and pepper in oil for 5 minutes or until tender. Add garlic; cook 1 minute longer. Add the tomato sauce, bay leaves, oregano, basil and sugar. Bring to a boil. Reduce the heat and simmer, uncovered, for 20-30 minutes or until thickened, stirring frequently.

■ Cook the pasta according to the package directions; drain. Discard bay leaves from sauce. Stir in the pasta, 5 cups of mozzarella cheese, pineapple and ham.

■ Transfer to a greased shallow 3-qt. baking dish. Sprinkle with remaining cheese. Bake, uncovered, at 350° for 30-35 minutes or until heated through.

Yield: 12 servings.

To cook pasta more evenly, prevent it from sticking together and avoid boil-overs, always cook it in a large kettle or Dutch oven. Unless you have a large kettle, don't cook more than 2 pounds of pasta at a time.

Smoked Pork Chops with Sweet Potatoes

Helen Sanders
FORT MYERS, FLORIDA

Apple and sweet potato flavors combine so nicely with pork. My troops always enjoy simple dinners like this one.

PREP: 20 min.
BAKE: 40 min.

- 6 smoked boneless pork chops (7 ounces *each*)
- 1 tablespoon canola oil
- 4 large sweet potatoes, cooked, peeled and cut lengthwise into thirds
- 1/2 cup packed brown sugar
- 1/8 teaspoon pepper
- 2 large tart apples, peeled and thinly sliced
- 1/4 cup apple juice *or* water

■ In a large skillet, brown the pork chops in oil on each side. Transfer to a greased 13-in. x 9-in. baking dish. Top with the sweet potatoes. Combine the brown sugar and pepper; sprinkle over sweet potatoes. Top with apples; drizzle with apple juice.

■ Cover and bake at 375° for 30 minutes. Uncover; bake 10-15 minutes longer or until a meat thermometer reads 160°.

Yield: 6 servings.

Chicago-Style Deep-Dish Pizza

Lynn Hamilton
NAPERVILLE, ILLINOIS

My husband and I tried to duplicate the pizza from a popular Chicago restaurant, and I think our recipe turned out even better. The secret is baking it in a cast-iron skillet.

PREP: 20 min. + rising ■ **BAKE:** 40 min.

3-1/2	cups all-purpose flour	1	can (8 ounces) tomato sauce
1/4	cup cornmeal	1	can (6 ounces) tomato paste
1	package (1/4 ounce) quick-rise yeast	1/2	teaspoon salt
1-1/2	teaspoons sugar	1/4	teaspoon *each* garlic powder, dried oregano, dried basil and pepper
1/2	teaspoon salt	48	slices pepperoni
1	cup water	1	pound bulk Italian sausage, cooked and crumbled
1/3	cup olive oil	1/2	pound sliced fresh mushrooms

TOPPINGS:

- 6 cups (24 ounces) shredded part-skim mozzarella cheese, *divided*
- 1 can (28 ounces) diced tomatoes, well drained
- 1/4 cup grated Parmesan cheese

■ In a large bowl, combine 1-1/2 cups flour, cornmeal, yeast, sugar and salt. In a saucepan, heat water and oil to 120°-130°. Add to the dry ingredients; beat just until moistened. Add the remaining flour to form a stiff dough.

■ Turn onto a floured surface; knead until smooth and elastic, about 6-8 minutes. Place in a greased bowl, turning once to grease top. Cover and let rise in warm place until doubled, about 30 minutes.

■ Punch dough down; divide in half. Roll each portion into an 11-in. circle. Press dough onto the bottom and up the sides of two greased 10-in. ovenproof skillets. Sprinkle each with 2 cups mozzarella cheese.

■ In a large bowl, combine the diced tomatoes, tomato sauce, tomato paste and seasonings. Spoon 1-1/2 cups over each pizza. Layer each with half of the pepperoni, sausage, mushrooms, 1 cup mozzarella and 2 tablespoons Parmesan cheese.

■ Cover and bake at 450° for 35 minutes. Uncover and bake 5 minutes longer or until lightly browned.

Yield: 2 pizzas (8 slices each).

Editor's Note: Two 9-in. springform pans may be used in place of the skillet. Place pans on baking sheets. Run knife around edge of pan to loosen crust before removing sides.

Ham Broccoli Bake

PREP: 15 min.
BAKE: 20 min.

- 1-1/4 cups uncooked elbow macaroni
- 1-1/2 cups chopped fresh broccoli
- 1 can (10-3/4 ounces) condensed cream of mushroom soup, undiluted
- 1 cup cubed fully cooked ham
- 1 cup (4 ounces) shredded cheddar cheese
- 1/2 cup shredded part-skim mozzarella cheese
- 1/2 cup milk
- 1 tablespoon dried minced onion
- 1/4 teaspoon pepper
- 1 cup crushed potato chips

■ Cook macaroni according to package directions. Meanwhile, in a large bowl, combine the broccoli, soup, ham, cheeses, milk, onion and pepper. Drain macaroni; add to ham mixture.

■ Transfer to a greased 8-in. square baking dish; sprinkle with the potato chips. Bake, uncovered, at 350° for 20-25 minutes or until bubbly.

Yield: 4 servings.

Jennifer Shiew
JETMORE, KANSAS

While trying to come up with a way to use leftover cooked broccoli, I adapted this recipe from a friend. My husband and brother-in-law thought it was great. The three of us had no trouble cleaning the pan! The crushed potato chips may seem old-fashioned, but they are delicious.

One-Dish Pork Chop Dinner

■ In a large resealable plastic bag, place 1/4 cup flour, salt and pepper; add the pork chops. Seal the bag; toss to coat. In a Dutch oven over medium-high heat, brown chops in butter on both sides. Remove pork chops; set aside and keep warm.

■ Stir the remaining flour into the pan drippings until blended. Gradually whisk in the apple juice. Bring to a boil and while stirring, cook for 2 minutes or until thickened.

■ Return chops to pan; add the potatoes, onions and carrots. Cover and bake at 350° for 30 minutes.

■ Top with cabbage; cover and bake for 50-60 minutes longer or until a meat thermometer reads 160° and the vegetables are tender, basting occasionally with juices.

Yield: 8 servings.

Pat Waymire
YELLOW SPRINGS, OHIO

This is a meaty main dish for any affair, but it's great for St. Pat's Day. Apple juice gives the chops a wonderful flavor, and the cabbage is mild so it appeals to a wide variety of tastes.

One-Dish Pork Chop Dinner

PREP: 20 min. ■ **BAKE:** 1-1/2 hours

1/3 cup all-purpose flour, *divided*

Salt and pepper to taste

8 boneless pork loin chops (1/2 inch thick and 4 ounces *each*)

1/4 cup butter, cubed

2 cups apple juice

2 pounds small red potatoes

1 pound *or* 1 jar (16 ounces) small whole onions, drained

1 pound carrots, cut into 3-inch pieces

6 to 8 cups shredded cabbage

To shred cabbage by hand, first, cut the head in half and remove the core, then cut into wedges. Place the cut side down on a cutting board and with a large sharp knife, cut into thin slices.

Christina Ingalls
MANHATTAN, KANSAS
This is my husband's favorite casserole, and he requests it often. He just loves the combination of zesty Italian sausage and the three types of cheeses.

Baked Ziti and Sausage

Baked Ziti and Sausage

PREP: 25 min. ■ BAKE: 30 min.

3 cups uncooked ziti *or* other small tube pasta

1/2 pound Italian sausage links

1/4 cup butter, cubed

1/4 cup all-purpose flour

1-1/2 teaspoons salt, *divided*

1/4 teaspoon plus 1/8 teaspoon pepper, *divided*

2 cups milk

1/2 cup grated Parmesan cheese, *divided*

1 egg, lightly beaten

2 cups (16 ounces) 4% cottage cheese

1 tablespoon minced fresh parsley

1 cup (4 ounces) shredded part-skim mozzarella cheese

Paprika

■ Cook the pasta according to package directions. Drain; place in a large bowl. In a small skillet, cook the sausage over medium heat until no longer pink; drain and cut into 1/2-in. slices.

■ In a saucepan, melt the butter. Stir in the flour, 1 teaspoon salt and 1/4 teaspoon pepper until smooth; gradually add milk. Bring to a boil; cook and stir for 2 minutes or until thickened. Remove from the heat; stir in 1/4 cup Parmesan cheese. Pour over pasta; toss to coat.

■ Combine the egg, cottage cheese, parsley, and remaining Parmesan cheese, salt and pepper. Spoon half of the pasta mixture into a greased 2-1/2-qt. baking dish. Top with the cottage cheese mixture. Add the sausage to the remaining pasta mixture; spoon over top. Sprinkle with mozzarella cheese and paprika.

■ Bake, uncovered, at 350° for 30-35 minutes or until a meat thermometer reads 160°.

Yield: 6 servings.

Oven-Baked Ribs

Eric Spencer
FRANKFORT, INDIANA
This recipe was developed by a college buddy of mine. I make it often for family and friends.

PREP: 20 min.
BAKE: 2-1/2 hours

4 pounds pork spareribs

2 medium oranges

1 bottle (28 ounces) barbecue sauce

1 cup coarsely chopped onion

2/3 to 1 cup packed brown sugar

1 tablespoon Worcestershire sauce

1-1/2 teaspoons chili powder

1 to 1-1/2 teaspoons hot pepper sauce

1/4 to 1/2 teaspoon cayenne pepper

■ Place the ribs in two foil-lined 15-in. x 10-in. x 1-in. baking pans. Bake at 325° for 2 hours; drain. Cut into serving size portions.

■ Place ribs in an ungreased 13-in. x 9-in. baking dish. Squeeze the oranges, reserving 1/2 cup juice and peel. Combine juice, barbecue sauce, onion, brown sugar, Worcestershire sauce, chili powder, pepper sauce and cayenne. Cut orange peel into large chunks and add to sauce; pour sauce over ribs.

■ Bake, uncovered, for 30-45 minutes or until ribs are tender and sauce is thickened, turning ribs several times to coat with sauce. Discard orange peel.

Yield: 4-6 servings.

Sausage Calzones

Janine Colasurdo
CHESAPEAKE, VIRGINIA

In these irresistible pizza turnovers, Italian sausage, ricotta, Parmesan, spinach and seasonings are all wrapped in homemade dough for a meal that tastes like it came from your favorite pizzeria.

PREP: 35 min. + rising ■ **BAKE:** 20 min.

- 1 package (1/4 ounce) active dry yeast
- 1/2 cup warm water (110° to 115°)
- 3/4 cup warm milk (110° to 115°)
- 2 tablespoons plus 2 teaspoons olive oil, *divided*
- 1-1/2 teaspoons salt
- 1 teaspoon sugar
- 3 to 3-1/4 cups all-purpose flour
- 1 pound bulk Italian sausage
- 1 package (10 ounces) frozen chopped spinach, thawed and squeezed dry
- 1 carton (15 ounces) ricotta cheese
- 1/2 cup grated Parmesan cheese
- 1 tablespoon minced fresh parsley
- 1/8 teaspoon pepper
- 2 tablespoons cornmeal
- 1/2 teaspoon garlic salt
- 1-1/2 cups pizza sauce, warmed

■ In a large bowl, dissolve the yeast in warm water. Add the milk, 2 tablespoons oil, salt, sugar and 2 cups flour; beat mixture until smooth. Stir in enough of the remaining flour to form a soft dough.

■ Turn onto a floured surface; knead until smooth and elastic, about 6-8 minutes. Place in a greased bowl; turn once to grease top. Cover and let rise in a warm place until doubled, about 1 hour.

■ Meanwhile, in a large skillet, cook sausage over medium heat until no longer pink; drain. Add the spinach, cheeses, parsley and pepper; mix well.

■ Punch dough down; divide into six pieces. On a floured surface, roll each piece into an 8-in. circle. Top each with 2/3 cup filling. Fold dough over filling; pinch to seal.

■ Place on greased baking sheets sprinkled with cornmeal. Brush tops lightly with remaining oil; sprinkle with garlic salt. Bake at 400° for 20-25 minutes or until golden brown. Serve with the pizza sauce.

Yield: 6 servings.

Fruited Pork Tenderloin

PREP: 15 min.
BAKE: 30 min.

- 1/4 cup dried cranberries
- 1/4 cup chopped dried apricots
- 3/4 cup boiling water
- 1/2 cup chopped onion
- 2 tablespoons butter
- 1/2 cup coarsely chopped pecans
- 2 pork tenderloins (1 pound *each*)
- 1/4 teaspoon salt
- 1/4 teaspoon pepper
- 1/3 cup apricot preserves, warmed, *divided*

■ Place cranberries and apricots in a small bowl; add boiling water. Soak for 8 minutes; drain. In a small skillet, saute the onion in butter until tender. Remove from the heat. Stir in the pecans, cranberries and apricots.

■ Make a lengthwise slit down the center of each tenderloin, cutting two-thirds of the way through the meat. Place on a greased rack in a broiler pan; open the tenderloins so they lie flat. Sprinkle with the salt and pepper.

■ Brush with half of preserves; top with fruit mixture. Bake at 375° for 30-35 minutes or until a meat thermometer reads 160°. Drizzle with remaining preserves.

Yield: 6 servings.

Taste of Home Test Kitchen

This recipe is versatile, because it comes together quick enough to make for a weeknight dinner. But it's also fancy enough to serve to special guests. Using the flat side of a meat mallet to flatten the pork tenderloin before baking will speed up the cooking process.

Hash Brown Pork Bake

Bacon Tomato Casserole

Mary McGair
MILWAUKIE, OREGON

This recipe from my mother is simple to make and can be an entree or side dish.

PREP: 30 min.
BAKE: 10 min.

 6 ounces uncooked egg noodles
 1 pound sliced bacon, diced
 1/3 cup chopped green pepper
 1/3 cup chopped onion
 1 teaspoon salt
 1/2 teaspoon dried marjoram
 1/2 teaspoon dried thyme
 1/8 teaspoon pepper
 1 can (28 ounces) stewed tomatoes
 1 cup (4 ounces) shredded cheddar cheese

■ Cook the noodles according to the package directions; drain. In a large skillet, cook bacon over medium heat until crisp. Remove to paper towels to drain, reserving 2 tablespoons drippings.

■ In the drippings, saute the green pepper, onion, salt, marjoram, thyme and pepper for 5 minutes. Stir in the tomatoes. Bring to a boil. Reduce the heat; simmer, uncovered, for 10 minutes. Stir in the noodles. Add half of the cooked bacon.

■ Transfer to a greased 2-qt. baking dish. Top with the cheese and the remaining bacon. Bake, uncovered, at 350° for 10-15 minutes or until the cheese is melted.

Yield: 4-6 servings.

Darlis Wilfer
WEST BEND, WISCONSIN

This comforting family-style casserole is so convenient since it uses frozen hash brown potatoes. Its creamy deliciousness will be popular with your family, too.

Hash Brown Pork Bake

PREP: 15 min. ■ **BAKE:** 1 hour

 2 cups (16 ounces) sour cream
 1 can (10-3/4 ounces) condensed cream of chicken soup, undiluted
 1 package (32 ounces) frozen cubed hash brown potatoes, thawed
 2 cups cubed cooked pork
 1 pound process cheese (Velveeta), cubed
 1/4 cup chopped onion
 2 cups crushed cornflakes
 1/2 cup butter, melted
 1 cup (4 ounces) shredded part-skim mozzarella cheese

■ In a large bowl, combine sour cream and soup. Stir in the hash browns, pork, process cheese and onion. Transfer to a greased 3-qt. baking dish.

■ Toss cornflake crumbs and butter; sprinkle over top. Bake, uncovered, at 350° for 50 minutes. Sprinkle with the mozzarella cheese. Bake 10 minutes longer or until bubbly.

Yield: 8 servings.

Church-Supper Ham Loaf

Rosemary Smith
FORT BRAGG, CALIFORNIA

Whenever there is any leftover ham, it gets ground up and used in this special loaf for a future meal. As the name suggests, it has made more than one appearance on a buffet table after church.

PREP: 10 min. ■ **BAKE:** 50 min. + standing

2 cups soft bread crumbs	1/8 teaspoon paprika
1 cup (8 ounces) sour cream	1 pound fully cooked ham, ground
2 eggs, lightly beaten	1 pound reduced-fat bulk pork sausage
1/3 cup chopped onion	
2 tablespoons lemon juice	SAUCE:
1 teaspoon curry powder	1 cup packed brown sugar
1 teaspoon ground ginger	1/2 cup water
1 teaspoon ground mustard	1/2 cup cider vinegar
1/8 teaspoon ground nutmeg	1/4 teaspoon pepper

■ In a large bowl, combine the bread crumbs, sour cream, eggs, onion, lemon juice and seasonings. Crumble ham and sausage over mixture and mix well.

■ Shape into 9-in. x 5-in. oval; place in a greased shallow baking pan. Bake, uncovered, at 350° for 30 minutes.

■ In a small saucepan, combine the sauce ingredients; bring to a boil. Pour over loaf. Bake, uncovered, 20-30 minutes longer or until no longer pink and a meat thermometer reads 160°. Let the ham loaf stand 10 minutes before slicing.

Yield: 6-8 servings.

When lemons are in season or you have extra lemons on hand, juice them and freeze the juice in ice cube trays. Measure 1 or 2 tablespoons of juice into each compartment in your ice cube tray. When frozen, remove the cubes and place them in resealable freezer bags. It's great to have the lemon juice already measured when you're in a hurry!

Ham and Swiss Casserole

Doris Barb
EL DORADO, KANSAS

When I prepare this casserole for gatherings, it's always a hit. It can easily be doubled or tripled for a crowd.

PREP: 15 min.
BAKE: 40 min.

1 package (8 ounces) egg noodles, cooked and drained

2 cups cubed fully cooked ham

2 cups (8 ounces) shredded Swiss cheese

1 can (10-3/4 ounces) condensed cream of celery soup, undiluted

1 cup (8 ounces) sour cream

1/2 cup chopped green pepper

1/2 cup chopped onion

■ In a greased 13-in. x 9-in. baking dish, layer half of the noodles, ham and cheese.

■ In a large bowl, combine the soup, sour cream, green pepper and onion; spread half over the top. Repeat layers. Bake, uncovered, at 350° for 40-45 minutes or until heated through.

Yield: 6-8 servings.

Dallas McCord
RENO, NEVADA

This lasagna-like entree takes me back to my childhood. A friend's mother used to fix it for us when we were kids. I made a few changes, but it's still quick and delicious.

Cheesy Sausage Penne

Cheesy Sausage Penne

PREP: 25 min. ■ **BAKE:** 30 min.

1 pound bulk Italian sausage	1 package (8 ounces) cream cheese, softened
1 garlic clove, minced	1 cup (8 ounces) sour cream
1 jar (26 ounces) spaghetti sauce	4 green onions, sliced
1 package (16 ounces) uncooked penne pasta	2 cups (8 ounces) shredded cheddar cheese

■ In a large skillet, cook the sausage over medium heat until meat is no longer pink. Add garlic; cook 1 minute longer. Drain. Stir in spaghetti sauce; bring to a boil. Reduce heat; cover and simmer for 20 minutes.

■ Cook pasta according to package directions; drain. Meanwhile, in a small bowl, combine the cream cheese, sour cream and onions.

■ In a greased shallow 3-qt. baking dish, layer half of the pasta and sausage mixture. Dollop with half the cream cheese mixture; sprinkle with half the cheddar cheese. Repeat layers.

■ Bake, uncovered, at 350° for 30-35 minutes or until bubbly.

Yield: 12 servings.

Pork Parmigiana

PREP/TOTAL TIME: 30 min.

1-1/3 cups uncooked spiral pasta
   2 cups meatless spaghetti sauce
   1 pork tenderloin (1 pound)
 1/4 cup egg substitute
 1/3 cup seasoned bread crumbs
   3 tablespoons grated Parmesan cheese, *divided*
 1/4 cup shredded part-skim mozzarella cheese

■ Cook the pasta according to the package directions. Place the spaghetti sauce in a small saucepan; cook over low heat until heated through, stirring occasionally.

■ Meanwhile, cut tenderloin into eight slices; flatten to 1/4-in. thickness. Place egg substitute in a shallow bowl. In another shallow bowl, combine bread crumbs and 1 tablespoon Parmesan cheese. Dip pork slices in egg substitute, then roll in crumb mixture.

■ Place on a baking sheet coated with cooking spray. Bake at 425° for 5-6 minutes on each side or until juices run clear. Drain the pasta; serve with the spaghetti sauce and pork. Sprinkle with the mozzarella and remaining Parmesan.

Yield: 4 servings.

Julee Wallberg
SALT LAKE CITY, UTAH

I bring home the flavors of Italy, including tomato sauce and Parmesan and mozzarella cheeses, with this tantalizing Parmigiana that uses only seven ingredients. Baked in mere minutes, the crispy yet moist pork tenderloin makes an easy, breezy dinner your family will love!

Fish & Seafood

233

227

228

For a break from meat and potatoes, try one of these hearty oven entrees made with fish or seafood. You'll find classic one-dish meals like tuna casserole, lasagna, rice hot dishes and jambalaya. What a great way to try a change of scenery at the dinner table!

Creamy Seafood-Stuffed Shells

Katie Sloan
CHARLOTTE, NORTH CAROLINA
Inspired by my love of lasagna, pasta shells and seafood, I created this recipe that's easy to make but special enough for company. I serve it with garlic bread and a salad.

Creamy Seafood-Stuffed Shells

PREP: 40 min. ■ BAKE: 30 min.

24 uncooked jumbo pasta shells
1 tablespoon finely chopped green pepper
1 tablespoon chopped red onion
1 teaspoon plus 1/4 cup butter, *divided*
2 cans (6 ounces *each*) lump crabmeat, drained
1 package (5 ounces) frozen cooked salad shrimp, thawed
1 egg, lightly beaten

1/2 cup shredded part-skim mozzarella cheese
1/4 cup mayonnaise
2 tablespoons plus 4 cups milk, *divided*
1-1/2 teaspoons seafood seasoning, *divided*
1/4 teaspoon pepper
1/4 cup all-purpose flour
1/4 teaspoon coarsely ground pepper
1-1/2 cups grated Parmesan cheese

■ Cook the pasta according to package directions. Meanwhile, in a small skillet, saute green pepper and onion in 1 teaspoon butter until tender; set aside.

■ In a large bowl, combine the crab, shrimp, egg, mozzarella, mayonnaise, 2 tablespoons milk, 1 teaspoon seafood seasoning, pepper and the chopped green pepper mixture.

■ Drain and rinse the pasta and stuff each shell with 1 rounded tablespoon of seafood mixture. Place in a greased 13-in. x 9-in. baking dish.

■ In a small saucepan, melt the remaining butter over medium heat. Whisk in the flour and coarsely ground pepper and gradually whisk in remaining milk. Bring to a boil; cook and stir for 2 minutes or until thickened. Stir in Parmesan cheese.

■ Pour over the shells. Sprinkle with the remaining seafood seasoning. Bake, uncovered, at 350° for 30-35 minutes or until bubbly.

Yield: 8 servings.

Instead of draining jumbo pasta shells in a colander (which can cause them to tear), carefully remove them from the boiling water with tongs. Pour out any water inside the shells and drain on lightly greased waxed paper until you're ready to stuff them.

Mary Beth Harris-Murphree
TYLER, TEXAS

If you enjoy Creole and Cajun dishes, you'll love this one. The seasoning and andouille sausage give it a terrific kick, and seafood fans will appreciate the shrimp. The cheese sauce adds a rich and upscale touch to this simple dish.

Cajun Shrimp Lasagna Roll-Ups

PREP: 30 min. ■ BAKE: 25 min. + standing

1-1/4 pounds uncooked medium shrimp, peeled and deveined
1 medium onion, chopped
2 tablespoons olive oil
4 medium tomatoes, seeded and chopped
2 tablespoons Cajun seasoning
3 garlic cloves, minced
1/4 cup butter, cubed
1/4 cup all-purpose flour
2 cups milk
1-1/2 cups (6 ounces) shredded cheddar cheese
1 cup diced fully cooked andouille sausage
12 lasagna noodles, cooked and drained
4 ounces pepper Jack cheese, shredded
1 teaspoon paprika

■ In a large skillet, saute shrimp and onion in oil until shrimp turn pink. Stir in tomatoes and Cajun seasoning; set aside.

■ In a large saucepan, saute garlic in butter for 1 minute. Stir in flour until blended. Gradually add milk. Bring to a boil over medium heat; cook and stir for 2 minutes or until thickened. Remove from the heat; stir in cheddar cheese until smooth. Add sausage; set aside.

■ Spread 1/3 cup shrimp mixture over each noodle. Carefully roll up; place seam side down in a greased 13-in. x 9-in. baking dish. Top with cheese sauce. Sprinkle with pepper Jack cheese and paprika.

■ Cover and bake at 350° for 15 minutes. Uncover; bake 10-15 minutes longer or until bubbly. Let stand 15 minutes before serving.

Yield: 6 servings.

Andouille sausage is a smoked sausage made of pork and garlic usually associated with Cajun dishes such as jambalaya and gumbo. The traditional sausage has a nice, spicy zip to it. If you are unable to find andouille, you can use kielbasa instead.

Potato Salmon Casserole

Laura Varney
BATAVIA, OHIO
I enjoy experimenting with cooking new things, which is how I came up with this tasty dish. It's a great way to work salmon into your menu.

PREP: 5 min.
BAKE: 35 min.

2-1/2 cups cubed cooked potatoes
2 cups frozen peas, thawed
1 cup mayonnaise
1 can (14-3/4 ounces) salmon, drained, bones and skin removed
5 ounces process cheese (Velveeta), cubed
1 cup finely crushed cornflakes
1 tablespoon butter, melted

■ Place potatoes in a greased 2-qt. baking dish. Sprinkle with peas; spread with mayonnaise. Top with salmon and cheese.

■ Bake, uncovered, at 350° for 30 minutes. Combine cornflake crumbs and butter; sprinkle over top. Bake 5-10 minutes longer or until golden brown.

Yield: 4-6 servings.

Val Keithley
HAMMOND, INDIANA

A friend gave me this recipe, and it's been a family favorite since the first time I made it. I find that the dish comes together easily and quickly.

Catfish Creole

Catfish Creole

PREP: 20 min. ■ BAKE: 15 min.

1/4 cup *each* chopped onion, celery and green pepper

2 teaspoons olive oil

2 garlic cloves, minced

3/4 cup chicken broth

1 tablespoon tomato paste

1/2 teaspoon salt

1/2 teaspoon *each* dried basil, oregano and thyme

1/8 teaspoon *each* white, black and cayenne pepper

Dash paprika

1/2 cup diced fresh tomato

1 pound catfish *or* orange roughy fillets

Hot cooked rice

Minced fresh parsley

■ In a small skillet, saute the onion, celery and green pepper in oil until tender. Add the garlic; cook 1 minute longer. Add broth, tomato paste and seasonings; bring to a boil. Reduce the heat; simmer, uncovered, for 5 minutes or until heated through. Stir in the tomato.

■ Arrange the fillets in a greased 13-in. x 9-in. baking dish; top with the vegetable mixture. Bake, uncovered, at 375° for 15-20 minutes or until fish flakes easily with a fork. Serve over rice; sprinkle with parsley.

Yield: 4 servings.

Shrimp Rice Casserole

PREP: 10 min.
BAKE: 30 min.

12 ounces cooked medium shrimp, peeled and deveined

2 cups cooked rice

1 can (10-3/4 ounces) condensed cream of mushroom soup, undiluted

1 can (4 ounces) mushroom stems and pieces, drained

1 cup (4 ounces) shredded cheddar cheese

4 tablespoons butter, melted, *divided*

2 tablespoons chopped green pepper

2 tablespoons chopped onion

1 tablespoon lemon juice

1/2 teaspoon white pepper

1/2 teaspoon ground mustard

1/2 teaspoon Worcestershire sauce

1 cup soft bread crumbs

■ In a large bowl, combine the shrimp, rice, soup, mushrooms, cheese, 2 tablespoons butter, green pepper, onion, lemon juice, pepper, mustard and Worcestershire sauce.

■ Transfer to a greased 1-1/2-qt. baking dish. Combine the bread crumbs and remaining butter; sprinkle over top. Bake, uncovered, at 375° for 30-35 minutes or until lightly browned.

Yield: 6 servings.

Marcia Urschel
WEBSTER, NEW YORK

I've been making this delicious casserole for more than 30 years, and it hasn't failed me once. It's fast to fix plus it always pleases family and friends. For a healthier version, use brown rice and reduced-fat soup and cheese.

Ruby Williams
BOGALUSA, LOUISIANA

My sister-in-law shared this recipe when I first moved to Louisiana. It's been handed down in my husband's family for generations. It's quick to prepare, nutritious and beautiful. I've passed it on to my children, too.

Blend of the Bayou

PREP: 20 min. ■ BAKE: 25 min.

- 1 package (8 ounces) cream cheese, cubed
- 4 tablespoons butter, *divided*
- 1 large onion, chopped
- 2 celery ribs, chopped
- 1 large green pepper, chopped
- 1 pound cooked medium shrimp, peeled and deveined
- 2 cans (6 ounces *each*) crabmeat, drained, flaked and cartilage removed
- 1 can (10-3/4 ounces) condensed cream of mushroom soup, undiluted
- 3/4 cup cooked rice
- 1 jar (4-1/2 ounces) sliced mushrooms, drained
- 1 teaspoon garlic salt
- 3/4 teaspoon hot pepper sauce
- 1/2 teaspoon cayenne pepper
- 3/4 cup shredded cheddar cheese
- 1/2 cup crushed butter-flavored crackers (about 12 crackers)

■ In a small saucepan, cook and stir the cream cheese and 2 tablespoons butter over low heat until melted and smooth; set aside.

■ In a large skillet, saute the onion, celery and green pepper in remaining butter until tender. Stir in the shrimp, crab, soup, rice, mushrooms, garlic salt, pepper sauce, cayenne and reserved cream cheese mixture.

■ Transfer to a greased 2-qt. baking dish. Combine the cheddar cheese and cracker crumbs; sprinkle over the top. Bake, uncovered, at 350° for 25-30 minutes or until bubbly.

Yield: 6-8 servings.

Shrimp are available fresh or frozen (raw or cooked, peeled or in the shell) or canned. Shrimp in the shell (fresh or frozen) are available in different varieties and sizes (medium, large, extra large, jumbo). Uncooked shrimp will have shells that range in color from gray or brown to pink or red. Fresh shrimp should have a firm texture with a mild aroma.

Walleye Veracruz*

Robert & Linda Nagle
PARK RAPIDS, MINNESOTA

Living in Minnesota lake country, we've naturally had to come up with a variety of recipes for fresh walleye. This is a tradition of ours that has Mexican flair. We like to sprinkle the fish with lemon-pepper, then top it with onion, green pepper and tomato.

PREP/TOTAL TIME: 30 min.

- 4 walleye *or* catfish fillets (6 ounces *each*)
- 2 teaspoons lemon-pepper seasoning
- 1 medium red onion, sliced and separated into rings
- 1 medium green pepper, sliced into rings
- 1 large tomato, sliced
- 1/4 cup sliced ripe olives

■ Place the fillets in a 13-in. x 9-in. baking dish coated with cooking spray. Sprinkle with lemon-pepper. Layer with the onion, green pepper, tomato and olives.

■ Cover and bake at 350° for 25-30 minutes or until the fish flakes easily with a fork.

Yield: 4 servings.

✱ Nutrition Facts: 1 serving equals 197 calories, 3 g fat (1 g saturated fat), 146 mg cholesterol, 396 mg sodium, 7 g carbohydrate, 2 g fiber, 34 g protein. **Diabetic Exchanges:** 5 very lean meat, 1 vegetable.

Taste of Home Test Kitchen
Since scallops will continue to release their cooked juices, drain the liquid before returning the scallops to the pan so that your sauce is thicker.

Scallops Au Gratin

Scallops Au Gratin

PREP/TOTAL TIME: 30 min.

- 3 tablespoons all-purpose flour
- 1 cup whole milk
- 1/2 cup heavy whipping cream
- 1/4 cup white wine
- 1 teaspoon Dijon mustard
- 1/4 teaspoon salt
- 1/4 teaspoon pepper
- 1-1/2 pounds bay scallops
- 1/2 cup chopped onion
- 2 tablespoons butter

- 1 jar (4-1/2 ounces) sliced mushrooms, drained
- 1/2 teaspoon dried tarragon
- 1-1/4 cups shredded Asiago cheese

TOPPING:
- 1/3 cup dry bread crumbs
- 2 tablespoons butter, melted
- 1 tablespoon grated Parmesan cheese

- In a large bowl, combine the flour, milk, cream, wine, mustard, salt and pepper until smooth; set aside.

- In a large skillet, saute scallops and onion in butter until scallops are opaque. Remove with a slotted spoon. Add milk mixture to the skillet. Bring to a boil; cook and stir for 2 minutes or until thickened.

- Drain scallops. Add the scallops, mushrooms and tarragon to the sauce; heat through. Stir in Asiago cheese until melted.

- Divide scallop mixture among four 10-oz. baking dishes. Combine the topping ingredients; sprinkle over scallop mixture. Broil 6 in. from the heat for 1-2 minutes or until golden brown.

Yield: 4 servings.

Baked Seafood Avocados

Marian Platt
SEQUIM, WASHINGTON
Everyone who tastes this simply wonderful luncheon dish is surprised that the avocados are baked.

PREP: 15 min.
BAKE: 25 min.

- 1 cup mayonnaise
- 3/4 cup chopped celery
- 1/2 cup thinly sliced green onions
- 1/8 teaspoon salt, optional
- 1/8 teaspoon pepper
- 1 can (4-1/2 ounces) crabmeat, drained, flaked and cartilage removed
- 1 can (4 ounces) medium shrimp, rinsed and drained
- 4 large ripe avocados, halved and pitted
- 1 to 2 tablespoons lemon juice
- 1/4 cup crushed potato chips, optional

- In a large bowl, combine the mayonnaise, celery, onions, salt if desired and pepper. Add crab and shrimp; mix well. Peel the avocados if desired. Sprinkle avocados with lemon juice; fill with seafood mixture. Sprinkle with potato chips if desired.

- Place avacados in an ungreased 13-in. x 9-in. baking dish. Bake, uncovered, at 350° for 25-30 minutes or until bubbly.

Yield: 8 servings.

Oven Jambalaya

Flounder Florentine

Bobby Taylor
MICHIGAN CITY, INDIANA

A mixture of garden vegetable cream cheese and healthy chopped spinach lends rich flavor to these tender fish fillets. You'll have an elegant meal on the table in just over 30 minutes.

PREP: 10 min.
BAKE: 25 min.

  1 package (10 ounces) frozen chopped spinach, thawed and squeezed dry

  1 carton (8 ounces) spreadable garden vegetable cream cheese, *divided*

  4 flounder *or* sole fillets (3 ounces *each*)

  2 tablespoons 2% milk

1/2 teaspoon lemon juice

1/8 teaspoon salt

1/8 teaspoon pepper

■ In a small bowl, combine the spinach and 3/4 cup cream cheese. Spoon onto each fillet; roll up. Place the seam side down in a greased 8-in. square baking dish.

■ Bake, uncovered, at 375° for 25-30 minutes or until fish flakes easily with a fork.

■ In a small microwave-safe bowl, combine the milk, lemon juice, salt, pepper and remaining cream cheese. Microwave on high for 30-60 seconds; stir until smooth. Spoon over fish.

Yield: 4 servings.

Ruby Williams
BOGALUSA, LOUISIANA

If you're looking for an easy but delicious version of the classic Louisiana stew, jambalaya, then this is it. The oven does the work for you.

Oven Jambalaya

PREP: 10 min. ■ BAKE: 1 hour

2-1/4 cups water

1-1/2 cups uncooked long grain rice

  1 can (10-3/4 ounces) condensed cream of celery soup, undiluted

  1 can (10-3/4 ounces) condensed cream of onion soup, undiluted

  1 can (10 ounces) diced tomatoes and green chilies, undrained

  1 pound smoked sausage, cut into 1/2-inch slices

  1 pound cooked medium shrimp, peeled and deveined

■ In a large bowl, combine the first five ingredients. Transfer to a greased 13-in. x 9-in. baking dish.

■ Cover and bake at 350° for 40 minutes. Stir in sausage and shrimp. Cover and bake 20-30 minutes longer or until the rice is tender.

Yield: 8-10 servings.

Seafood Enchiladas

- In a large saucepan, cook onion in butter over medium heat until tender. Add garlic; cook 1 minute longer. Combine sour cream and flour until smooth; gradually add to onion mixture. Stir in broth, chilies, coriander and pepper. Bring to a boil. Reduce the heat and simmer, uncovered, for 2-3 minutes or until thickened. Remove from the heat; stir in 1/2 cup cheese.

- Place crab in a small bowl; stir in 1/2 cup sauce. Spoon equal amounts on tortillas; roll up tightly. Place seam side down in an 11-in. x 7-in. baking dish coated with cooking spray. Top with remaining sauce.

- Cover and bake at 350° for 30 minutes. Uncover; sprinkle with the remaining cheese. Bake 5 minutes longer or until cheese is melted. Let stand for 5 minutes. Top with tomato, green onions and olives.

Yield: 8 servings.

*Nutrition Facts: 1 enchilada equals 243 calories, 11 g fat (5 g saturated fat), 53 mg cholesterol, 662 mg sodium, 21 g carbohydrate, 1 g fiber, 16 g protein. **Diabetic Exchanges:** 1 very lean meat, 1-1/2 starch, 2 fat.

Donna Roberts
MANHATTAN, KANSAS
I received this recipe from an old friend of the family many years ago, and my gang still loves it today. The crab makes it a wonderful change of pace from other weeknight fare.

Seafood Enchiladas*

PREP: 30 min. ■ BAKE: 35 min.

1/2 cup chopped onion
1 tablespoon butter
1 garlic clove, minced
1 cup (8 ounces) reduced-fat sour cream
3 tablespoons all-purpose flour
1 cup reduced-sodium chicken broth
1 can (4 ounces) chopped green chilies
1 teaspoon ground coriander

1/4 teaspoon pepper
1 cup (4 ounces) shredded reduced-fat Mexican cheese blend, *divided*
2 cups coarsely chopped real *or* imitation crabmeat
8 flour tortillas (6 inches), warmed
1/2 cup chopped tomato
1/2 cup chopped green onions
1/4 cup chopped ripe olives

Imitation crabmeat, also called surimi, is fish that is shaped, flavored and colored to resemble crab. It is often made from Alaskan pollock, a lean firm fish with a mild flavor. Both natural and artificial flavors, as well as artificial coloring are used.

Suzanne Zick
OSCEOLA, ARKANSAS

This dish is so easy to fix, and the flavor is better than any tuna helper I've ever tried. It was a staple when I was in college since a box of macaroni and cheese and a can of tuna cost so little.

Macaroni Tuna Casserole

Macaroni Tuna Casserole

PREP: 10 min. ■ BAKE: 20 min.

- 1 package (7-1/4 ounces) macaroni and cheese
- 1 can (10-3/4 ounces) condensed cream of celery soup, undiluted
- 1 can (6 ounces) tuna, drained and flaked
- 1/2 cup milk
- 1 cup (4 ounces) shredded cheddar cheese

Minced fresh parsley, optional

■ Prepare the macaroni and cheese according to the package directions. Stir in the soup, tuna and milk. Pour into a greased 2-qt. baking dish. Sprinkle with the cheese and parsley if desired. Bake, uncovered, at 350° for 20-25 minutes or until cheese is melted.

Yield: 4 servings.

It's easy to change up Macaroni Tuna Casserole to suit your taste. Try using mozzarella cheese, or substitute half the cheese with Pepper Jack for some zip.

Tomato and Onion Salmon

Lillian Denchick
OLMSTEDVILLE, NEW YORK

Tomatoes, onions and lemon juice make this moist, flaky salmon something special. My husband and I really like salmon cooked this way. A salad and rolls round out the menu nicely.

PREP/TOTAL TIME: 30 min.

- 4 salmon fillets (5 ounces each)
- 2 teaspoons olive oil
- 1/4 teaspoon dill weed
- 1/4 teaspoon pepper
- 2 medium tomatoes, thinly sliced
- 1 medium onion, thinly sliced
- 4 garlic cloves, minced
- 1/2 cup reduced-sodium chicken broth
- 1 tablespoon lemon juice
- 2 tablespoons minced fresh parsley

■ Place the salmon in a 13-in. x 9-in. baking dish coated with cooking spray. Drizzle with oil; sprinkle with dill and pepper. Top with tomatoes; set aside.

■ In a small skillet coated with cooking spray, saute onion and garlic. Add the broth, lemon juice and parsley. Bring to a boil; cook for 2-3 minutes or until most of the liquid has evaporated.

■ Spoon over salmon. Cover and bake at 350° for 13-18 minutes or until the fish flakes easily with a fork.

Yield: 4 servings.

Creamy Halibut Enchiladas

Jenifer Rohde
YUMA, ARIZONA

Reeling in compliments is easy when you serve a rich and mouthwatering entree like this.

PREP: 15 min. ■ **BAKE:** 30 min.

4 cups water
2 pounds halibut, cut into 1-inch cubes
2 packages (3 ounces *each*) cream cheese, softened
2/3 cup sour cream
3 tablespoons mayonnaise
2 cans (4 ounces *each*) chopped green chilies
1 can (4-1/4 ounces) chopped ripe olives, drained
4 green onions, chopped
1-1/2 teaspoons ground cumin
1/2 teaspoon salt
1/4 teaspoon pepper
8 flour tortillas (8 inches)
1-1/2 cups (6 ounces) shredded pepper Jack *or* Monterey Jack cheese
1/3 cup shredded Parmesan cheese
1-1/2 cups heavy whipping cream
1/2 cup salsa

■ In a large saucepan, bring water to a boil. Carefully add fish; reduce heat. Cover and simmer for 5 minutes or until fish flakes easily with a fork; drain well. In a large bowl, combine the cream cheese, sour cream, mayonnaise, chilies, olives, onions, cumin, salt and pepper. Fold in fish.

■ Place 1/2 cup down the center of each tortilla; roll up. Place enchiladas in a greased 13-in. x 9-in. baking dish. Sprinkle with cheeses; drizzle with cream.

■ Bake, uncovered, at 350° for 30-35 minutes or until bubbly. Serve with the salsa.

Yield: 8 servings.

When buying fresh fish fillets or steaks, look for firm flesh that has a moist appearance. Don't purchase fish that looks dried out. Whole fish should have bright clear eyes that are not sunken and a firm body that is springy to the touch. Fresh fish should have a mild aroma, not a strong odor.

Tuna Crescent Ring

PREP/TOTAL TIME: 30 min.

1 tube (8 ounces) refrigerated crescent rolls
1 can (12 ounces) white water-packed solid tuna
1 cup frozen peas and carrots
1/2 cup shredded cheddar cheese
1/4 cup mayonnaise
1 tablespoon Dijon mustard
1-1/2 teaspoons dried minced onion
1 teaspoon Italian seasoning

■ Unroll the crescent dough and separate into triangles. Place on an ungreased 12-in. pizza pan, forming a ring with pointed ends facing the outer edge of pan and wide ends overlapping. Lightly press wide ends together.

■ In a small bowl, combine the remaining ingredients. Spoon over wide ends of ring. Fold the points over the filling and tuck under wide ends (filling will be visible).

■ Bake at 375° for 15-20 minutes or until golden brown and the filling is hot.

Yield: 4 servings.

Julia Bivens
MARTINSBURG, WEST VIRGINIA

This is really easy to throw together, and I often use it when I am too tired to fix anything else. I usually have the ingredients on hand, and from beginning to finish, it takes me only half an hour. Plus, it's always popular with my family.

Alaskan Halibut Lasagna

- In a large skillet over medium heat, melt 2 tablespoons butter. Add halibut and thyme. Cook until fish flakes easily with a fork, about 10 minutes. Add garlic; cook 1 minute longer. Remove and set aside.

- Add the remaining butter to the skillet. Stir in flour and salt until smooth; cook and stir until golden brown. Gradually add broth and cream. Bring to a boil; cook and stir for 2 minutes or until thickened.

- In a greased 13-in. x 9-in. baking dish, layer half of the noodles, halibut, white sauce and cheese. Repeat the layers. Cover and bake at 350° for 20 minutes. Uncover and bake 20 minutes longer or until bubbly. Let stand 15 minutes before serving. Sprinkle with parsley if desired.

Yield: 8 servings.

Evelyn Gebhardt
KASILOF, ALASKA
Even "meat and potatoes lovers" compliment this delectable white lasagna's great taste. You can substitute cod or chicken for the halibut if you like.

Alaskan Halibut Lasagna

PREP: 35 min. ■ BAKE: 40 min. + standing

6 tablespoons butter, *divided*	1-1/2 cups chicken broth
1-1/2 pounds halibut steaks, bones removed and cut into 1-inch cubes	1 cup heavy whipping cream
3/4 teaspoon dried thyme	8 ounces lasagna noodles, cooked and drained
2 garlic cloves, minced	2 cups (8 ounces) shredded Swiss cheese
1/3 cup all-purpose flour	Minced fresh parsley, optional
1/2 teaspoon salt	

Dried herbs don't spoil, but they do lose flavor over time. You may want to replace herbs that are over a year old. Store dried herbs in airtight containers and keep them away from heat and light. Don't put them in the cupboard above the stove.

Dona Grover
ROCKWALL, TEXAS

I'm asked to fix this dish over and over, so there's no doubt it's worth sharing. The creamy sauce combined with the crab and pasta makes for a rich and satisfying meal.

Padre Island Shells

Padre Island Shells

PREP: 20 min. ■ BAKE: 25 min.

- 1/2 cup chopped green pepper
- 2 tablespoons thinly sliced green onion
- 4 tablespoons butter, *divided*
- 2 tablespoons all-purpose flour
- 1/2 teaspoon salt
- 2 cups milk
- 1 large tomato, peeled and chopped
- 2 tablespoons minced fresh parsley

- 1-1/4 cups shredded pepper Jack cheese, *divided*
- 3-1/2 cups medium shell pasta, cooked and drained
- 3 cans (6 ounces *each*) crabmeat, drained, flaked and cartilage removed *or* 1 pound imitation crabmeat, flaked
- 1/2 cup dry bread crumbs

■ In a large saucepan, saute the green pepper and onion in 2 tablespoons butter until tender. Stir in flour and salt until blended. Gradually stir in milk. Bring to a boil; cook and stir for 2 minutes or until thickened. Stir in the tomato and parsley.

■ Remove from the heat; stir in 1 cup of cheese until melted. Stir in pasta and crab. Transfer to a greased shallow 2-1/2-qt. baking dish. Cover and bake at 350° for 20 minutes.

■ Melt the remaining butter; toss with bread crumbs. Sprinkle over the casserole. Top with the remaining cheese. Bake, uncovered, for 5-10 minutes longer or until golden brown.

Yield: *6-8 servings.*

New Haven Clam Pizza

Susan Seymour
VALATIE, NEW YORK

This appetizer is always a big hit with our family and friends.

PREP: 20 min. + rising
BAKE: 20 min.

- 1 package (1/4 ounce) active dry yeast
- 1 cup warm water (110° to 115°)
- 1 teaspoon sugar
- 2-1/2 cups all-purpose flour
- 1 teaspoon salt
- 2 tablespoons canola oil
- 2 cans (6-1/2 ounces *each*) chopped clams, drained
- 4 bacon strips, cooked and crumbled
- 3 garlic cloves, minced
- 2 tablespoons grated Parmesan cheese
- 1 teaspoon dried oregano
- 1 cup (4 ounces) shredded part-skim mozzarella cheese

■ In a large bowl, dissolve yeast in water. Add sugar; let stand for 5 minutes. Add flour, salt and oil; beat until smooth. Cover; let rise in a warm place until doubled, 15-20 minutes.

■ Punch dough down. Press onto the bottom and up the sides of a greased 14-in. pizza pan; build up edges slightly. Prick dough several times with a fork.

■ Bake at 425° for 6-8 minutes. Sprinkle remaining ingredients over crust in order listed. Bake for 13-15 minutes or until crust is golden and cheese is melted. Cut into wedges.

Yield: *8 servings.*

Slow Cooking 101

The original slow cooker, called a Crock-Pot®, was introduced in 1971 by Rival®. Today, the term "slow cooker" and the name Crock-Pot® are frequently used interchangeably, however, in actuality Crock-Pot® is the brand and slow cooker is the appliance.

Most slow cookers have two or more settings. Food cooks faster on the high setting, however, the low setting is ideal for all-day cooking or for less tender cuts of meat. Use the "warm" setting to keep food hot until it's ready to serve. The slow cooker recipes in this book refer to cooking on either "high" or "low" settings.

Some newer slow cookers seem to heat up faster than older ones. If you have an older model and a recipe directs to cook on low, you may want to set the slow cooker on the highest setting for the first hour of cooking to be sure the food is thoroughly cooked.

ADVANTAGES of Slow Cooking

CONVENIENCE. Slow cookers provide people with the convenience of safely preparing meals while being away from home. The appliances are readily available and budget-friendly.

HEALTH BENEFITS. As more people make better food choices to improve their overall health, slow cooking has gained popularity. Low-temperature cooking retains more vitamins in the foods and healthier cuts of lean meat will become tender in the slow cooker without using extra fats. Many slow cooker recipes call for condensed soups, but lower sodium and lower fat versions can be used. And, for many busy folks, knowing that a healthy meal is waiting at home helps home cooks to avoid less-healthy, "fast-food" meals after work.

Cranberry Pork Roast

Nutrition Facts:
5 ounces cooked pork with 1/2 cup sauce equals 294 calories, 11 g fat (3 g saturated fat), 68 mg cholesterol, 110 mg sodium, 21 g carbohydrate, 3 g fiber, 27 g protein.

Southwest Beef Stew

Nutrition Facts:
1 cup equals 228 calories, 6 g fat (3 g saturated fat), 42 mg cholesterol, 482 mg sodium, 26 g carbohydrate, 4 g fiber, 17 g protein.

The recipes above are just a sample of 50+ recipes in this cookbook that include Nutrition Facts and Diabetic Exchanges. It's easy to see how much fat, sodium, fiber, protein and more is in each serving of these dishes, helping you and your family maintain a healthier diet.

FINANCIAL SAVINGS. A slow cooker uses very little electricity because of its low wattage. For instance, it would cost roughly 21 cents to operate a slow cooker for a total of 10 hours. If you roast a pork roast for 2 hours in the oven instead of using the slow cooker for 10 hours, you would spend $2.51 to operate an electric oven or $1.49 to operate a gas oven. Plus, slow cookers do not heat the home as ovens do, providing summertime savings in home-cooling costs.

TIPS FOR TASTY OUTCOMES

- No peeking! Refrain from lifting the lid while food cooks in the slow cooker, unless you're instructed in a recipe to stir or add ingredients. The loss of steam can mean an extra 20 to 30 minutes of cooking time each time you lift the lid.

- Be sure the lid is well-placed over the ceramic insert, not tilted or askew. The steam during cooking creates a seal.

- When food is finished cooking, remove it from the slow cooker within 1 hour and promptly refrigerate any leftovers.

- Slow cooking may take longer at higher altitudes.

- Don't forget your slow cooker when you go camping, if electricity is available. When space is limited and you want "set-it-and-forget-it" meals, it's a handy appliance.

- Reheating food in a slow cooker isn't recommended. Cooked food can be heated on the stovetop or in the microwave and then put into a slow cooker to keep hot for serving.

- Use a slow cooker on a buffet table to keep soup, stew, warm dips or mashed potatoes hot.

know when it's DONE!

145°F
- Medium-rare beef and lamb roasts
- Fish

160°F
- Medium beef and lamb roasts
- Pork
- Egg Dishes

165°F
- Ground chicken and turkey

170°F
- Well-done beef and lamb roasts
- Chicken and turkey that is whole or in pieces

WHEN USING YOUR SLOW COOKER...

- Slow cookers come in a range of sizes, from 1-1/2 to 7 quarts. It's important to use the right size for the amount of food you're making. To serve a dip from a buffet, the smallest slow cookers are ideal. For entertaining or a potluck, the larger sizes work best. Check the chart below to find a useful size for your household.

- To cook properly and safely, manufacturers and the USDA recommend slow cookers be filled at least half full but no more than two-thirds full.

- With many slow cooker recipes, the ingredients are added at once and are cooked all day. For make-ahead convenience, place the food items in the crock the night before, cover and refrigerate overnight (the removable stoneware insert makes this an easy task). In the morning, place the crock in the slow cooker and select the temperature.

- Do not preheat your slow cooker. An insert that has been in the refrigerator overnight should always be put into a cold base unit. Stoneware is sensitive to dramatic temperature changes, and cracking or breakage could occur if the base is preheated.

- After the recipe is finished cooking, if there are any leftovers, allow them to cool, then refrigerate. Slow cookers should not be used to reheat leftovers. Instead, use a microwave, stovetop burner, or oven to reheat foods to 165°. This ensures that the food has been thoroughly heated and it is safe to eat.

- Following a power outage of less than two hours, you can finish cooking food from your slow cooker on the stovetop or microwave. If it's been more than two hours or you are unsure how long the power has been out, discard the food for your safety.

SLOW COOKER SIZE

HOUSEHOLD SIZE	SLOW COOKER CAPACITY
1 person	1-1/2 quarts
2 people	2 to 3-1/2 quarts
3 or 4 people	3-1/2 to 4-1/2 quarts
4 or 5 people	4-1/2 to 5 quarts
6 or more people	5 to 7 quarts

A MELTING POT OF INGREDIENTS

BEANS. Minerals in water and variations in voltage affect different types of dried beans in different ways; therefore, dried beans can be tricky to work with in the slow cooker. As a result, dried beans should always be soaked before adding to a slow cooker recipe. To soak beans, place them in a Dutch oven or stockpot and add water to cover by 2 inches. Bring to a boil, and boil for 2 minutes. Remove from the heat, cover and let stand for 1 hour. Drain and rinse the beans, discarding the liquid. Sugar, salt and acidic ingredients, such as vinegar, have a hardening effect on beans and prevent them from becoming soft and tender. It's best not to cook beans with these flavorings, but to add them only after the beans are fully cooked. Lentils and split peas do not need to be soaked.

COUSCOUS. For the best results when preparing couscous, cook on a stovetop instead of in a slow cooker.

DAIRY. Milk-based products tend to break down during slow cooking. Add items like milk, sour cream, cream cheese or cream during the last hour of cooking unless the recipe instructs otherwise. Cheeses don't generally hold up over extended periods of cooking, so they should be added near the end of cooking. Condensed cream soups can be cooked in slow cookers for extended periods of time with minimal curdling concerns.

FISH & SEAFOOD. Since fish and seafood cook quickly in a slow cooker and can break down if cooked too long, they are often added toward the end of the cooking time.

MEATS. For enhanced flavor and appearance, meat may be browned before going into the slow cooker. Browning, although not vital, may improve the color and flavor of meat. When cooking a roast over 3 pounds, be sure to cut it in half before placing it in the slow cooker to ensure that it thoroughly cooks. Frozen meats should be completely thawed before being placed in a slow cooker. Trim excess fat from meat or poultry before placing in a slow cooker. A slow cooker retains heat, and large amounts of fat could raise the temperature of the cooking liquid, causing the meat to overcook and become tough.

OATS. Quick-cooking and old-fashioned oats are often interchangeable in recipes. However, old-fashioned oats hold up better in a slow cooker.

PASTA. If added to a slow cooker when dry, pasta tends to become very sticky. It's best to cook it according to the package directions and stir it into the slow cooker just before serving. Small types of pasta, like orzo and ditalini, may be cooked in the slow cooker. To keep them from becoming mushy, add during the last hour of cooking.

RICE. Converted rice is ideal for all-day cooking. If using instant rice, add it during the last 30 minutes of cooking.

VEGETABLES. Vegetables, especially potatoes and root vegetables (such as carrots), tend to cook slower than meat. Place these vegetables on the bottom and around the sides of the slow cooker and put meat on top of the vegetables. Add tender vegetables, like peas and zucchini, or those you'd prefer to be crisp-tender, during the last 50 to 60 minutes.

COOK TIMES

CONVENTIONAL OVEN
15 to 30 minutes

SLOW COOKER
Low: 4 to 6 hours
High: 1-1/2 to 2 hours

CONVENTIONAL OVEN
35 to 45 minutes

SLOW COOKER
Low: 6 to 8 hours
High: 3 to 4 hours

CONVENTIONAL OVEN
50 minutes or more

SLOW COOKER
Low: 8 to 10 hours
High: 4 to 6 hours

When a range in cooking time is provided, this accounts for variables such as thickness of meat, how full the slow cooker is and the temperature of the food going into the cooker. As you become more familiar with your slow cooker, you'll be better able to judge which end of the range to use.

CONVERTING RECIPES FOR THE SLOW COOKER

Almost any recipe that bakes in the oven or simmers on the stovetop can be easily converted for the slow cooker. Here are some guidelines.

- Before converting recipes, check the manufacturer's guidelines for your particular slow cooker. Find a recipe that is similar to the one you want to convert and use it as a guide. Note the amount and size of meat and vegetables, heat setting, cooking time and liquid.

- Since there is no evaporation, adjusting the amount of liquid in your recipe may be necessary. If a recipe calls for 6 to 8 cups of water, try starting with 5 cups. Conversely, recipes should include some liquid. If a recipe does not include liquid, add 1/2 cup of water or broth.

- In general, 1 hour of simmering on the range or baking at 350°F in the oven is equal to 8-10 hours on low or 4-6 hours on high in a slow cooker. Check the chart, top left.

- Flour and cornstarch are often used to thicken soup, stew and sauce that are cooked in a slow cooker.

Useful Handles for Lifting Food

Layered dishes or meat loaves, such as Slow-Cooked Taco Meat Loaf (page 33), are easier to get out of the slow cooker using foil handles. Here's how to make and utilize them:

1. For a 3-qt. slow cooker, cut three 20- x 3-inch strips of heavy-duty foil (or 25- x 3-inch strips for large slow cookers). Or cut 6-inch wide strips from regular foil and fold in half lengthwise. Criss-cross the strips to resemble spokes of a wheel.

2. Place the foil strips on the bottom and up the sides of the ceramic insert. Let the strips hang over the edge. To prevent food from sticking to the foil, coat the foil strips with cooking spray.

3. Place food in the order suggested by the recipe in the center of the foil strips and lower until the food rests on the bottom of the slow cooker.

4. After the food cooks, grasp the foil strips and carefully lift the food from the ceramic insert. Remove the foil strips from the food before serving.

HINTS FOR CLEANING SLOW COOKERS

- Removable stoneware inserts make cleanup a breeze. Be sure to cool the insert before rinsing or cleaning with water to avoid cracking. Do not immerse the metal base unit in water. Clean it with a damp sponge.

- Wash the insert in the dishwasher or in warm soapy water. Avoid using abrasive cleansers since they may scratch the stoneware.

- To remove mineral stains on a ceramic insert, fill the cooker with hot water and 1 cup white vinegar; cover. Set the control to high and allow to "cook" for 2 hours. Discard liquid, and when cool, wash with hot, sudsy water. Rinse well and dry.

- To remove water marks from a highly glazed crockery insert, rub the surface with vegetable oil and allow to stand for 2 hours before washing with hot, sudsy water.

General Recipe Index

Alphabetical Recipe Index